8 Cashel Blue
   (& Crozier Blue)
9 Celtic Promise
10 Colston Bassett
   Stilton
11 Coolea
12 Cornish Yarg
13 Doddington
14 Dorset Blue
   Vinny
15 Duckett's
   Caerphilly
16 Dunlop
17 Durrus (& Dunmanus)
18 Edmund Tew
19 Flower Marie
20 Gorwydd Caerphilly
   (& Pitchfork Cheddar)
21 Gubbeen
22 Hafod
23 Hawes Wensleydale
24 Isle of Mull Cheddar
25 Keen's Cheddar
26 Kirkham's Lancashire
27 Lanark Blue (& Maisie's Kebbuck, Corra Linn)
28 Lincolnshire Poacher
29 Lord of the Hundreds

A Cheesemonger's History
of the British Isles

Cheshire cheese-press.

'We are taught in school that history is about kings and queens
and posh people sitting on horses, but Ned Palmer teaches us
that in fact, correctly understood, history is mainly about cheese.
I hugely enjoyed his engaging, learned, funny, surprising book.
Palmer wears his extraordinary range of knowledge lightly,
but he is serious too. His book is history from below, from the
perspective of daily life; it talks about the food and the life and
the needs of unfamous people. *A Cheesemonger's History of the
British Isles* is the best kind of social history, the kind you can eat.'
John Lanchester

First published in Great Britain in 2019 by

Profile Books
3 Holford Yard, Bevin Way
London WC1X 9HD

www.profilebooks.com

1 3 5 7 9 10 8 6 4 2

Typeset in Sina
to a design by Henry Iles.

A CIP catalogue record for this book is available from the
British Library.

ISBN 978-1788161183
e-ISBN 978-1782834755

Printed and bound in Great Britain by Clays Ltd, Elcograf S.p.A.
on Forest Stewardship Council (mixed sources) certified paper.

A Cheesemonger's History of the British Isles

NED PALMER

P

PROFILE BOOKS

For Imo, my constant solace

and in memory of
Mary Holbrook 1938–2019

Contents

INTRODUCTION

Fresh out of Red Leicester

WORKING AS A CHEESEMONGER, you get to hear the Monty Python cheese sketch a lot. You know the one: John Cleese attempts to buy cheese and reels off a list of forty-three varieties, only to be cheerfully rebuffed on each request by Michael Palin as Mr Wensleydale the cheesemonger ('I'm afraid we're fresh out of Red Leicester, sir'). People often feel moved to perform a bit of it when they enter a cheese shop. Fair enough – some of them do it quite well, and I'm happy to wait. But the curious thing is that, when the sketch was first performed in 1972, it wasn't far off the mark.

For, back in the Dark Ages of the early 1970s, you would have been hard-pressed to buy a decent piece of British cheese. Of course, there was Stilton for Christmas, and blocks of Cheddar the rest of the year, maybe even some Cheshire or Lancashire. But that was pretty much your lot. British cheese had become virtually extinct, as had the tradition of 'farmhouse' dairies. Stilton aside, the cheese of Britain and Ireland was virtually all factory produced – acceptable perhaps for a Welsh rarebit, or as a cube on a cocktail stick poised between a bottled olive and a pineapple chunk. But if you wanted 'fancy cheese', for a cheeseboard, it was French or Italian – and even then only half a dozen kinds.

Which makes this book something of a miracle. The British Isles today boasts more than eight hundred named cheeses, from soft cheeses like the fresh and delicate goat's milk Perroche to full-on, funky washed-rinds like the aptly named Renegade Monk.

Renegade is also a great example of a new current in cheesemaking – as a combination of washed-rind and blue, it's a modern mash up of two distinct cheese styles. At the same time there has been a revival of some classic farmhouse varieties, which had all but disappeared. Rich, smooth and earthy, Sparkenhoe Red Leicester is a great example of this resurgence of tradition. You can buy these local, artisanal cheeses at farmers' markets and dedicated cheese shops, and there are decent arrays at any respectable supermarket. Charles de Gaulle famously asked, 'How can you govern a country that has two hundred and forty-six varieties of cheese?' Well, we too have become that country.

But how did all this happen? How did we create dozens of regional varieties, in farmhouses across the British Isles? How did the first British cheese get made, for that matter? How was the world of cheesemaking revolutionised in the Middle Ages by the labours of monks? Why did we then allow our cheeses to disappear, in the first half of the twentieth century, and just how did we get them back in its last decades? That is the subject of this book, and, as you read on, I hope to reveal that its title is not as fanciful as it might first appear. You can, in a very real sense, explore the history of the British Isles through the cheeses its people have made, from the arrival of farming in Neolithic times right through to the present.

I have divided the history of the British Isles into ten periods, each of them accompanied by a cheese that characterises the era. Of course, I'm not saying that Stilton is the only cheese that mattered in the eighteenth century, nor that the only way to look at the Industrial Revolution is with a ploughman's lunch of Cheddar. But the cheese that heads each chapter has something to tell you about that time. I'll recount the stories of how these cheeses came to be, why they were popular at that time, how they might have tasted or looked, who made them, who ate them, what those people's lives might have been like, and how they and their cheeses were shaped by the currents of history, religion, war, plague, supermarkets and the Milk Marketing Board.

Along the way, we'll meet cheeses that have been lost and found, revived, reinvented, industrialised, or returned to farmhouse traditions. I'll share my own cheesemonger lore and show how to pick a really great example of a particular cheese – and what you might want to consider drinking with it to enhance its flavours. I will also, I hope, explain something of the magic of cheesemaking. How a liquid as bland as milk can be transformed into a rich, savoury and complex food that has graced the tables of the British Isles for thousands of years.

G.K. Chesterton lamented that 'poets have been mysteriously silent on the subject of cheese', but one at least wasn't. In November 1935, T.S. Eliot wrote to The Times in response to a letter by John Squire, suggesting that a statue be erected to the inventor of Stilton cheese. While Eliot appreciated Squire's 'spirited defence of Stilton', he thought that putting up a statue was not going far enough. 'If British cheese is to be brought back from the brink of extinction, a Society for the Preservation of Ancient Cheeses must be formed without delay', he wrote. Eliot was a big Cheshire fan, prizing a 'noble Old Cheshire' against a Stilton any day, but quite rightly he finishes his letter with this stirring call: 'this is no time for disputes between eaters of English cheese. The situation is too precarious and we must stick together.' Happily for us, the situation is no longer quite so precarious...

CHAPTER ONE

Sleightlett

Neolithic feasting

4000 BCE–43 CE

ONE WET AND WINDY FEBRUARY AFTERNOON, I found myself standing on a hill in Wiltshire holding a piece of fresh goat's cheese. Not just any hill. I was shivering in the rainy shadow of Stonehenge, trying to pay homage to the earliest cheesemakers of Britain, while ignoring the onset of hypothermia.

I was also reflecting on the journey that had brought me – and the cheese – to this place. A journey that began nearly twenty years ago in London's Borough Market. I had found myself short of a job, having exhausted the possibilities of a philosophy degree, and discovered from a stint in Australia that only the most fortunate can make a living as a musician. Which was why I was helping my friend Todd Trethowan sell his Gorwydd Caerphilly cheese. Never having tasted proper cheese before, let alone sold any, the first thing I had to do was to try some, and as the complex, intriguing and delicious flavours unfolded across my palate I experienced what I can only call an epiphany. This might seem a disproportionate reaction to eating a piece of cheese, but proper Caerphilly, as made by Todd on his family farm in Wales, is one of the world's great cheeses.

It is made from unpasteurised milk (also known as raw milk) to provide a more complex flavour; it tastes of lemon, butter and earth; and its texture varies from a moistly crumbly centre to a rich creamy outer layer, with a grey and white mould rind that has the feel of soft felt. I started asking Todd a lot of questions: 'How does milk turn into this?' and 'Why doesn't all cheese taste this good?' Todd did his best, but in the end, perhaps to stop me bothering him, he recommended me for a job at Neal's Yard Dairy, a shop famous since the 1980s for its range of British and Irish cheese.

In my interview for the Dairy, I was careful to make it clear that this would only be a temporary thing, as I would soon be resuming my career as a jazz pianist. And then I ended up working at the Dairy for six years. I worked on the retail counter, and did time in the cellars, turning the cheeses. I also began visiting some of the great cheesemakers of Britain and Ireland, and – by making cheese with them – began to understand how flavours are influenced not just by technique but by what a French winemaker would call terroir – the soil, the local climate and the culture of the people who make the cheese.

That might explain how I ended up at Stonehenge, but not how the cheese got there. To do so we will have to go back several millennia to the Middle East, where cheesemaking was invented – or perhaps it would be more truthful to say, discovered.

The earliest direct evidence for cheese appears in what is now northern Turkey, in archaeological finds from 6500 BCE, in the form of milk fat deposits on potsherds. That means cheesemaking began soon after the domestication of animals, but about *a thousand years before* adult humans developed the ability to digest milk. The first evidence for this trait, known as adult lactase persistence (lactase is the enzyme needed to digest milk) appears in what is now Hungary in around 5500 BCE. So perhaps cheese was, at its onset, a way of making milk digestible to humans – a neat trick that resulted from a combination of prehistoric appetite, inquisitiveness and ingenuity.

The earliest cheeses were probably made from goat's milk, since goats were among the first animals to be domesticated. But how did anyone figure out the steps that are necessary to convert the milk they could not tolerate into the tasty cheese they could happily consume? I have an answer – a story I like to call the 'Foolhardy Herder'. Picture, if you will, a goatherd hanging out with his newly domesticated companions somewhere on a rocky plateau in the Zagros Mountains (which border Iran, Iraq and Turkey), eight or nine thousand years ago. It's hot and he's been on his feet all day. He's hungry and thirsty, so he decides to drink some goat's milk – even though it's always made him sick before. The milk he tries has been sitting around for a while and when he drinks it he notices a slightly thicker texture and a pleasingly refreshing sourness. What he notices next is…nothing. No discomforting side effects. Rushing back to the family cave, he overcomes the scepticism of his siblings and parents and they set out on a programme of empirical research to figure out what is going on, i.e. they drink a lot of milk. After a few false starts, they realise they can drink the milk if it's gone a bit sour. What's happened is that the lactophilic bacteria hanging about in the vicinity have converted the lactose in the milk into lactic acid; this coagulates the milk which, if drained, becomes a form of ur-cheese.

Ur-cheese, or cream cheese to give it its modern name, is not the complex and delicious foodstuff that has inspired this book. Cream cheese isn't very long-lasting; all the moisture means that it goes off in a matter of days. So, to make it last, and develop more flavour, you need a little more accidental science. You need to dry your curd using some kind of coagulant. Happily for the ur-cheesemakers this coagulant existed in the stomachs of the animals they were herding, a substance called rennet, which encourages milk proteins to knit together while allowing the liquid whey (which is mostly water) to escape. And, beyond that, there is just one final step in cheesemaking – adding salt, which provides taste, draws more moisture and, happily, adds another element of protection from the wrong sort of bacteria.

So cheese is really just milk that has used three classic ways of preserving food – pickling, drying and salting. Each of which could be discovered, over a millennium or two, by accident.

Farming – including dairying and cheesemaking – was part of the 'Neolithic package' that gradually spread out from the Fertile Crescent (modern Iran, Syria and bits of Turkey and Iraq) and up through Northern Europe, arriving in the British Isles around 4000 BCE. This was a thousand years before the main phase of building at Stonehenge began, which was fortuitous to say the least. Cheese, as a portable protein and mineral-rich foodstuff, enables people to travel and settle beyond their own lands. It must also have been incredibly handy for Neolithic builders dragging those big stones about.

Back to the field in Wiltshire, then. I had decided, despite persistent cold rain, to approach the stone circle on foot – as the people who built it and worshipped there would have done. On the outskirts of Amesbury, I abandoned the road for a long, straight prehistoric track which took me through fields of turnips and sheep towards the crest of a hill. Stonehenge was frustratingly hidden from view, but as I walked up the track, with larks ascending around me, it was easy to imagine the ancient pilgrims walking this same road. When I reached the crest, I found myself among a cluster of grave mounds, with gnarled trees crowning them. And then I caught a first view of the henge, about a mile away across a valley. Even through a mizzle of sleety rain it's quite a sight, and it must have made an almighty impression on those neolithic folk, when the freshly cut circle of stones were a dazzling feat of engineering. And all the more amazing when the sun came up at the summer solstice.

Stonehenge in the nineteenth century with a visiting shepherd.

Having communed with the stones, I headed off to the visitors' centre, where I had an appointment with some Neolithic farmers, in a manner of speaking. Jill and Mark Hatch are historical re-enactors with a special interest in food and I had been introduced to them by my friend Jess, who was by happy coincidence both the PR manager for Stonehenge and married to Todd Trethowan (he of the Gorwydd Caerphilly). In the world of cheese, everything is connected. Jill and Mark were to be found sitting beside a small campfire making Neolithic cheese, dressed in leather jerkins and woollen clothes. Jill was beating some greyish, milky liquid in a clay pot with a wooden pestle, making butter, while Mark was giving a quarter- turn to a blackened bell-shaped pot full of milk nestled next to the fire. In other words, a Neolithic cheese vat.

Without standing on ceremony, I produced my cheese for them to take a look at. It was a small round of Sleightlett, a very simple fresh cheese, which you could make with a couple of bowls, a colander and a spoon. I wanted to know if Jill and Mark thought this was the sort of thing that people had been making about five and a half thousand years ago. 'Absolutely,' said Jill. 'I mean, it's not as if they'd have been Cheddaring. They wouldn't have had all that sort of kit.' Cheddaring is a thing that you do to make Cheddar and other hard cheeses: it requires big steel vats and curd mills, among other things.

That settled, and because we were all British, we started talking about the weather. Jill pointed out that it's unlikely Neolithic dairy farmers would have made cheese in the winter. For a start, there wasn't much milk around. At the onset of winter, you slaughtered the animals you thought wouldn't make it through to spring (this was before farmers wintered their stock on root crops and silage) and the ones that remained lived on short commons – too short to keep them producing milk. 'Also,' said Jill, pointing accusingly at the pot by the fire, 'it's too cold. Look at this! No one in their right mind would be trying to do this in winter.' The milk was resolutely not turning into cheese. It was simply too cold for the bacteria to get on with their job of souring the liquid; they were hibernating.

Mark also wondered if there was much feasting and celebration at Stonehenge in the summer. 'You've got loads to do, then, if you're a farmer,' he said. 'You're far too busy for messing about with pilgrimages and feasting. But in the winter there isn't much to do, and by winter solstice you're probably wondering if the sun is ever going to come up again, so you might well want to do some sort of ritual to help it on its way.'

He might be onto something. The pigs whose bones have been found in feasting pits near Stonehenge were slaughtered at around nine months old. Since piglets are born in spring, that would make the time of their slaughtering around December: perfect for a big midwinter feast. And, as pigs love whey and thrive upon it, so summer cheesemaking would also help produce nice fat juicy porkers for your winter feasting.

🐷 🐷 🐷

I had wondered if cheese was a staple or a feasting food for the Neolithic people. At Salisbury Museum you can see the skeletons of a group of four people: a woman aged around forty-five and three children, buried together around 3300 BCE in Monkton-up-Wimborne, about twenty-five miles from Stonehenge (an early version of which would have just about got going at that time). Analysis of the children's bones shows that they all had iron deficiency, suggesting a low meat diet, but that their diet contained a lot of protein – quite probably from dairy products. Might this indicate that meat was a high-status food saved for special occasions, but that dairy was an everyday food? Of course we're speculating, but one thing we can say with something approaching certainty is that cheese was being made.

This certainty is quite recent. For a long time, the evidence for prehistoric cheesemaking in the British Isles was indirect. All we knew was that at places like Hambledon Hill in Dorset, where archaeologists found cattle bones dated to the middle of the fourth millennium BCE, these tended to be from older female cows. It was assumed that the cattle were being kept mainly for their milk rather than their meat. Given that at this time the majority of adults in Britain and Ireland were still likely to be lactose intolerant, the only sensible reason to keep all this milk would have been to make cheese with it. Nevertheless, this interpretation was, one might say, a bone of contention, until in 2003 a group of research scientists at Bristol University published a paper called 'Direct Chemical Evidence for Widespread Dairying in Prehistoric Britain'.

In this study, the authors described a process whereby it is possible to distinguish between animal and dairy fats in residues left on ancient potsherds. The process is called stable isotope analysis and it is explained with a nice series of cartoons in the Stonehenge Exhibition Centre, if you'd rather forgo the pleasure of reading the bioarchaeological paper. Essentially, the findings rest on differences in Carbon 13 values, which are lower in dairy than in animal fats. The scientists announced that for dairy products at all Britain's Neolithic, Bronze Age and Iron Age settlements they had 'direct evidence for the exploitation of domesticated ruminant animals'.

Further studies were carried out in Scotland and Ireland and, as I promised, we can now say with some certainty that cheesemaking began in the British Isles at the same time as the arrival of farming, around 4000 BCE. That is four thousand years before the Romans.

This was something of a revelation to the whole cheese history community, who had previously accepted that the Romans had introduced cheesemaking (as well as roads, irrigation, public baths, etc.) to Britain. This patronising attitude towards our native

Neolithic cheesemaker Jill Hatch with some stubborn milk.

foodways was summed up by the description of ancient Britons by the Romano-Greek historian Strabo in his *Geographica*:

> Their habits are in part like those of the Celti, but in part more simple and barbaric – so much so that, on account of their inexperience, some of them, although well supplied with milk, make no cheese; and they have no experience in gardening or other agricultural pursuits.

Strabo also mentioned that the Irish ate their parents, which I don't believe either.

Of course, the 'Direct Chemical Evidence' paper is not suggesting that the Neolithic British or Irish invented or stumbled upon cheesemaking on their own. What seems likely is that cheesemaking, along with arable and pastoral farming, developed in the Fertile Crescent and spread from there. There is, however, much debate about whether it was the farmers or the idea of farming that spread. At present, based on genetic studies, opinion is leaning towards the idea that farming people replaced the indigenous hunter-gatherers, and cheese may have played a role in this. The ability to make a concentrated, preserved and portable foodstuff from milk would have helped one culture to outperform or indeed conquer the other, and it also seems that the gene (or, more correctly, *allele*) for adult lactase persistence seems to have followed the spread of cheesemaking. So perhaps cheesemaking plus adult milk-drinking played a part in the farming culture's success over the hunter-gatherer – what you might call dairy imperialism.

It seems that there was a pause between the farming culture arriving on the shores of the Channel and North Sea and it hopping over to the British Isles. The distinctive pottery taken as a sign of Neolithic farming culture, known as Linearbandkeramik, appears in Holland around 5300 BCE, and almost a thousand years later in Britain and Ireland. There's a bit of argument over the reason for this hiatus. Some suggest that the Neolithic people moved easily along the river valleys of Europe, taking their farming practice with them, but that they slowed or stopped when they got to the sea. Another argument, espoused by the forthright sheep farmer and archaeologist Francis Pryor, is that the British and Irish didn't need to take up farming, because the bounty of their forests and shores was sufficient for their needs.

There is a wider question here about why anyone would take up farming in the first place. The archaeological record shows that populations that made the shift to farming became less healthy, less tall, shorter-lived, and began to show evidence of injuries sustained from a lifetime of repetitive toil. But I know why they did it, and I am happy to dissolve this controversy here and now: they developed a taste for beer and cheese.

Here's what I think happened. Natives of Britain or Ireland, picking a sunny calm day in which to make the crossing, popped over the Channel in one of their excellent dug-out log boats to visit their continental cousins. On this visit their friends and relations introduced them to a delicious and intoxicating liquid – beer – and a delicious, creamy, satisfying food – cheese. The Brits and Irish were all like, 'I've got to get me some of that!' Perhaps they extended their stay to pick up a few pointers on the production of grain and milk and the fermentation of both, or perhaps they invited some of their relatives to come and settle on the islands, promising to trade their knowledge of hunting and gathering grounds for training in brewing and dairying.

Seriously, some prehistorians do believe that people began to settle and domesticate crops so that they could brew more beer, and others contend it was the domestication of ruminant animals to get more milk for cheese that drove the move towards a farming lifestyle. And, according to the timeline on the wall of the visitors centre in Stonehenge, brewing and cheesemaking turn up around the same time, well before baking. These Neolithic people had their priorities right.

Standing around outside the visitors' centre was beginning to get chilly. Seemingly more so for me in my modern nylon walking jacket than for Mark and Jill in their wool and leather. But that was okay, because I had a bit of a walk in front of me to see the feasting pits I mentioned earlier. These were not at Stonehenge itself but at a nearby Neolithic settlement where the people who built the circle lived – a place now known as Durrington Walls.

I had decided I had to stand in the very place where the earliest evidence of cheesemaking in Britain was found. So, bidding farewell to my new Neolithic friends, I trudged off back down the

Avenue, wondering (as we cheesemongers are prone to do) what modern cheese would be closest to the Neolithic experience. I had always imagined it would be something soft, fresh and made of goat's milk, like Sleightlett. But, as the sleet tore down, I found my thoughts turning to the Orkneys, and to Seator's, a fresh and crumbly cheese from those islands that has become a bit of a favourite of mine. It is a cow's milk cheese and this would fit the bill in these parts, for archaeologists have found at Durrington a preponderance of cattle bones.

Made by Anne Seator at Grimbister Farm, Seator's comes in pale yellow cylinders about eight inches high and six across. Although you could mature it (I have seen one on the counter at Iain Mellis's cheese shop in Edinburgh with a mould rind, looking much like a Wensleydale), for me the joy of a Seator's is to eat it within days of its making. At this age, it has a moist, giving texture with just a bit of crumbliness, and the flavour is milky and clean with a gentle refreshing acidity. It is mild and delicate, and the enjoyment of a mild cheese is a pleasure that grows upon you. A mild cheese also takes considerable skill to get right: there's nowhere to hide, as every element of its flavour must be just perfectly in balance.

Aside from being made with cow's milk, another thing Seator's has in common with whatever sort of cheese was being made at Neolithic Durrington is that it was originally made without a starter culture. Back when Anne's mum Hilda was making Seator's, her unpasteurised milk from the family farm already had enough naturally occurring lactophilic bacteria to to get the ball rolling. She would collect the milk from cows that she knew by name and let it sour naturally until it was acidic enough for the rennet to start working. This is an ancient way to make cheese. It's slow and gentle, which milk likes, and in using the indigenous bacterial cultures of your farm you are giving the cheese a unique character, a bit like that French concept of *terroir*. As the exact population of lactic bacteria will vary from day to day, so will your cheeses change in flavour and texture. That, to me, is something to celebrate, but

Seator's Orkney cheese – best eaten fresh for the true Neolithic experience.

I can understand you may need a bit more consistency if you're running a business. For this reason Anne does add some lactophilic bacteria, or 'starter culture', at the beginning of the cheesemaking season, just to get things going and provide a sort of core family of bacteria to establish the cheese's essential character.

There were probably Neolithic cheesemakers in the Orkneys, making cheese the Seator's way. After all, the island is the home of Skara Brae, a coastal village occupied from 3100 to 2500 BCE, the same time the people of Durrington Walls were making gigantic stone monuments (and cheese). The people of Skara Brae ate shellfish, hunted deer and seals, and kept cattle and sheep, so it's reasonable to think that they were partial to a nice bit of cheese.

Like Skara Brae, Durrington Walls was a cluster of round houses, which were set in a round bowl, sheltered from the wind (a fine example of Neolithic town planning). Unlike at Skara Brae, there are no remains at Durrington, but there are some fine replicas near the visitors' centre, made from cob – a mixture of dung, mud and brushwood that the people of south-west Britain were still using as a building material in the nineteenth century. They look just like the huts in *Asterix* comics, so it was easy enough to imagine a cluster of these huts and the people sitting in them making cheese. I found myself speculating that, if they had pots for dairying, perhaps the people of Neolithic Durrington might have had other cheesemaking equipment too, like wicker moulds, or strainers to drain off whey, or wooden discs (known as followers) to press the curd and make firmer cheeses. Of course, if these things were made of less durable materials than clay, it explains why they didn't survive; as archaeologists like to say, 'The absence of evidence isn't evidence of absence.'

Given the diversity of cultures in Britain and Ireland – from widely dispersed smallholdings to more densely packed communities – it's perfectly possible that these different cultures made different varieties of cheese. Without being too speculative, and based on the cheesemaking technology we have found (smallish clay pots), simple soft cheeses seem a plausible candidate for at least one of these varieties. It also looks like there were plenty of cows around, and in quite large herds too.

That said, I had chosen Sleightlett – a goat's cheese – to take to Stonehenge, and as my signature cheese for this chapter, because I think the first cheeses ever made by humans were most likely to have been made from goat's milk. Also I like goats. They are curious, gregarious and independent. Much like cheesemakers.

Goats were probably the first livestock animal that humans domesticated, around ten thousand years ago, and this may be due in part to their temperament. The natural habitat of the undomesticated wild goat, *Capra aegagrus hircus* to its Latin friends, was the Zagros Mountains range, where I imagined the Foolhardy Herder discovering cheesemaking. There, in cosy and well-situated caves lived Mesolithic (middle Stone Age) tool-using humans, hunting and gathering, though not really into farming or livestock-rearing just yet. A fluffy version of the story might have the inquisitive goats popping into these caves for a look at these odd bipedal creatures, and gregariously sticking around, until by mutual agreement they decided to move in. But perhaps there was more guile from the hunters, realising that they wouldn't have to run about after agile mountain goats so much if they could get some to come and live with them.

Goats turned up in the British Isles, along with sheep and cattle around 4000 BCE, signalling the beginning of the Neolithic period in Britain and Ireland. Some of their descendants have gone feral and still hang on in the craggy hills of Northumberland, north Wales and the steeper bits of Ireland. In County Kerry, on each 10th of August, the Puck Fair takes place – *Aonach an Phoic* in Gaelic, meaning 'Fair of the He-Goat'. This involves a bunch of brave and foolhardy folk going up into the hills to kidnap a feral goat and bring it down to the village. There it presides over the Fair in a position of honour (if a cage can be called honourable), before being released back into the wild when the Fair is done. If you are thinking the cage seems a bit overly cautious for a nice friendly goat by the way, I suggest you take a look at a picture of one.

There were then no animals larger than wild pigs indigenous to Ireland, which had become separated from mainland Europe in around 12,000 BCE, a good six thousand years before Britain did the same. This means that, to get started with dairying, the people who brought farming to Ireland also had to bring their goats and their cattle with them. I have been sailing in the Irish Sea in a small wooden boat, and it was hairy enough with just my grumpy dad for company. I can't imagine what it would have been like sharing a small wicker and hide boat in that choppy water with a grumpy cow and a goat or two. But somehow the intrepid Neolithic settlers of Ireland managed this feat.

When I have written 'goat' in this chapter, I ought really to have written 'goat/sheep', which is how the animal is referred to in every single book and paper I have read about the archaeology of the period. I spent a painfully long time trying to figure out what this slash meant. Was it that these archaeologists weren't that interested in goats? Or was the lack of distinction between the two animals such a basic assumption that no one bothered to explain it? Then at last I found a phrase in an article about faunal remains (bits of bone) that alluded to the extreme difficulty of distinguishing between the bones of the two animals. I let out a triumphant yawp at this finding – in the Rare Books Reading Room of the British Library, which is a very quiet room indeed, and must have startled my fellow readers.

I was reading up, at the time, on the Céide Field System on the coast of County Mayo, which Irish archaeologist Seamus Caulfield believes was established by 3500 BCE. Five miles square, it is the oldest known field system in the world and contained hundreds of individual farms. Although the soil there is too acidic for bones to survive, Caulfield theorised that the system had been set up to manage dairy herds, an idea backed up by Irish finds of pottery sherds on which traces of milk fat still remain. If this was the case, the Céide Fields might be evidence of a Neolithic Irish cheesemaking culture. Take that, Strabo.

But to return to Sleightlett. What is it like? And might Neolithic cheeses have been essentially similar?

Well, Sleightlett cheeses are white discs, about three inches across and about one fat inch high, coated in a light dusting of ash. Being young, they have a delicate simple flavour, fresh acidity, and a mouth-filling moussy texture. They are, oddly enough, not goaty. The goatiness of goat's cheese can be problematic and some people have been put off for life by a ripe specimen. Sleightlett is not problematic. One reason for its lack of goatiness is that the cheese is so young that it hasn't had time to develop those more powerful flavours. The other reason is that it is made with gentleness and patience.

But what is it that makes a goat's cheese taste goaty, if that is not too obvious a question? I found the answer to this in a paper from the University of Iran on the composition of goat's milk (they've got a lot of goats in Iran). It turns out that the elements responsible for the goaty flavour are short-chain fatty acids called capric, caproic and caprylic acids (any Latin speakers will see where they're going with that). These short-chain fatty acids are relatively fragile and, if stirred vigorously or heated quickly, the chains break apart, releasing their goaty flavours. So, you see, if the cheesemaker lacks gentleness, and stirs the milk too hard, or lacks patience and heats the milk too fast, the goatiness will ramp up. If the capric and other acids are allowed to break down more slowly over time, you are more likely to get that balanced mix of flavours.

Eaten at a few days to a week old, Sleightlett will not challenge you with its goatiness. However, as a young, fresh goat's cheese, it's only going to be available during the goat's cheese season, early spring to late autumn. Goats are much less amenable than cows to being milked all year round, so their milk is mostly only available during that period. You might get older cheeses out of season, but for something young and fresh that's your window of opportunity. That's okay, though, because the delicate flavour and refreshing acidity of a young goat's cheese is just what you want in the warmer weather.

Pairing delicate cheese with drinks can be a bit of a challenge. My fundamental principle is that the intensity of the cheese and the drink should be about the same. There's no point in drinking a delicate Chenin Blanc with a hint of elderflower while eating a great grunty Cheddar like Lincolnshire Poacher – the poor wine will just get knocked about all over the place. Also, I'm not always a fan of pairing red wines with cheese – which I know will sound counterintuitive to many readers. Reds can often be quite tannic – and the tannins in the wine can react with the fat in cheese, creating a bitter flavour.

That said, one must be nothing if not inconsistent, and what I like most with Sleightlett is a big, brash, Aussie, sparkling Shiraz called The Full Fifteen. Why? Because the acidity in the cheese brings out the fruit in the wine – it's like having cherry compote with crème fraîche. Also because of the mouth-feel – having soft moussy cheeses with sparkling wines creates a lovely sparkly texture in the mouth, a bit like Sherbet Dip Dabs.

Sleightlett is made on Sleight Farm, which sits on a hill outside the village of Timsbury in West Somerset. It was the creation of Mary Holbrook, who started making cheese here in the late 1970s and is considered one of the harbingers of the renaissance in cheesemaking that got going around that time. She was also the first cheesemaker I ever encountered.

I'd only been at Neal's Yard Dairy a few months when the owner, Randolph Hodgson, found me having a stretch after a long day of turning cheese in the cellar. 'Do you like all this, then?' he asked.

By 'this', he was referring to the whole cheesemongering lark, which he signified by an airy wave of the hand taking in counter, shelves and cellar full of ripening cheeses. I told him I did, which was true but perhaps odd, as I was just about to spend the next hour scrubbing a load of mould-encrusted wire racks. Still, I must have sounded genuine because he offered me the chance to go and stay on Mary's farm for a week or two and make cheese with her.

I already knew and loved Mary's cheeses – her washed-rind Cardo, her Old Ford (a hard goat's cheese) and Tymsboro, her best known cheese, a salty-peppery, ash-covered pyramid. So I was eager as a puppy when Mary picked me outside Bath station in her little van. There was no room in the front and I took my chances in the back with a rather pointy bit of agricultural equipment. The roads of that part of Somerset are small and winding, and it was quite an adventure in the pitch-black back end of the van.

When we arrived at the farm gate, I got out to open it, and opted to walk up to the farm. The road spirals around a short steep hill, at the top of which are the farmhouse and barns, and on the way up I enjoyed the view of a patchwork of small fields and hills, with the houses and church spire of Timsbury in the middle distance. The view was occasionally interrupted by the presence of defunct and rusting bits of agricultural machinery, some so ancient that they seemed to have come from the dawn of the machine age – an aesthetic shared by farms all over Britain and Ireland and, I suspect, the world. I don't think it is carelessness, quite the opposite. It's a frugal and prudent attitude, never throwing anything away in case it turns out to be useful. By the looks of things on Mary's farm, they made tractors out of cast iron and oak in the 1900s, and these ancient behemoths seem set to outlast this century.

I met up with Mary again in the farmhouse, with its grey, stone walls and mullioned windows, perched on the brow of the hill. Putting the kettle on, she explained that it was probably a Victorian dower house, and might have originally been situated down in the village then taken apart, stone by stone and timber by timber, to be put back together here.

The kitchen was a treat, its shelves stuffed with a historical collection of jam saucepans, meat grinders, earthenware bowls, cheese moulds, slightly terrifying knives, and things whose use I can only guess at. I also noted an alarming medicinal bottle of something called 'Black Drink (Not for Human Consumption)'. And there were books everywhere – about Victorian women travellers, Byzantine church frescoes and German Enlightenment scientific instruments, plus some excellent fiction and such farmhouse classics as *Diseases of Sheep* and *On the Curing of Meat*.

Another pleasure of Mary's kitchen was the 'Freezer Lucky Dip'. At some point during that first evening I must have started looking hungry, which prompted her to say, 'Oh – here's a torch, pop down to the cellar and dig something out of the freezer, doesn't matter what.' Which was fortunate advice, for the freezer was rammed

Mary Holbrook in her dairy with a tray of her distintive pyramid-shaped Tymsboro cheeses.

with large chunks of frozen meat in unlabelled bags. Not only did I have no idea what part of a beast I was holding, I didn't even know what animal it had come from. Which led to conversation openers like: 'Oooh, that's a pig spleen. There's a recipe for that in *Nose to Tail*. Always wanted to try that!' Or: 'Ah, that was one of those deer that kept nibbling the shoots of the saplings in Low Field, so we had to shoot a few to discourage the others. Still, he ought to taste good!'

I can't remember which of those we had for dinner that first night. What I do remember is that, as a novice cheesemonger,

I had no idea about the early starts required in cheesemaking, and stayed up too late, drinking too much. The next morning, addressing my breakfast coffee and slice of cold meat, I felt distinctly bleary. Mary, of course, was absolutely fine. Farming people are tough.

Thankfully, the commute from kitchen to dairy was not too arduous. Through the back garden with its planters of kitchen herbs and a gate into the yard, then past an open doorway to the milking parlour. It takes about two minutes. Or it ought to. I was distracted, by the Inquisitiveness of Goats. I'd never seen so many goats so close before and couldn't help making eye contact with a few. This was a mistake, as they and all their friends came over to have a look at the new guy, causing a goat-jam and making Kay, Mary's farm manager, cross.

⟐ ⟐ ⟐

The first thing you do when making Sleightlett is mix the morning milk, which has come straight from the milking parlour (and is warm), with the evening milk which has been sitting in the milk tank (and is cold). If you get the proportion just right, the milk is exactly at the temperature for making Mary's soft cheeses – about 22° C (or what older folks call 'seventy-one'). Getting the temperature right at this point is crucial, and when I messed up during my stint and the milk was 23–24° we had to wait until it cooled. Tiny variations at this stage of the process can lead to dramatic outcomes as the cheese matures. The cool milk from the previous night comes out of the milk tank, a steel-jacketed vat the size of a hot tub. The warm morning milk has come straight from the goats and is pumped in from the milking parlour to a separate vat. You dip the milk out of tank and vat with a steel pail and mix it in big plastic tubs in the cheesemaking room. If, like me, you're inexperienced, you tend to end up quite milky.

Having mixed the milk in the right proportions, we added starter to the milk. In modern cheesemaking, it is common to use a bought culture that comes as a freeze-dried powder. Mary, for most of the cheesemaking season, used whey saved from the previous day's cheesemaking, which contains live cultures. This is a much more traditional method and, as the cultures evolve over time, it will lead to strains that are unique to the dairy, so the cheese becomes a unique expression of a particular place and time. However, the results are much less predictable, both in the end results and during the make itself. This is the same issue that confronts the Seators up in Orkney when using no starter at all to make their cheese. Some cheesemakers would consider this to be a pain, and some would consider it rather fun and interesting. Mary was very definitely one of the latter.

I stirred the whey into the milk in a very gentle motion and with a degree of thoroughness beyond anything I had ever done before. I was a keen apprentice and prepared myself to learn, on this first outing, something of the technical aspects of cheesemaking – how to test the acidity of the curd, when to add rennet, and how much to use.

'I reckon it's time to add the rennet now,' Mary said after a bit.

'How do you know?' I asked.

'Oh, you know.' she said, dipping her finger into the curd and trying it. 'It tastes about right.'

This is not the way of factory cheesemaking. Nor, I now know, the way of many cheesemakers, who will test the pH or (believing that inaccurate) the titratable acidity, using various bits of kit, some of which look like Apple has got into cheesemaking. One thing Mary did measure, though, was the *amount* of rennet. Rennet is so powerful that 50ml will coagulate a 2,700-litre vat of milk, albeit quite slowly.

Measured and added, the rennet required some more thorough stirring from me. That concluded, we had a pause, or at least the day's batch of cheese had a pause, while the milk set into curd. For the kind of cheese we were making on that day – a lactic-set soft cheese, the very Sleightlett I had brought as homage to the cheesemakers of Stonehenge – the curd takes about twenty-two hours to set as the starter culture does its work, coagulating the milk with the lactic acid it produces. (By contrast, the curd for Cheddar, which uses much more rennet, sets in a matter of hours.) Hence 'lactic-set' as opposed to 'rennet-set'. This style of cheesemaking is also called a 'punctuated make', which means that stages when you need to do something, like adding starter or rennet, cutting and ladling curd, are punctuated by breaks.

Which doesn't mean the end of a cheesemaker's day. Far from it. The main job of the day is ladling the curd that started setting the previous day into the moulds – little plastic strainers that allow the whey to drain off and give shape to the cheese. The moulds for Sleightlett are, as I mentioned, cylinders, about six inches high and a few inches across. This is an old form and indeed I have seen clay moulds identical in size and shape in the archaeological museum in Lisbon. These were dated to the Chalcolithic (Copper) period, which kicked off in Europe around 3500 BCE.

Ladling curd into moulds is one of those jobs that looks effortless when it is being done by someone who has forty years' practice. It is not effortless. You have to be gentle, but you can't be too slow. The curd is acidifying all the time, and if it hangs about too long in the vat the cheese will end up too sharp, hard and dry. You also need to be consistent. The moulds should fill up at the same rate to the same height, or your cheese will be all different sizes. And you need to move steadily around the vat as you work. If you dig all your curd out from one side, the curd from the other side will acidify for longer and make different cheeses.

After that first session of ladling, my wrist, shoulder blade and lower back were stiff and aching. Mary, by contrast, looked as if she had done a gentle stretch. But then she ladled all day, day after day; it's not as if the goats won't give you milk on a Sunday.

For all the aches, though, I loved ladling – and still do. It is meditative to an almost Zen-like degree, and it instills good posture and slow, controlled movements, so that you feel relaxed and attentive at the same time. And the atmosphere in a small dairy like Mary's, making soft cheese, adds to the contemplative mood, suffused as it is with warmth and the comforting smell of freshly soured milk. This effect is particularly noticeable when you are ladling at night and the only sound is the trickling of whey from the moulds and occasional hoot of an owl.

More often than not you will end up ladling at night when you are making soft lactic-set cheese. The curd takes a while to settle in the mould, so you can't ladle it all at once, but you still need to get it all out of the vat by the end of the working day. The time it takes to ladle an entire batch of curd will change across the season as the milk changes in character and behaviour. As the proportion of solid to liquid increases, so does the time it takes to drain. The rhythm of a small-scale cheesemaker's life is dictated by the curd: when you get up and go to bed, when you eat and when you do the many other jobs that are required. If a cheesemaker says of another that they 'make cheese by the clock, not the curd', it is a grievous insult.

One way that you might try to flatten out some of this variation is to alter the feed of your animals, perhaps adding some maize or cattle cake to supplement their forage. Some farmer-cheesemakers pay great attention to the composition of their milk – largely the fat to protein ratio – and change the feed to optimise this relationship. I asked Mary if she ever did this with her goats. 'I'm not a technical farmer,' she laughed. 'You try and get a goat to eat something it doesn't want to. They're very discerning eaters. Sometimes they'll cross a whole field without eating anything in it to get to something they do want on the other side.'

Mary Holbrook started making cheese in 1978 ('Or was it 1979?' she wondered) and hadn't expected to become a farmer, let alone a cheesemaker. But the farm was in her late husband John's family, and when they decided the manager they were paying to run the place wasn't doing a good job, they decided to take over.

At first, Mary had tried to make a sort of goat's milk feta. Feta is a crumbly soft white cheese but her first attempts came out as a hard cheese, so she called it Mendip and sold it as that. 'Sometimes you have to let the milk tell you what to make,' she explained. 'I've never sat down and said, "I'm going to make a cheese like this". Things come along by accident.'

At the end of a day's cheesemaking Mary liked to have a walk around the farm, making a circuit of some of the more distant fields. Walking around with her and listening to her talk made me think about something the archaeologist Francis Pryor said about 'the landscape of the mind' of prehistoric farmers, and how they would have been 'steeped in the history of the countryside around them.' I think Pryor meant that for those people the land was intimately bound up with their family histories and their cultural and spiritual beliefs. He also talks about the 'working landscape', an eminently pragmatic way of looking at landscape as a set of parts that must function together to produce your crops, milk and meat. Both attitudes must have created a sense of stewardship among the early farmers, looking after the land so that it kept them and their families and also for future generations.

In one field Mary had planted a load of saplings. 'I won't be around to see them when they're trees,' she said, 'but you've got to put something back in, haven't you?' Mary was not a particularly sentimental person: I doubt you can be as a livestock farmer. But she had a feel for her land, as its temporary custodian.

On the way back down to the farmhouse that evening, we stopped off in another field to pay a visit to 'the girls', as Mary called her goats. As gregarious and inquisitive as ever, they all came up to say hello and crowded around me.

'They're very friendly,' I said.

'Look down,' replied Mary, and I did, to see one of them chewing contentedly on the hem of my woolly jumper. I suppose she'd seen it from the other side of the field and decided she fancied it.

Coming back down the hill we were confronted by a view of little patchwork fields divided by hedgerows and punctuated by the short sharp hills of this part of Somerset. As often as not the whole was partly hidden by a cosy blanket of mist. Sleight Farm is a small mixed farm, which is rare in these days of large-scale specialised agriculture. Mary kept goats, pigs, some years a small herd of bullocks, some chickens, a goose or two, living side by side. This created views straight out of a Ladybird book of the farmyard.

This way of farming is elegant. You use the milk from your goats to make cheese, feed the whey to the pigs, whose dung feeds the fields and makes the good grass that feeds the goats that give you milk. I think this rhymes in Old English. It is certainly an ancient way of farming. Timothy Darvill, in his book *Prehistoric Britain*, wrote that 'Many of the settlements and farmsteads discussed here must have been surrounded by garden plots, paddocks, grazing areas, and of course patches of woodlands.'

He could have been describing Mary's farm.

I mentioned earlier that rennet is an animal product – to be more exact, it is derived from the abomasum or fourth stomach of a ruminant animal, and in most cases comes from a calf or kid. That's one of the less romantic aspects of cheesemaking.

There are, however, vegetarian alternatives. A more traditional option is a thistle native to Portugal called a cardoon. To turn this into a rennet-like substance, the cheesemaker traditionally soaks a bag of thistles in water and then wrings it out, making use of the resulting liquid. This is as painful as it sounds, and when I asked Mary about it she kindly let me have a try (she was using thistle juice in her Cardo cheese). More modern vegetarian rennet substitutes are also available, derived from a specially grown fungus, or from a process where genetic material from cattle produces chymosin, the main active ingredient in rennet.

As an ex-vegetarian (from my sixteenth to my twenty-sixth birthday), I am aware of the moral issues around eating animal products. These days I try just to eat as ethically as possible, mindful of how meat and dairy products are farmed. The hard fact is that if you consume dairy products you are to some extent involved in the death of animals. Calves, lambs and kids are, to put it bluntly, surplus to requirements in a dairy herd unless they are needed to replace a milking animal that has retired.

There are some positives, though. To make really good cheese you need really good milk, and to make really good milk you need happy, healthy, unstressed animals. Small-scale, high-quality cheese is about as ethical as farming gets. Also, cheesemakers (like most farmers) are decent human beings. I would almost go so far as to say that you can't make really good cheese if you are not.

And they aren't just nice to their animals for selfish reasons. Mary Holbrook called all her 'girls' by name and showed considerable affection for all her animals. Julie Cheney, who produces a small fudgey textured cow's milk cheese called St Jude, has a painting of her favourite dairy cow on her kitchen wall. And the Jones brothers, who make Lincolnshire Poacher, have a happy-cow scratching machine outside their milk parlour. There's a nice video of this on YouTube (search for 'happy cow' and 'poacher'), showing the cows forming a queue as they wait for their turn to step up and have a nice scratch. I can highly recommend it for our troubling times.

☙ ☙ ☙

CHAPTER TWO

Spenwood and Wigmore

What the Romans did for our cheese

43 CE–1066

THE BRITISH MUSEUM HOLDS SOME OF THE WORLD'S great treasures – the Rosetta Stone, the Sutton Hoo helmet, the Elgin Marbles. But I went there to see a cheese mould. Should you wish to do the same, it's to be found in Room 49, the Weston Gallery, along with other finds from Roman Britain. On the day I visited, the room was full of children chattering beside displays of swords and helmets. It was a bit less busy around the cheese mould case.

The mould is a small clay pot, reddish-brown, about eight inches across and three inches high, with holes in the bottom. It was found in 1882 amongst the remains of a Roman villa near Lower Halstow in Kent and I hope the archaeologist who discovered it was properly celebrated. The mould is in perfect condition and must look exactly as it did some one and a half to two thousand years ago, when a Romano-Kentish cheesemaker ladled curd into it before going off to have a cup of ale while waiting for the whey to drain off.

My quiet veneration was tinged with a little worry, though. The mould has a pronounced circular ridge in the bottom. And I could

The treasures of the British Museum – an actual Roman cheese mould.

not help thinking what a pain it would be to get it clean. You'd think, given their roads, aqueducts and other triumphs of civil engineering, that the Romans would have come up with a mould that was easier to wash.

This isn't just a rogue mould, either. I've seen quite a few of them now from villas and Roman army sites across Britain, and they are interestingly standardised, all the same shape and size and all with that ridge in the bottom. I really don't get what that is there for. Not only would it make washing up hard, but it would leave a groove in the top and bottom of the cheese (because you flip the cheese in the mould halfway through the making process), which would attract all sorts of mould and cheese mites. Perhaps that was the idea – both mould and mite can be used to ripen cheese. French affineurs have a method of cheese ripening that involves encouraging them. The well-known Mimolette is a result of this, a rock-hard orange cheese shaped like a flattened cannonball whose pockmarked rind is a result of mites eating away. Personally, having spent a significant part of my mongering career brushing mites off cheese, I'm not that keen on them.

The mould in the British Museum is labelled as a 'cheese press', but I've seen them referred to as cheese-strainers and, memorably, in an article about Roman army rations, a cheese squeezer. Ask any modern cheesemaker or monger, however, and they'll call it a mould – a way of shaping the curd as it drains. Moulds come in all sorts of shapes and sizes, from tall cylinders for Stilton, little round pots for St Jude and truncated pyramids for Tymsboro. They are mostly made from plastic these days, although I've heard of wicker ones still in use in the more remote bits of Spain.

☁ ☁ ☁

After a couple of false starts in 55 and 54 BCE under Julius Caesar, the Roman invasion of Britain really got going in 43 CE, under the Emperor Claudius. Two years earlier, the Praetorian guard had (quite understandably) murdered Claudius's psychotic nephew Caligula, and put Claudius on the throne without the blessing of the Senate. So he was in need of a win – and conquering Britain seemed like a good bet. Claudius duly sent over some legions and, three or four months later, the Emperor himself arrived to lead his troops into Camulodunum, modern Colchester. Thus began the Roman period, or occupation if you prefer, which lasted until the early fifth century.

The Romans never made it over to Ireland, at least as far as we know, and the Irish cheesemakers, free from Roman interference, carried on making their indigenous cheeses. As for Britain, we are all familiar with what the Romans brought over – roads, aqueducts, baths, centralised administration, taxes, etc. – but the burning questions for any decent historian of the period must be what sort of cheeses the Romans made in Britain, and how much they influenced British cheesemaking culture of the subsequent centuries.

The Romans were keen on cheese and thankfully some of them wrote about it in enthusiastic detail. Pliny the Elder, in his encyclopedic *Naturalis Historia*, written towards the end of the first century, celebrates the medical qualities of cheese, particularly in the treatment of tuberculosis and stomach ulcers, and claims that goat's cheese is more digestible than cow's milk cheese. He was possibly correct in this assertion – fat particles in goat's milk are smaller and more varied in size, making them easier to break down in the human digestive system.

Pliny describes some of the most popular cheeses consumed by the Romans. As ever, the cheeses of France, or – to be less anachronistic – Gaul, get a lot of love: 'the kinds of cheese most esteemed in Rome come from Nemausus, particularly Lesura and Gabalis', he writes. Nemausus is now known as Nîmes; Lesura and Gabalis are Lozère and Gévaudan. All are located in the Occitanie, in south-west France, whose most famous cheese is the mighty Roquefort, a blue sheep's milk cheese. Some of its makers have, as you might expect, claimed that theirs is the cheese Pliny was alluding to. I'm not entirely convinced, as Pliny continues: 'its excellence is only very short lived and it needs to be eaten while it is fresh'. Roquefort is a blue cheese, and the blue takes some weeks to develop, so it is hardly a fresh cheese.

I think a more plausible candidate for 'most esteemed in Rome' would be a soft goat's cheese like Pélardon, also produced in the Occitanie region, which might be ready to eat at one week old, and which you wouldn't want to keep for much longer than three weeks. According to Orbis – an incredibly cool piece of software that allows you to calculate journey times in the Roman world – the trip from Nemausus to Ostia, the port for Rome, would have taken seven and a half days, so the cheese could have arrived on the cheese counters of Rome in peak condition.

Pliny also mentions a cheese called Vatusican from the Centronian Alps, the modern Savoie region. Given that this would have had to make an arduous and bumpy journey down an Alp and along Gaulish roads to a Mediterranean port such as Massilia (modern Marseilles), it must have been something large enough to be worth shipping, and durable enough to survive, which immediately brings to mind Beaufort, a raw cow's milk cheese still made to this day in the region. These formidable cheeses are almost a metre in diameter and weigh about forty-five kilos, or ninety pounds. They belong in the Alpine family of cheeses and are not a million miles distant from the ever-more-popular Comté –

A cellar of Beaufort cheeses cared for by their affineur. The cheeses are being ripened in a manner described in the first century by Columella.

though their flavour is more intense, with notes of white chocolate and, oddly, liver.

The fact that Romans were consuming fancy imported cheese from the Alps and southern France suggests that cheese was a high-status food as much as a staple. *Apicius*, a first-century cookbook for the wealthier Roman, which survives in medieval manuscript copies, has a recipe for a chicken liver salad containing grated hard cheese, capers and pine nuts, with extra cream cheese in the dressing, and a cheese dip with fig syrup, fish sauce and wine. The pinnacle of Roman cheese cookery was known as the placenta, a two-foot-long pastry enclosing fourteen pounds of cheese. Those Romans knew how to live. Martial, another great Roman writer of the first century, includes some particularly prized cheeses like Vestina, a mild breakfast cheese, and Velabrum, a smoked cheese, in his list of appropriate gifts for the festival of Saturnalia.

Romans not only came up with medicinal uses, recipes and this year's must-have cheeses, they also wrote down how to make it. The most detailed recipes are in *Res Rustica* ('On Agriculture'), a manual of farming written by Lucius Junius Moderatus Columella, also in the first century. This devotes eight hundred words (in Book VII) to cheesemaking and it's clear that what it is describing is a full-on commercial operation, on a much grander scale than the sort of cottage industry I imagine was going on in Britain at the time.

Res Rustica explains the basic economics of cheesemaking, explaining that it can be a good way of making money if your farm is too far from a market where you could sell liquid milk; that if you make fresh soft cheese, you'll need to sell it quickly 'while it is fresh and still retains its moisture'; and that harder cheeses, of a 'rich and thick consistency', can not only keep for longer, but 'this kind of cheese can even be exported beyond the sea'.

Columella also understands the importance of good quality fresh milk and lists some vegetable products that you can use to coagulate milk, such as fig sap, safflower and thistle juice (which, as we noted earlier, Mary Holbrook adopted for her Cardo), but writes that the rennet of lambs or kids is better. He is very specific about the amount of rennet you need, which is one denarius' weight for every pail of milk, or about three and a half grams.

Once set, Columella instructs that the curd should be ladled into wicker cheese moulds to drain. He understands the importance of getting the whey off quickly and talks about how 'countryfolk' press the cheese under weights. When firm, the cheeses are turned out onto 'very clean boards' (showing that even then the importance of good hygiene was well understood) before being salted and pressed for nine days. At the end of this period the cheeses are washed and laid out on wicker trays to dry, taking care that they are not touching each other. Then, finally, comes a ripening phase, in which, 'so that the cheese may remain the more tender, it is closely packed on several shelves in an enclosed place which is not exposed to the winds.' It is hard to fault Columella's technique, which is almost identical to the way cheese is made today.

The ripening of cheese is a skilful and valuable craft that, a little shamefully, doesn't have a name in English. We borrow the French term, *affinage*, to describe it and refer to the person who practises it as an affineur. There couldn't be a clearer illustration of the different value placed on cheese in French and British cultures than this, although the fact that we have found the need to borrow the term tells you that things are getting better. I spent some of my happiest years in the cellar of Neal's Yard Dairy's Covent Garden shop learning how to be an affineur, and it's nice to think that on the whole, my forefathers in affinage would have recognised what we were doing.

Columella also talks about cheese flavoured with pine kernels or thyme, and cheeses that have been smoked and coloured over apple wood. As a younger monger, I didn't hold with the flavouring and smoking of cheese. I thought you should just make good cheese and not mess about with it. Having learnt that these practices have such a venerable history, I feel a bit less opposed to them. In fact, I admit one of my favourite soft sheep's milk cheeses, Lingot St Nicolas, made by an Orthodox monk called Père Gabriel in the south of France, is flavoured with thyme, and one of my favourite British cheesemakers, Tom Calver, smokes some of his Westcombe Cheddar in a smoker that he made himself out of an old telephone box.

Looking at Columella's recipe for a pressed and salted cheese made me think of a hard sheep's milk cheese called Spenwood, which is produced in Berkshire by Anne Wigmore. Berkshire (or at least the area we call Berkshire) was at the heart of Roman Britain and, by happy coincidence, Spenwood could almost have come out of that mould in the British Museum. It comes in discs that are about six inches across and two deep. Hard sheep's milk cheeses like Spenwood were made for the legionaries' rations, and I have to say that if rations were as good as Anne's cheese, with its sweet milky flavour and fruity acid notes, I'd have been tempted to join up. As long as they could give me something clerical to do, with no outdoor work, no heavy lifting and absolutely zero chance of being attacked by barbarians.

By the time the Spenwood cheeses arrive in Neal's Yard Dairy, they have already gone through their drying phase. Our job was to give them a final maturation that would allow them to express their full complex flavour. To do this, we packed them closely on shelves in the cellar of the Covent Garden shop – 'an enclosed place which is not exposed to the winds', in Columella's words. When they arrived as young cheeses, they were a pale ivory colour and slightly springy to the touch. A few weeks later, when they were ready to eat, they had developed an off-white rind and were much firmer, though not too hard or dry, remaining 'the more tender', just as Columella instructed.

Alongside the size, shape and texture, the other reason I am so confident in identifying Spenwood as the sort of cheese that would have been made in those ubiquitous Romano-British cheese moulds is that it is very similar to harder types of Pecorino sheep's milk cheese made in Italy today. Pecorino and its Spanish and Basque cousins, Manchego and Ossau Iraty, are – as smallish hard sheep's milk cheeses – a truly ancient style, getting a mention in 700 BCE or thereabouts in Homer's *Odyssey*, no less. When Odysseus and his shipmates hide in the cave of Polyphemus the Cyclops, they realise that, as well as being a one-eyed giant, he is a cheesemaker – and a good one at that. The Greek sailors notice that his cheeses are neatly laid out on racks to dry, and the whey (which would make a refreshing drink in the hot Mediterranean summer – or could be used as a starter culture) carefully stored. The narrative is thus one of the earliest written accounts of cheesemaking in European literature, a fact that unaccountably doesn't get much mention in the commentaries on Homer. Yet it is replete with detail. The Cyclops coagulates his milk (probably with fig sap, which was locally available) and presses the cheese lightly in wicker baskets, producing small cheeses that in the humid and cool conditions of his cave would have dried at just the right rate to produce a complex-flavoured cheese like Spenwood.

You might have noticed that in both Columella and Homer the cheese moulds are made of wicker and not clay. So why am I talking about clay moulds and not wicker ones? Well, one reason is that the clay ones survive for thousands of years, to end up in a museum on show to curious cheesemongers. The other is that you can press a cheese much harder in a clay mould than in a wicker one. The harder you press a cheese, the more moisture you will expel and the harder the resulting cheese will be, so it will keep longer and be more durable. These are both good qualities for a cheese if you want to sell it far afield. Dryness and durability are also useful in a cheese if you want to feed it to soldiers, as it will keep nicely in their packs, while they are yomping across the damper parts of Scotland.

In the last chapter I said that making cheese is a way of making milk digestible by converting lactose into lactic acid. But it's also a way of preserving milk by making it more acidic, and making milk portable by getting rid of all that heavy and non-nutritious water. These factors make cheese an excellent food for explorers and soldiers. In fact, throughout human history, cheese has been an important part of a soldier's ration. Hittite texts from the second millennium BCE mention 'aged soldiers' cheese', which historians have interpreted as a mature hard cheese for soldiers still young and hardy enough to gnaw on it, rather than a soft cheese for toothless old veterans.

Four thousand years later, the cheesemakers of Normandy generously supplied every French soldier fighting on the Western Front in the First World War with a Camembert. Not only was this an act of patriotic generosity, it was also a marketing strategy of genius –Camembert can trace its national fame in France from this period. It was a daring act, though, and one that showed the French are never shy of confirming to their national stereotype, favouring gourmandising over practicality – for Camembert is actually a soft, plump, creamy cheese, not particularly suited for trench life despite being enveloped in a delicate, velvety white rind. But that's exactly the point. It has a complex, piquant flavour reminiscent of cabbages, cream and pepper, and I like to think of a homesick poilu (a French Tommy) consoling himself with a morsel of Camembert, with a swig of rouge from his canteen, no matter how squishy the cheese had got.

British troops carry cheese in their ration packs today, although sadly they don't get a beefy Somerset Cheddar or a creamy morsel of Stilton. Jamie Davies, who runs The Cheese & Wine Shop in Darlington and used to be a soldier before he became a cheesemonger, told me that the army labels the foodstuff as 'cheese, processed'. Although he and his mates thought the stuff was so awful they called it 'cheese possessed'. That made me think that, given the choice, I'd rather join the French army, until I checked

French poilus enjoying a bit of Camembert in the trenches.

their current rations and found that the luscious Camembert has been replaced with triangles of *Vache qui rit* (those little silver triangles of *Laughing Cow* processed cheese). I think on balance I'll stick with the cheesemongering.

That the Roman army ate cheese made in moulds like the one at the British Museum is no idle speculation on my part. One was found at the fort of Corbridge in Northumberland just south of Hadrian's Wall, and another at Holt in north Wales, at the site of a legion's pottery and tile works, which suggests standardised moulds were produced for making army-issue cheese. A particularly well-preserved cheese mould turned up at Balmuildy Fort on the Antonine Wall, which marked the furthest Roman penetration into Scotland. So, you see, they were fuelling their Pict subjugation, such as it was, with cheese.

Archaeological finds also show that the Roman army was provided with some pretty decent wines. One of the most prized was Falernian from Surrentum (now Sorrento) in south Italy, where they still produce wines from the Falanghina grape. With their full-bodied, off-dry flavour, these make an excellent partner for certain cheeses. In fact, they would go beautifully with Spenwood, which also has a slightly caramelly sweetness. I imagine, in Roman times, the mature Falernian was largely reserved for the officers. The men got what is often described as 'sour' wine. This is a little unfair on the wine, for what they were really describing is young wine, which by virtue of its youth is sharp but also very refreshing – just the thing after a long dusty march along Watling Street.

The troops, like all soldiers before or since, were fond of their beer, too, as we can see in a letter found at Vindolanda, a major fort on Hadrian's Wall. In this missive, Masculus, a cavalry decurion, asks his commanding office Flavius Cerialis about troop dispositions for the following day but swiftly gets to the nugget: 'My fellow soldiers have no beer. Please order some to be sent.' That's the sort of officer I'd like to serve under.

Perhaps Flavius Cerialis would have ordered the beer from Tertius the Brewer, whose name appears on one of the writing tablets found at a Roman army site fort in Carlisle and also on a tablet found in a recent dig in the City of London, prior to the building of the Bloomberg banking HQ. The Bloomberg tablets are a breathtaking find, comprising the wooden backing tablets on which wax would be laid for document-writing. Faint traces of words scratched into the wax still remain in the wood, giving us a tantalisingly personal glimpse into life in early Roman London. The most significant tablet is a contract between two freed slaves, Tibullus and Gratus. It is the oldest dated document to be found from Roman Britain, which makes it the oldest document in Britain. Written on 8 January 57 CE, it's an IOU from Tibullus to Gratus for the sum of '105 denarii from the price of the merchandise which has been sold and delivered'. Sadly it doesn't stipulate what merchandise, so I am going to please myself by imagining that part of the delivery was excellent Spenwood-style cheeses.

The army was 'responsible more than anything else for those defining characteristics of Romanisation', contends Guy de la Bédoyère in his book, *Roman Britain*. That being the case, it is worth asking how much, as keen makers and eaters of cheese, the Roman army influenced the course of British cheese history. It's important not to think of the Roman army as like modern armies, which aren't much involved in everyday civilian life. In Roman Britain you might meet legionaries acting as policemen or tax collectors, or working as civil engineers and builders on the roads, aqueducts and, more importantly, the forums and basilicas, the market-places and seats of local government. Around permanent forts, like Vindolanda and Birdoswald on Hadrian's Wall, civilian settlements called vici developed as locals realised there was money to be made providing food, drink and whatever else a legionary on leave might want to spend his hard-won denarii on. With legionaries and local labourers working together and swapping their packed lunches, we can assume the locals must have tried Roman-style cheese. Maybe the army cheesemakers hired local help from the vici. Since the locals had already been making cheese for four thousand years, it wouldn't have been hard to train them up to more technical cheesemaking.

The first steps of making a cheese like Spenwood are just the same as for a soft fresh cheese like Sleightlett, souring milk with lactophilic bacteria and adding rennet to coagulate it. However, to make a harder, more durable and longer-keeping cheese, extra steps are required. The curd is cut while still in the vat, allowing more of the liquid whey to be released, and is heated and stirred

51

after cutting. I wouldn't for a moment say that fresh cheesemakers lack skill, but these more technical steps do require that the cheesemaker knows what size the morsels of cut curd should be and has the skill to cut cleanly and consistently, and the experience (especially before thermometers) to know how much to heat the curd and how long to stir it, before going back to another of the steps common to all cheesemaking, draining off the whey.

If the British cheesemakers were used to making simpler, fresh cheeses, it must have been an eye-opener to see their Roman counterparts using curd knives and large metal vats to heat curd to the higher temperatures and make the amounts required to service the army's requirements. They must, after all, have had to make a lot of cheese. The first-century historian Livy says that the cheese ration for a legionary was one ounce (twenty-eight grams) per day. For a legion at its full strength of five thousand men, that's a hundred and forty kilos of cheese a day, or seventy whole Spenwoods. But then, of course, they'd only be making cheese in the spring and summer, when the animals were giving milk. So to tide the army over the autumn and winter, you'd need to make something like a hundred cheeses a day. This raises the intriguing thought that it was the Romans who introduced large-scale standardised cheesemaking to Britain and are ultimately responsible for block Cheddar. Thanks, Romans.

Since the army recruited from all over the Empire, other cheese cultures might also have found their way to Britain. Dacian auxiliaries were stationed on the Wall for most of the second and third centuries, giving them plenty of time to hang out with the locals and share their cheese. The Dacians, from modern Romania, might have brought their Brinza Burduf ('bellows cheese'), a rural sheep's milk cheese still made in the mountains of Transylvania and hung in a sheep- or goatskin bag to mature. Brinza is a *pasta filata* or stretched-curd cheese, where the curd is set into a firm rubbery texture and pulled and stretched, a bit like making noodles or toffee. It's possible that the Romans learnt the *pasta filata* method

Roman cheesemaking techniques still in use for Spenwood: cutting, heating and stirring the curd to make harder cheeses.

after their invasion of Dacia, resulting ultimately in one of the most famous Italian cheeses – mozzarella.

Another way that Roman cheese culture might have influenced that of the British Isles would be the adoption of Roman practices to display social status. It seems that the people of south-east Britain were the most Romanised in the period leading up to the invasion, a time known to archaeologists as the Late Pre-Roman Iron Age or LPRIA. Finds of Mediterranean amphorae – in the words of Guy de la Bédoyère, 'the cardboard box, oil drum and packing case of its age' – tend to cluster in this part of Britain. These were the people that Caesar describes as being most civilised, where 'most civilised' really means 'most like us'. So, by the time of Claudius's invasion, the Briton upper classes already sent gifts to Roman emperors and went to them with their problems. Indeed, it was an internal coup against the Roman client king Verica that provided a pretext for the 43 CE invasion.

Not that the Romans were ready to accept the Britons as equals. The historian Tacitus wrote scathingly about the adoption of Roman culture by the local British elites: 'a liking sprang up for our style of dress, and the toga became fashionable. Step by step, they were led to things which dispose to vice, the lounge, the bath, the elegant banquet. All this in their ignorance, they called civilisation, when it was but a part of their servitude.'

A lot of this disposition to vice was going on in the villas of the wealthy upper-class Romano-Britons. The most complete of these to have been unearthed is Fishbourne in West Sussex, which by 75 CE or so was a palace of four wings around a garden, covering ten acres. Someone really important must have lived here – one candidate is the British client king Tiberius Claudius Togidubnus, who had been brought up in Rome and may have succeeded Verica. If Togidubnus wanted to entertain his friends and relations in high Roman style, he might have laid out a nice cheeseboard of fancy foreign imports – perhaps Vatusican, the Beaufort ancestor from the Savoie, or Cantal, a large, hard, aggressively flavoured cow's milk cheese from the Auvergne. There might have been some home-produced offerings too – cheese was made in these villas, as the discovery of a cheese mould in the Lower Halstow villa attests.

And remember that Columella referred to cheese flavoured with pine nuts or other flavourings – these might, as softer cheeses, have been made in wicker baskets, along with smoked cheeses, neither of which would show up in the archaeological record. So Tiberius's cheeseboard is starting to look a bit more respectable – a couple of foreign imports, a nice soft cheese rolled in Kentish cob nuts, some smoked sheep's cheese. Maybe he brought out some of that famous Falernian to accompany it. A late-harvested wine (meaning that the grapes have shrunk and the sugar concentrated), Falernian was aged in amphorae for up to twenty years, a process which would have made it taste much like Madeira or sherry. That sweet and oxidised flavour would have made the wine a great partner for cheese, and the ageing process would have made it impressively expensive. For a modern-day equivalent, you might try the orange wines of Georgia, which are still fermented in gigantic amphorae buried in the earth.

I imagine some of Tiberius's British clients, possibly distant relatives, subservient to him and reliant on his patronage, arriving at the entrance to the villa. They would have been led through the formal gardens to the reception hall, marvelling at the complex mosaics and brightly painted stucco. Later on, they might have found themselves in the triclinium or dining room, feeling slightly uncomfortable lying on the unfamiliar couches – Romans considered it a mark of civilisation to eat lying down – surrounded by wall paintings of sylvan scenes, with nubile nymphs pursued by priapic satyrs. If this assault on the visual sense wasn't enough, after dinner or before, when their appetites were sharp, they might have been offered that cheeseboard of which we spoke so highly. For a palate used to simple soft fresh cheese and ale, it must have been overwhelming and wonderfully exciting. I like to imagine these clients, heading back under the stars, to their village of wattle and daub huts, a little unsteady on their pins and also drunk on flavour. Just as I was on my first day at Neal's Yard Dairy, when I tasted all sixty cheeses on the counter and a door opened onto a marvellous new world.

Romano-British towns – with their populations of artisans, shop-keepers, labourers and farmers coming in to sell their produce – would also have been a place where locals could have tried some Roman-style cheeses. Perhaps not the fancy imported stuff, but at least the locally made ones. Cheese and other dairy products would have been on sale in the forum, which in the larger towns

Supine Romans enjoying their cheeseboard – as imagined by the Victorians.

would have contained a macellum, a covered market. Examples have been found at Leicester, Wroxeter, Colchester and St Albans (Verulamium). Most tantalising for the historically minded cheesemonger is a find at Silchester, a village in Hampshire known to the Romans as Calleva Atrebatum. It is thought that one of the buildings discovered in its forum might have been a dairy, with a milking parlour out the back and a cool room with a stone slab on which cheese and other dairy products might have been kept. Maybe that was where Tiberius Claudius's chef bought his cheese.

So, as assistant cheesemakers in army dairies, as guests at the dinner table of a villa, or as customers at Calleva's forum, the British were exposed to Roman cheese and cheesemaking. What I'm curious about is how thoroughly people took up Roman culture and how much this changed British cheesemaking.

Fortunately, it turns out that someone has asked this question before – albeit about Rome's effect on British foodways in general rather than specifically about cheese. The study is a PhD thesis submitted by Gillian Hawkes at the University of Leicester and it takes archaeological reports from high- and low-status sites in central Britain, occupied both before and during the Roman period, and looks at what these suggest about changes in food culture. Concentrating on the East Midlands, and a people called the Corieltauvi, the study found that high-status sites were more likely to show the adoption of Roman foodways than low-status ones, and urban sites more than rural, which isn't too surprising.

These findings were largely based on changes in the material culture at the sites – that is, changes in the kinds of equipment used for preparing and serving food. So, if you find that people swapped their grandmother's saddle quern for a mortarium, a characteristically Roman sort of mortar, you can infer that they were adopting Roman foodways. But at all levels of society, rural and urban, the British picked and chose what they wanted from the Roman cultural package, maintaining much of their core culture. It appears, for example, that even high-status Corieltauvi remained largely beer drinkers rather than moving to wine, and that they kept on with the native practice of hunting and eating wild game. If what you eat is more a part of your essential core culture than how you prepare and serve it, then this shows the persistence of a native culture under a veneer of the Roman.

Roman cheesemaking (and cheese-eating) in Britain went on for almost four hundred years – or roughly twelve generations of Romano-British cheesemakers. Then in 410 CE the Emperor Honorius wrote to the Britons to tell them that from now on they were on their own regarding the defence of Britain, as he was too busy with the Visigoths, who in August of that year went on to sack Rome itself, accelerating the decline of the western Roman Empire.

A prevalent image of the transition from the Roman period in Britain is that it was swift, comprehensive and violent, with Romano-British aristocrats cowering in the ruins of their villas, besieged by marauding bands of unsubdued Picts and opportunist Saxons. Meanwhile the decaying towns were deserted by their barely civilised inhabitants, who, having thrown off the shackles of urban life, joyfully returned to their muddy villages of round wattle and daub huts. In truth, it seems the change from Roman to self-rule may not have been as sudden as this view suggests.

A fascinating account of the transition from a Romanised society to, well, something else, is given by Tony Wilmott in an article titled 'Roman Commanders, Dark Age Kings'. Wilmott excavated Birdoswald, the most significant fort on Hadrian's Wall, and discovered a granary that during the zenith of Roman rule would have contained grain for the garrison's rations, but was re-purposed some time in the late fourth or early fifth century. A hearth was built at one end and near to it some high-status objects were found – a ring, an earring and a late Roman silver coin. The building in this incarnation looks a lot like a chieftain's hall. Wilmott sees in this sequence the metamorphosis of a Roman commander, who may have already become something like a local governor or magistrate, into a local chief or king, and suggests that the legion or cohort that he commanded, which by then might have had a generous proportion of local lads, had become his private army.

This might seem to us like a step back, from the orderly centralised government of Rome to something with more than a hint of Mad Max about it. But there are other ways of looking at this change. There is an idea that the final end of Roman rule in Britain was partly brought about by a revolt of the Romano-British elite who were tired of paying taxes to a distant authority that had, to be frank, not been doing a very good job, as border raids culminated in 367 with the 'barbarian conspiracy' in which Picts, Scots, Franks and Saxons raided and plundered across Britain and Gaul. In this light you could see this local leader, his men and

A Roman mortarium, made in Britain and stamped on the rim with the name of its manufacturer, Sollus. A useful addition to the Romano-British kitchen.

the local people, not as the last remnants of a Romanised society forlornly banding together to resist the barbarian tide, but as a bunch of scrappy independent-minded people, happy to go their own way.

An alternative view to this idea of sudden and catastrophic urban decay is that towns had been decreasing in importance in Roman Britain as power centres moved to the villas. It is possible, then, to see the decline of towns in the fifth and sixth centuries as part of a longer process and not of a sudden collapse of society.

Of course, there was a great change in society as Roman central government faded away, characterised by a process referred to as 'radical material simplification' by Paul Freedman, Professor of Medieval History at Yale. What this means is that there is suddenly (in archaeological terms) a lot less stuff. You can see the process as you walk from one room in the British Museum to another. The Roman Britain room is full of everyday objects and tools which are movingly familiar: scissors, tweezers, spoons and bowls, saws, picks and hammers, and, of course, cheese moulds. But go into the 'early medieval' room next door and you notice there are far fewer everyday objects. What has survived is much more high-status: jewellery, religious art and artefacts and weapons.

Two things notably disappear from the archaeological record in the fifth century: coins and pottery. Coin finds tail off in Britain from the late fourth century as Rome's grasp on the province becomes more tenuous, and pottery, as a product of a centralised, cash economy, follows. So, I hear you say, thanks for the history lesson, but what has this got to do with cheese? Well, what I'm getting at is that just because we stop finding Roman pottery cheese moulds, it doesn't mean that people stopped making cheese in Britain in 410, or even that they stopped making Roman-style cheese. The cheese industry, producing military rations, must have disappeared. But local cheesemaking probably continued, albeit less often using clay moulds, which when they broke were probably replaced with locally made wicker or wooden versions.

If there is one figure who personifies early medieval Britain, it is King Arthur. The image of Arthur has changed considerably over the centuries and even in my own lifetime. The idea of a chivalrous knight in a Disney castle, familiar to those of us who saw John Boorman's *Excalibur* when we were kids (I was nine), has given way to a picture of a shaggy ex-Roman war-leader or *dux bellorum*, spending his evenings indulging in a little decorous carousing with his war band in a prototype mead hall.

If this sounds familiar, it is because the hall and its occupant in Birdoswald fort would make a great candidate for this sort of Arthur. Especially given that the few contemporary texts that do mention a possible Arthur tend to place him in the north rather than the sites with which he is associated – Tintagel and Glastonbury – in south-west England.

If there was an Arthur, based in Birdoswald, Catterick, Colchester or indeed Tintagel, what sort of cheese would he have eaten? Or, to put it another way, what did Britain do to Roman cheese?

My answer is mould-ripened cheese. This is not a cheese that has been ripened in a mould – but cheese that has been ripened with mould. The mould rind is encouraged to grow on the cheese as it matures and contributes significantly to the flavour and texture of the cheese. The moulds and yeast on the rind actually change the cheese itself, growing tiny roots into the paste called cilia, which break down the structure of the firm young cheese, lowering acidity, making it more creamy and finally liquid. Imagine a very ripe Camembert which, when you cut it, splurges out across your cheeseboard. Also, notice the sharp aroma and peppery flavour. This is largely down to the production of ammonia – a side effect of this ripening process. But it is also due to the micro-organisms of the moulds and yeast, which have their own flavours, from a slightly astringent flavour of the white mould *Penicillium camemberti* to the cabbagey flavour of the yeast *Geotrichum*.

Camembert may be the best-known example of a mould-ripened cheese, and people tend to think of it as a French style. Brie is also a member of this family. However, there are plenty of modern examples made in the British Isles. One that I like is Tunworth, made by Stacey Hedges in Hampshire. This is actually directly inspired by Camembert – so much so that French chef Raymond Blanc once described it as the best Camembert in the world.

If you are unfortunate enough to have only tried these sorts of cheeses in their more industrial form, you might be wondering why I'm talking about them with such enthusiasm. Appearing on the shelves of supermarkets and, in the case of Brie, often pre-cut into single wedges completely covered in a mould rind, these snowy white smooth-surfaced cheeses don't have the sort of intensity and complexity of flavour that I celebrate in a Tunworth or its French uncle, Camembert. This is partly due to their smooth white rind, *Penicillium camemberti*, the mould formerly known as *Candidum*, which more industrial cheesemakers like to use in great quantities, since it produces an unchallenging and uniform appearance and a more consistent if less interesting flavour. It's also easy to deal with just one mould rather than an unruly population of competing moulds, yeasts and bacteria that might otherwise come along to join the party.

More adventurous cheesemongers like to seek out the ugly fruit of the mould-ripened family – farmhouse-style Camemberts, or Tunworth itself. Here, the white *Candidum* is joined by the wrinkly textured *Geotrichum*, 'the mould that wants to be a yeast', as it has been memorably described, and the orange colour of some *Coryneform bacteria*. These helpful micro-organisms confer complexity, adding those cabbagey notes I mentioned, perhaps a tinge of sulphur and an edge of washed-rind funk. These multicultural populations take a bit more looking after, which is where the skill of the affineur comes in, creating conditions amenable to all, not allowing one

Tunworth, baked and served with sourdough. A meal fit for a king – or a Romano-British warlord.

micro-organism to dominate the others, so ending up with a much more complex and interesting cheese.

Like so many aspects of cheesemaking, including its very discovery, I am pretty sure that mould-ripened cheeses originated by accident. And I think it happened in North European countries that had adopted Roman cheesemaking methods. Remember Columella, he of the authentically detailed Roman cheese recipes? He also has a recipe for a soft cheese which he calls 'hand pressed cheese', in which the curd is broken up in the vat and washed in hot water, then shaped by hand or pressed into wooden moulds. As this cheese isn't pressed and salted repeatedly, it would end up soft and creamy; in fact, the washing of the curd would create a particularly silky unctuous texture.

In a warm Mediterranean climate you would need to eat softer cheese within a few days, before it went rancid, which is just what Columella says about the kind of cheese you would get using this method. It would have been eaten fresh and young. However, if you were making a cheese like this in a cooler climate, you could ripen it for longer, allowing the development of a nice, interesting rind made up of whatever indigenous moulds and yeasts were living in your dairy or cellar. I imagine that, although the very first mould-ripened cheeses would have looked pretty gnarly and tasted quite wild, a bit of trial and error over a few batches would have set the cheesemaker on the right path towards an acceptably consistent and tasty product.

🧀 🧀 🧀

As if by happy accident, Anne Wigmore, who makes Spenwood, descendant of the legionaries' cheese, also makes a soft mould-ripened cheese – the eponymous Wigmore – and, as if she had designed it to fit in this chapter, is is also a washed-curd cheese just like the one in Columella's recipe.

Anne began making her cheese in 1986 in the prosaic location of a 'garden outbuilding' or shed in Spencers Wood, near Reading. Anne has an interesting background for an artisanal cheesemaker in that she originally worked as a microbiologist at the National Institute for Research in Dairying. She began her cheesemaking career in their research dairy and set up her own operation, Village Maid Cheese, in 1986. Most artisan cheesemakers I know either fell into the trade from something completely different and had to pick up the craft of cheesemaking as they went along, like Mary Holbrook, or grew up in a cheesemaking family, like Quinlan Steele, maker of the rambunctious Milleens cheese. It is a very different path to begin from a background of scientific knowledge and rigorous empirical cheesemaking in a research dairy and then to develop that into a more craftsmanlike style of cheesemaking ... and to make such delicious, complex and fascinating cheese.

The reason that Anne makes sheep's milk cheese is also interesting, as it tells us something about the state of artisanal cheesemaking in Britain in the 1980s. Back then, the hand of the Milk Marketing Board lay heavily on the shoulders of farmhouse cheesemakers: the MMB bought their milk and then sold it back to them to make cheese. The problem was, if you were a small-scale cheesemaker, the MMB might refuse to sell you any milk, since it was deemed inefficient to deal with small producers. However, they were only bothered with cow's milk. If you wanted to make a sheep's milk cheese, you were a lot freer to operate.

Anne had another reason for using sheep's milk, and one that in its eccentricity and adventurousness is typical of so many cheesemakers. Around the time that she began to think about making her own cheese, some friends invited her to sail to Australia with them on their home-built yacht. Stopping off along the way in Sardinia, Anne tried the native cheese, Pecorino Sardo, and on her return to Britain after six months of nautical adventures she decided to try making something similar. Pecorino Sardo is a hard sheep's cheese, in size and shape much like the cheese I believe

Anne Wigmore, looking after her Spenwood cheeses. Like many British cheese pioneers, she began in the late 1980s.

would have come out of those Roman moulds and also much like the cheese that Odysseus found the Cyclops making.

Wigmore, the soft washed-curd cheese I mentioned earlier, was developed after Anne's business had outgrown its original site and moved to larger premises in nearby Riseley. Neal's Yard Dairy were looking for a soft, mould-ripened sheep's milk cheese to fill a gap in their range and encouraged Anne to make one. After months of development, which I imagine involved a few sub-par batches and some very happy pigs (pigs love cheese and are not too discerning about its quality), Wigmore was born. As a washed-curd cheese, it has a silky texture quite different from the more mouth-coating heavy creaminess of something like a Camembert.

It's important not to confuse curd-washing with rind-washing. The trick with curd-washing is that, while the curd is still in the vat, some of the whey is drained off to be replaced with hot water (which ultimately creates that lovely silky texture). As we saw from Columella's recipe, this method has been around for at least a couple of thousand years. Rind-washing is another thing altogether, as we will explore in the next chapter. It's also worth noting from Columella's recipe that you wouldn't need a lot of sophisticated equipment to make this sort of cheese. So, if you were living in a culture that had just undergone 'radical material simplification', this would be a cheese to go for.

It pains me to say such a thing, but I suspect that cheesemaking innovation wasn't high on people's list of priorities in post-Roman Britain. In 450 CE, the Saxons turned up in force and these war-like pagans wiped out the indigenous Christian Britons, driving their remnants into Wales and over the channel to Western France (hence 'Brittany'). Or at least this is what the sixth-century Christian writer Gildas tells us, and many historians to this day have followed his narrative – one of invasion, conquest and the whole-sale replacement of one population with another.

Gildas is also one of the near-contemporary writers to mention an Arthurian candidate, a Romano-British war leader called Ambrosius Aurelianus, who, he writes, briefly stemmed the Saxon tide at the battle of Mount Badon around 500 CE. Sadly, Gildas didn't think to mention what kind of cheese Ambrosius liked.

There is a conflicting account of the Saxon takeover of Britain, which, like the end of Romano-Britain, argues that the Saxon arrival was not so sudden nor so catastrophic. Saxon warrior bands did come over, then unseat and replace the British aristocracy, but the rest of the British people weren't driven off or killed, or at least not to the devastating degree that Gildas would have us believe.

However genocidal it was, the Saxon takeover was certainly thorough. In the words of the brilliant medieval historian Janina Ramirez, 'it was to transform the complexion of the British Isles permanently'. As a measure of how thorough this change was, Ramirez points out that Modern English, for all its Latin, Scandinavian and French influences, has almost no trace of the earlier British language; in her words, 'a linguistic cleansing' took place.

Things nonetheless settled down into a rough-and-ready stability, such that by the end of the fifth century there were seven Saxon kingdoms: East Anglia, Essex, Kent, Mercia, Northumbria, Sussex, and Wessex. A sign of increasing stability is that, by the end of the seventh century, coins – silver pennies called sceattas – start appearing once more in the archaeological record. Another sign of stability that makes the historian of cheese sigh with relief is that people started to write things down again.

What writings that survive to shed even the dimmest light on cheesemaking are largely legal documents, laws and charters, and medical texts. One of the earliest of the legal documents is the Laws of Ine, King of Wessex, inscribed between 688 and 726. One entry stipulates the land rent payable to the king for an estate of ten hides:

> Ten vats of honey, three hundred loaves, twelve ambers of Welsh ale, thirty of clear ale, two full-grown cows or ten wethers, ten geese, twenty hens, ten cheeses, an amber-full of butter, five salmon, twenty pound-weights of provisions and one hundred eels.

At first glance this may not seem to tell us much about seventh-century Wessex cheese, but actually this passage does contain

The science of cheesemaking – Anne Wigmore testing the acidity of her curds.

some interesting information if you tease it apart a bit. The first thing that strikes me is that cheese is considered a worthy rent for a king, or at at least for a king's household. Another thing is that whoever wrote these laws down didn't feel the need to say anything about how big these cheeses should be or whether they are hard or soft. Notice there is some detail about the cows, which must be fully grown, and the ale, Welsh or clear. This lack of detail about the cheese suggests to me that there was some standardisation in cheesemaking and the lawmaker is confident that everyone will know what is meant by 'ten cheeses'. Remember that standardisation was a concern for Roman cheesemakers, whether they were making cheese on an estate for sale in local markets or for the army. So perhaps the Anglo-Saxon cheesemakers of seventh-century Wessex were still making a Roman-style cheese, or at least one that had its roots in a Roman style, even if two hundred years later the recipe and the cheese itself may have mutated a bit.

Welsh kings, it appears, were not averse to a bit of cheese either. Hywell Dda ruled most of what is now modern Wales between 942 and 950. His name meant 'Hywell the Good', so named because his laws were considered to be just and fair, and these laws have a couple of things to say about cheese. Like Ine, Hywell was happy to have land rents paid to him in the form of cheeses, although he, a sensible man indeed, stipulated that cheese be part of the *dawnbwyd*, or food gift, in the summer, when it would be nice and fresh. Hywell's laws are not only comprehensive but impressively enlightened when it comes to the rights of women, in marriage and divorce. The laws list those things that a wife can give away without the consent of her husband, and these include cheese, butter and milk. In case of divorce, the woman is entitled to 'all the cheese which shall be in brine and unsalted'.

One thing this tells us is that the Welsh cured their cheeses in a brine bath a thousand years ago, just as the Trethowan family still do with their Gorwydd Caerphilly cheese today. Another thing it reveals is that the dairy was the province of women, and that if cheese was a food of some importance, worthy of a gift for a king, then dairy women probably had some social status in their communities. These laws weren't created out of nowhere by Hywell, but based on existing custom, which tells us that cheesemaking and dairying had been the province of women for some time. Other texts of the time confirm the place of women in both making and selling cheese. The *Rectitudines Singularum Personum* is a manual of Anglo-Saxon estate management, the surviving Old English version of which was written down in the late eleventh or early twelfth century. It lists the duties and rights of the workers on an estate, of whom the only female is the cheesemaker. Here is what she got:

> The cheesemaker is entitled to a hundred cheeses and is to make butter for the lords table from the whey, and she is to have all the buttermilk except the herdsmans share.

A hundred cheeses seems like a pretty good wage to me. And the buttermilk is a nice perk, too.

We also know that not only were there cheesemongers in London in the tenth century, but that they were women, too. Aethelred, who was king of Mercia from 978 to 1013, taxed the women cheesemongers of London a penny a week in the lead up to Christmas. That may not sound like a lot, but here are some things you could buy with a single penny according to Regia Anglorum, the Early Mediaeval Re-enactment Society: fifteen chickens, one-twentieth of a pig; one-tenth of a sheep; half a kilo of corn; a cow's eye. Apart from what this tells us about cheesemongers in London, what in heaven's name were they doing with the cow's eyes that made them worth fifteen chickens?

This was a higher tax than at other times of year, so clearly Christmas was a good time for the cheesemongers of London, a fact which hasn't changed in a thousand years. At Neal's Yard Dairy, Christmas was such an important time for us that we started planning for it in January. Also, if profits were higher in the lead-up to a major festival, cheese must have been a luxury item as well as a staple, with some cheeses more highly prized than others. Sadly, laws and charters aren't overly concerned with what kind of cheese the king is getting as rent or what kind of cheese his tax-paying cheesemongers are selling from their London stalls.

Cheese also makes the occasional appearance in Anglo-Saxon leechbooks, or medical texts. Goat's cheese, when directly applied to the afflicted part, was reckoned good for hot and itchy eyes, headaches and diseases of the feet. Cheese boiled in honey was good for lung disease, which recalls Pliny's advice to treat tuberculosis with cheese. Hallowed bread and cheese will cure 'a wit sick man' and 'new cheese' shredded into boiling water, made into little cakes and tied to the eyes, 'will be a remedy for eyes that have been struck or are bleared'. The leechbooks also contain some helpful advice on the interpretation of dreams of cheese. If you dream of being given new cheese, you are going to come into some money, but if the cheese is salty, you're going to get into an argument. (If – and this has nothing to do with cheese, but is too good not to share – you dream of camels and are odious to them, you are also going to get into an argument.)

Sadly for the British, or Anglo-Saxons, and by extension for the Scots, Welsh and Irish, after the Saxon consolidation and a brief period of Vikingless stability, things were about to get rough again, as 1066 and its concomitant Normans loomed on the horizon. Thankfully, for the history of cheesemaking, there was the fringe benefit of monks.

🧀 🧀 🧀

Milleens

The benefit of monks

1066–1348

IT'S A TOUGH LIFE BEING A CHEESE HISTORIAN. The research can take you all over the place – like a farmhouse on the Beara Peninsula, in County Cork, where I found myself eating one of Ireland's most famed cheeses, while admiring the dramatic, sea-girt landscape. For a Londoner like me, this was about as remote as it gets, and the cheese – a soft, pink washed-rind called Milleens – was fabulous.

Washed-rinds are the Marmite of the cheese world. Their flavour can have a savoury (or, as we cheesemongers say, umami) note and a smoky element that can make you think of smoked bacon or even peanuts. Some people consider their rambunctious flavour to be a peak gourmet experience; others wonder why you would put something quite so stinky in your mouth. I am, of course, in the former camp, and I do believe that a taste for washed-rinds is one that you can acquire. For example, you could – and perhaps should – start by trying a gentle Gubbeen, then progress to a more earthy Durrus, before moving on to a Milleens. All of these cheeses are made not far from each other in County Cork and this is no accident. Being on the Atlantic coast, it's a wet and salty place, conditions that favour the making of washed-rind cheeses.

The three I've mentioned are all products of a renaissance of Irish cheesemaking that began in the 1970s, but it's possible that cheeses very much like them were made here a long time ago, for washed-rind cheeses are widely believed to have been discovered or invented by monastic cheesemakers in medieval Europe. Classic, ancient examples like Munster from Alsace-Lorraine and Époisses from Champagne-Ardennes seem to back that up, and their fame means that washed-rinds tend to be thought of as a Northern European style. However, I'm convinced that washed-rind cheeses also have a much longer history in Ireland and Britain, one that begins in the very earliest medieval monasteries.

It's possible that washed-rind cheeses were actually invented in Ireland, and that their secret was taken by missionary monks to continental Europe in the evangelising missions of the sixth century. Some authorities – and Veronica Steele, progenitor of Milleens, was one – say that Alsace Munster got its name from the Irish province where it was originally made. It's a decent story, if unlikely to win you many friends among the cheesemongers of France.

When first made, washed-rind cheeses are – like all very young cheeses – white and firm with not much flavour. If you left them to their own devices in a cellar, they would grow white or greyish rinds and become mould-ripened cheeses like Wigmore. Their magical washed-rind transformation is effected by making a gentle brine solution of about three per cent salt, moistening a cloth with it, and giving each cheese a rub on one side, then flipping it over and doing the other, not forgetting to give the edges a quick go too. The applied salt discourages the moulds from growing and at the same time creates ideal conditions for one of my favourite families of bacteria, *Brevibacterium linens*, or *B. linens*. This bacterium grows into a rind which varies between pink and orange in colour and

Two local schoolchildren help judge Britain's smelliest cheese at the Royal Bath and West Show, 2009. The winner was Charles Martell's Stinking Bishop, made at his farm in Dymock.

imparts those flavours characteristic of the washed-rind style – its noted funkiness and umami. The rind can also help to break down the firm texture of the paste – the cheese inside the rind. These cheeses can range from quite firm examples like Gubbeen, to creamier Milleens and the oozing Stinking Bishop made over the Irish Sea in Gloucestershire.

B. linens is a naturally occurring bacterium, and in the fertile conditions of a medieval cheese cellar, once you had created an amenable environment for the cheese, it would have moved right in. In the more sterile atmosphere of a modern dairy, it might need a little help. One way to do this is to wash some of the older cheeses first and transfer the *B. linens* onto the younger ones on the cloth you use to wash them with, a process analogous to using whey from the previous day to start your cheese-make, or adding yeast from yesterday's brew to get today's going.

Washing cheeses is about the most dramatic transformation an affineur can impose on a young cheese. It's quite exciting to see the cheese's colour change over a few days from white to pink and the texture break down to soft and creamy. I remember in my early days as a monger feeling drunk with power, wanting to wash every cheese in the cellar. There's a bit of skill to it, though. You don't want your cheese to come out too wet and sticky, so a bit of restraint with the wetting of the cloth is required. And, as with all the tasks of the affineur, you must be alert and alive to the variation between types of cheese like Milleens and Gubbeen, and even between different batches of the same cheese. Some cheeses need to develop on their own for a bit longer before they're washed, or be washed more frequently as the pink rind begins to develop. This takes some experience, as well as a willingness to experiment.

The amount of attention that washed-rinds require is one reason for believing that these cheeses originated in the monasteries. In the post-Roman world, it seems likely that most, if not all, cheesemaking was on a small scale – peasant cheesemaking, in fact. Traditionally, the peasant cheesemaker was the the woman of the household, who had to find time for it alongside spinning thread, baking bread, brewing beer and looking after the pigs, chickens and children. A method like that for Mary Holbrook's Sleightlett would fit best into that kind of working day – a punctuated make, where, after adding rennet, there would be a long stretch of time to do other things while the milk set. Cheeses eaten fresh don't require much looking after, nor do older cheeses left to grow a rind, other than a bit of turning and rubbing now and then.

In a medieval monastery, with plenty of hands available, work was divided up in such a way that monks specialised in certain tasks, and it's easy to imagine someone having the time and mental space to devote to washing cheeses. Another part of the monastic origin story is that the monks liked the rich, meaty flavours of washed-rind cheeses as a replacement for meat on fast days. But I don't think this bit is plausible. Cheese was considered to be a meat, albeit a 'white meat', and was banned on fast days.

Also, it would be wrong to think of washed-rind cheese as the only form of monastic cheese. In the great houses of the Benedictines and Cistercians, some monks were much more equal than others. If these full-flavoured and high-maintenance washed-rinds were made in the monasteries of Britain and Ireland, I think they would mostly have been consumed by the abbot and the senior monks, while the rank and file, known as the choir monks, would have eaten simpler fare. These were probably harder cheeses made from skimmed milk where the cream had been taken off to make butter for the abbot's table.

🧀 🧀 🧀

The influence of the monasteries on cheese in the British Isles goes beyond the introduction of a single type like washed-rinds. Monasticism, particularly in the centuries after the Norman Conquest, had a huge effect on agriculture, and thus on our cheese. Almost all monasteries had connections with their parent orders in Europe, and this led to an exchange of ideas about agriculture, and of course cheese production. Of the monastic orders, it was the Cistercians, whose HQ was the abbey of Cîteaux near Dijon, who had the most influence on cheesemaking, with their huge flocks of sheep and commercial cheese operations on a scale to rival the Romans. But before we get to them I want to first explore the more humble beginnings of monasticism and early cheesemaking in Ireland.

Christianity, according to tradition, was brought to Ireland by Saint Patrick in the fifth century. The early Irish church was largely monastic in nature and the first monastery was probably that of St Enda on the Aran islands, established around the

Looking out from the medieval monastery on Skellig Michael to the austere pinnacles of Skellig Beag – a challenging place to make cheese.

year 450. Britain had, by this time, largely reverted to paganism and illiteracy, under the yet-to-refine Saxons, and Ireland was a reservoir of Christianity, with its monasteries also serving as banks of knowledge. The monks preserved and copied out secular books, as well as religious texts, including useful Latin treatises on agriculture.

Saint Finnian, one of the founding monks of the Irish Church, had studied at the monastery of Saint Martin at Tours, and around 520 established an influential house at Clonard, in County Wexford, whence many monks would establish houses of their own. These monasteries were not like the great houses of Fountains and Rievaulx and Mellifont, whose ruins haunt the landscape of Britain and Ireland. The early Irish houses consisted of a collection of huts or cells, a refectory where the monks would come together to eat and a chapel. If you want to see one for yourself, you could do no better than visit Skellig Michael, sited on a rock to the west of County Kerry. It was one of those founded by Saint Finnian, and its huddled collection of stone beehive huts, on a steep rock in the Atlantic, was later the retreat of Luke Skywalker.

The lives of the Skellig monks were probably as austere as their surroundings. Saint Finnian's monasticism was steeped in the traditions of the Desert Fathers, who sought an ascetic life in the Egyptian desert in the third century. They were keen on mortifying the flesh through such practices as not eating very much, not enjoying anything they did eat (one monk covered his food in a bitter powder to prevent sinful pleasure) and, in the case of Simeon the Stylite, living on top of a pillar.

The Irish monks, however, did eat cheese. It's mentioned in the ninth-century rule of the monastery of Tallaght, as a condiment, which suggests it was a bit of a treat. But I imagine cheese was generally more of a staple in their diet. Dairy products were favourite foods of the secular Irish, which is not surprising when you think of those Bronze Age farms in County Mayo, while cheese-related place names suggest a long history of cheesemaking. Muine

Making the washed-rind Mont d'Or cheese. Did the French get their techniques from Irish medieval cheesemakers?

Maothail in Limerick may mean 'thicket of the cheese,' coming from a root word for 'soft' and also for *beistings*, the last creamy drawings from a cow's udder. Senadh Mheidhg in Galway and Muileann an Mheidhg in Wicklow both come from the root word for 'whey'.

Tragically, all the traditional cheeses of Ireland have long disappeared and the blame for this devastating loss must be laid at the feet of the English, whose conquests of Ireland in the sixteenth and seventeenth centuries not only initiated centuries of oppression and suffering but wiped out cheesemaking along with much indigenous Irish culture. That is the view of Irish historian Mícheál Ó Sé, and I'm not about to argue with it.

However, tantalising glimpses of a cornucopia of cheese varieties and some sophisticated cheesemaking techniques remain, for which we have to thank Ó Sé and his 1948 article, 'Old Irish Cheeses and Other Milk Products', for the Cork Historical and Archaeological Society. Ó Sé opens with a discussion of Cais, from the Latin *caseus*, which can be a generic word for cheese or refer to hard pressed cheese (and is now the name of the Irish farmhouse cheese association). Then he writes of Tanag, a hard skimmed-milk cheese, which, being modest in nature, may have been just the thing the monks were eating in their little stone refectories, before moving on to *Faiscre grotha*, meaning 'pressed curds'. These were small cheeses, pressed in moulds and probably eaten fresh, and a clue to their size appears in the story of an attempt to poison Saint Patrick with cheeses smuggled into the saint's house under a woman's cloak. Another clue is a lovely ninth-century wooden cheese mould, found in an archaeological dig at a site in County Fermagh, which would have made cheese about six inches across. It was carved from a single piece of willow and had a cross cut into the base which would have left its mark on the cheese. This might suggest a monkish end-user or a form of protection agains malign supernatural interference in cheesemaking. (This will not, by the way, be the last time in this book that you hear about the role of the black arts in cheesemaking.)

The most intriguing sentence in Ó Sé's article is: 'Is ann fuair an mnai ag tath an grotha', a line he quotes from a twelfth-century saga, 'The Death of Fin Mac Cumaill'. For those of you not fluent in Irish Gaelic, I will translate: 'There he found the woman sticking together the curds.' This could refer to a sophisticated method of cheesemaking where the curds are heated and stirred. It's how you make famous Alpine cheeses like Comté, Gruyère and Beaufort, and it is responsible for their hard yet supple texture and their sweet and nutty flavours. Next time you are eating one of these, stop and ponder: you might be experiencing the flavour of a medieval Irish cheese!

But did the Irish invent this art and export it to the Alps? It's a tempting idea and not impossible. For in 590 or thereabouts Saint Columbanus set off from Ireland with twelve other monks to evangelise in France. They brought their learning, too, with manuscripts from the Irish monasteries that were copied for the libraries of the hundred or so monasteries that they established in what are now France, Italy and the Swiss Alps. If you catch an Irish cheesemaker on a good night, as I have, they might tell you that these monks also brought an indigenous Irish cheesemaking practice, uncontaminated by Roman occupation.

Whatever the truth of all this, the connection between Irish cheesemaking and Irish monks on the continent is nicely enshrined in a feisty modern cheese called St Gall, made in County Cork by Gudrun Shinnik. Gudrun learnt her craft in Switzerland, and based

The feisty St Gall, made in County Cork, by way of Switzerland, and commemorating a close encounter with a bear.

her cheese on Appenzeller, an alpine style named after its home canton. But she adopted its name from the larger surrounding canton – which is named after the monastery established in memory of Gallen, a charismatic Irish preacher who followed Saint Columbanus to the continent and was canonised after a miraculous encounter with a bear. Hard, sweet and supple like a mountain cheese, St Gall has a funky, peppery flavour gained by washing the rind in brine – another hint at its monastic origin.

☁ ☁ ☁

Irish monasticism reached its apogee in the sixth century, when under Saint Columbanus its monks established houses across the north of England and Scotland – most notably, in 563, at Iona, off the west coast of Scotland. The Iona monastery became the burial place of kings of Scotland such as Donnchad mac Crínáin and Mac Bethad mac Findlaích, better known to southerners as Duncan and Macbeth.

The Irish tradition, in the guise of the rule of Saint Columbanus, might have become the dominant form of Christianity in the British Isles if it hadn't been for the appearance of a rival tradition more closely connected to the pope in Rome. In the middle of the sixth century, the Italian monk Benedict of Nursia wrote a set of rules for monastic life, which formed the *Regula Benedicti*. These rules were a set of instructions for how to live harmoniously together in communities, rather than alone in a cave or on a pillar, and established a life of prayer, hard work and frugal simplicity rather than one of penitential asceticism. Benedict saw the latter as dangerously close to spiritual pride.

Benedict gave his name to the first great order of monks, the Benedictines, whose original abbey in Britain was established by the first Archbishop of Canterbury and apostle to the English, Saint Augustine, in 597. For the next thirty years or so, Irish and

Roman Christianity co-existed somewhat uneasily in Britain. But in 664, Oswiu, King of Northumbria, decided to move his ecclesiastical capital from Lindisfarne, off the Northumbrian coast, to York, thereby giving the dominance of the Roman tradition in Britain and Ireland a powerful boost. But, whatever their flavour, the monks of the British Isles were soon to face a far greater (and hairier) threat. In 793, Vikings raided the monastery of Lindisfarne, carrying away its treasures to adorn their halls and its monks to be their slaves. Two years later, Ireland suffered its first Viking raid on a church called Rathlin. The next two hundred years were marked by much Scandinavian-induced chaos and suffering across the British Isles. Particularly for the monks, who had plenty of loot and made docile slaves. And perhaps cheesemakers.

Washed-rind cheeses, though, may not have been to the Vikings' taste. They had their own cheese, which is still made in Norway today, although hard to get anywhere else. It's called Gamalost and if you fancy some you should visit Sognefjord for the goat's version or Hardangerfjord for the cow's milk one. It is a gnarly-looking cheese, dark brown with a paste that looks more like deeply grained wood than a foodstuff. The milk is skimmed, then soured for days before cheesemaking begins, and the curd is heated. This makes for a rock-hard cheese, excellent for taking on those long and wet voyages. And if you happened to forget your axe, you could always beat your enemies to death with your packed lunch.

The chaos eventually dissipated, partly through Viking settlement and civilisation, and partly (in the English narrative) through the leadership of Alfred the Great and his grandson Athelstan, who defeated the Vikings at York in 927 to become the first king of England. Scotland remained independent, for the time being. In Ireland, meantime, the Viking period ended when they were decisively beaten at Clontarf in 1014 by King Brian Boru. Tragically for Boru, and for the Irish people, the warlike

Gamalost, old cheese from Hardangerfjord, little changed since Viking times. Perhaps this is why they went raiding.

high king of Ireland was killed in his moment of triumph by a retreating Viking.

Getting rid of the Vikings made building monasteries much easier, and by 1066 there were about forty new Benedictine monasteries in England, all south of the River Trent.

🧀 🧀 🧀

As we all know, in 1066 William the Bastard (soon to be renamed the Conqueror) turned up and killed Harold Godwinson at the Battle of Hastings. In 1072, the Normans invaded Scotland and forced King Malcolm II to accept William as overlord. By 1094, most of Wales was under Norman control and, though Ireland was at first spared their attention, Diarmait Mac Murchada, deposed as king of Leinster in 1166, committed what was in hindsight the staggeringly unwise act of inviting the Normans over. In 1170,

Richard fitz Gilbert, Earl of Pembroke, aka Strongbow, took up the invitation and seized Dublin. The next time Ireland was to rule itself was 1922.

The Norman Conquest changed the course of history for the British Isles in ways so profound that adjectives like 'cataclysmic' and 'catastrophic' seem apt, certainly for the Anglo-Saxons, whose ruling class and church were replaced by the Normans, and whose native language was made subservient to the tongue of the rulers, Norman French.

But just because there was great change, it doesn't mean there was no continuity and you can see that in the Domesday Book. This astonishing document, completed in 1086, surveyed all the land in England south of the River Tees and the Westmoreland fells, listing estates, manors, towns and villages, their extent, land and livestock holdings and all the agricultural equipment needed to farm it. Crucially for William, it told him how much all this was worth, and what he could expect in tax, or geld as they called it.

Twenty years after Hastings, of the one hundred and eighty larger tenants in chief, i.e. those that held the land as tenants for their feudal lord William I, only two are English and, of fourteen hundred lesser tenants in chief, only one hundred are English. When you get down to the more lowly subtenancies, the proportion of English tenants increases considerably, and many of these were people who had owned their land before the Conquest. But the Normans were the landlords now, and held all the power.

What barely changed was who farmed the land – the free peasants and unfree villeins who actually did all the work. As much as their lives must have become harder and poorer under the feudal regime of the Normans, their working practices and customs probably changed very little. Oddly, what you won't find in the Domesday Book is any mention of Cheshire cheese. This came as a bit of a surprise to me, as it is a truth universally acknowledged, at least among British cheesemongers, that Cheshire is the first named British cheese and appears in Domesday. As a younger

The Domesday Book entry for Cheshire. See any cheese?

monger I was as guilty as anyone of propagating this myth, which is slightly shaming. Sadly for us (and for them), William's auditors weren't interested in cheese. When cheese does appear, it is only as an oblique reference to some cheesemaking kit appearing in the possessions of a manor, such as moulds or salting cloths. And I've searched and failed to find any mention of equipment like that in the Domesday entries for Cheshire.

Of course, I may have blinked and missed it. Domesday is quite a demanding read.

While it may have been bad news for many, 1066 signalled the beginning of a boom time for monasticism in Britain and Ireland. Between 1066 and 1154 the number of monasteries for men went from fifty to five hundred, and the monastic population (which includes both monks and nuns) increased seven- or eightfold.

All these monks and nuns needed feeding, so the growth in monasticism caused growth and change in agriculture and its produce – including, of course, cheese. It was the Cistercians who had the most transformative influence on cheese. The order, whose first house was established in 1098 at Cîteaux, were founded in reaction to what were perceived as the prideful excesses and secular dabbling of the Benedictines. The Cistercians wanted to go back to basics: prayer, seclusion, self-sufficiency and manual work. They looked different too. Their undyed woollen habits bleached in the sun and led to their being called the Whitefriars; the Benedictines, by contrast, wore black.

The first Cistercian abbey in the British Isles was founded at Waverley in 1128, followed within a decade by Tintern in Wales and the great northern abbeys of Fountains and Rievaulx, and Melrose in Scotland. The first Cistercian abbey in Ireland was founded in 1142 at Mellifont in County Lough.

The Cistercian surveyors were very specific about the sites they chose. They looked for narrow valleys with a river to carry away waste and pasture land for sheep. These remote locations were challenging places in which to live and work. A Carthusian monk at Witham in Somerset in the later twelfth century described his home as 'a horrible place, an empty solitude inhabited only by wild animals'.

Jervaulx Abbey in North Yorkshire was originally founded at a place called Fors, but the monks could not sustain themselves there and after enduring 'great hardships and misery' they moved sixteen miles down the valley to East Witton, where the ruins now stand. And it is a site with a particular place in British cheese history. It was here that Wensleydale, that quintessentially British cheese, is said to have been created by the monks, to a recipe brought from their parent house in France. I've read that this original recipe was for something like Roquefort, a very creamy and spicy blue sheep's milk cheese. How this might have evolved into Wensleydale, a hard cow's milk cheese, modest, restrained, with its delicate flavour and hard, yet moist and creamy texture, is a topic for later.

I visited Jervaulx on a beautiful early summer day, and the first thing I noticed was a stone trough, contemporary with the monastery, with a spring bubbling forth. I dipped my wrists into the clear dales water, closely observed by the field's other occupants, a flock of fat white-faced Cheviot sheep. The Cistercians reintroduced large-scale sheep farming to Britain – after its demise with the departure of the Romans – probably because sheep, being hardy and agile animals, suited the remote and hilly sites of the monasteries. Exporting wool to Flanders also made fortunes for the Cistercians, particularly for the great northern houses like Fountains and Rievaulx. And, along with the wool, all those sheep provided a lot of tasty lamb and mutton and a lot of cheese.

The Cistercians preferred to run their farms directly so as not to have to deal on a day-to-day basis with spiritually unclean secular types, and to have more control over their enterprises. This led to the creation of a Cistercian institution: a directly managed farm, usually close to the monastery, called a grange. Cistercians also liked to consolidate disparate landholdings they had been gifted into larger more efficient granges. It was this new scale and efficiency that really changed agriculture in the British Isles. Rather than individuals farming their own patches and looking after a few animals, these carefully managed farms took advantage of the learning of their monks and a depth of experience spanning Europe to increase production and innovate, not least in the making of cheese.

A peasant cheesemaker might have only one cow and, before the advances in cattle breeding of the eighteenth century, yields of milk were much smaller, so it wouldn't have been worth the cheesemaker's while to make a single small cheese from one day's milk. It's likely that the peasant women saved the product of a few days' milking, perhaps in a cool cellar or outbuilding, before they had enough to make cheese from. During this time the milk would have been acidifying as the naturally occurring lactic bacteria had their way. This more acidic milk wouldn't have been an attractive environment for any wandering *B. linens* type bacteria to settle down in, so these peasant cheese would have tended towards a mould-ripened style.

For the monks, their large flocks of sheep meant a lot of milk was available immediately. Not having time to acidify, this 'sweet milk' would have made low-acid cheeses to which passing members of the *B. linens* family would have flocked in their droves. Perhaps the monks looking after these cheeses knew perfectly well what the appearance of a pinkish shade on their cheese implied and began happily mixing up a batch of brine to continue that process, or looked on in wonder, courageously tasted the strangely coloured cheese, and began experimenting. But, either way, the conditions for cheesemaking on monastic farms were ripe for washed-rinds.

When I think of monasteries making cheese, I have a mental image of a rotund and jolly monk, the sleeves of his habit rolled up and his arms deep in a vat of curd. But, pleasing as this scene of monk-ish life might be, it is probably a bit suspect. For the cheesemak-ers were almost certainly part of the grange set-up, and Cistercian granges were staffed by lay brothers. These were men who had taken the vows of poverty, chastity and obedience and lived in the precincts of the monastery but were not actual monks.

At Jervaulx, as I left the field of sheep to enter the ruins of the monastery, the lay brothers' infirmary was the first building I came to. There was little left of it beyond a rectangle of well-kept turf and a trio of pillars but more exciting ruins awaited right next door.

These, the signs indicated, were the lay brothers' frater or refectory, where they ate their simple meals of bread, fruit, vegetables and cheese. In one wall I could make out the serving hatches from the kitchen, one for the lay brothers and another for the choir monks, who had their own refectory. This separation continued throughout the monastery; the lay brothers slept in a separate dormitory and even at prayer in the church were kept apart from the choir monks by a screen.

The more I found out about how the work of these lay brothers, the choir monks and the obedientiaries (the more senior office-holding monks) was divided up, the more I realised that that my picture of a jolly monk with his hands in a vat of curd was a fiction. In order to maintain a complete separation from the distractions and temptations of the secular world, the choir monks did not leave the precinct of the monastery. So, if the animals were being looked after and milked on a grange outside, it wouldn't have made any sense to transport volumes of liquid milk to the monastery for the choir monks to make cheese from. No, it was the lay brothers that were my cheesemaking antecedents.

Here is a list of lay brothers' duties from the Priory of Shene in London:

> The master of the Sheape shall also be master of the Goates.

> The Sheepe Master and his fellows, when neyde requyreth, muste turn and make the Cheese, and carefully take heede that they be not empared.

> Ever when the Seepe are milked, one of the Bretheren muste be present: He hym self also with other muste mylke them, make and keep the cheese.

There are a few things about this passage that stand out for me. One is the phrase 'master of the Goates'. Anyone who thinks they can master goats probably hasn't met any. Another is the myriad ways a medieval monk had for spelling 'sheep'. But more pertinent

Cheviot sheep having a drink at their forefathers' trough at Jervaulx.

for us is that the lay brothers were clearly making cheese as part of their agricultural duties. The phrase 'when neyde requyreth' suggests to me is that there were other people making cheese – actual professional cheesemakers – as well as lay brothers doing some cheesemaking when needed. I imagine this meant at the high point of the summer, when the animals were giving large volumes of milk and the cheesemaker was getting a bit overwhelmed. Or that on the smaller granges there wasn't enough income to justify a separate professional cheesemaker.

There were certainly professional cheesemakers in the high days of English monasticism. The job title *caseator* (cheesemaker in Latin) appears in the accounts of various monastic dairies. One such, in a grant of land, mentions a man called Richard of Hoddesdon (a town in Hertfordshire). But that word *caseator*, with its male ending, is rare, and it seems that the majority of cheesemakers at the granges were women. They were referred to as *deyes* in the monastic accounts, a word that originally meant female servant. But the close association between women and cheesemaking meant they gave their name to the place they worked – the dairy. I like to think that these professional women managed to cast off the low status implied by the origin of their title. After all, the *deyes* often ran the dairy and had staff working for them. The *deye* of one sixteenth-century grange owned by Sibton Abbey, a Cistercian house in Suffolk, was called Katherine Dowe and under her were her assistant, Alice Harys, and three servants. In 1507, Katherine earned one pound for her yearly salary, Alice ten shillings, and the servants eight shillings each. This was a decent wage. And I love knowing the name of an actual cheesemaker and her assistant from five hundred years ago.

Katherine and her team were obviously good at their jobs. Over a period of six years, the number of cows Katherine and Alice were looking after increased from sixty-six to a hundred and sixty-six. The cattle were a breed called Countryware, which had been crossed with Northernsteers, suggesting that a breed from the north was being used to improve an East Anglian stock. The improving of livestock breeds is most commonly associated with the eighteenth-century Enlightenment, so it's interesting to note the Cistercians had already got going with the project five centuries earlier.

There are other indications that Katherine Dowe was a conscientious cheesemaker. Walter of Henley, author of a contemporaneous treatise on farming, tells us that one could get about a hundred and twenty-eight pounds of cheese from one cow per year and six gallons of butter. Katherine and her staff got a hundred and fifty-six pounds of cheese and three gallons of butter. This could be a peculiarity of the milk produced by a particular breed, but I like to think that, as an expert cheesemaker, Katherine skimmed less cream off her milk to make butter with, preferring to make richer cheese of higher quality.

The employment of women in monastic dairies was widespread enough for some of the more uptight abbots to worry that their presence might tempt the lay brothers to break their vows of chastity. In fact the very statutes of the Premonstratensians (one of the more severe orders) stipulate that women employed on their granges should be 'such of whom no possibility of suspicion could possibly be entertained'. For what they meant by that, we might look to the fourteenth-century Prior of Malhamdale, in North Yorkshire, who decreed that only 'old and ill favoured' women should be employed in the priory dairies.

Whatever the truth of this, the monasteries, by employing people from the secular population, were providing a conduit for cheesemaking knowledge and practice to filter out into the wider world. And this transmission of knowledge was to dramatically expand when, after 1536, Henry VIII dissolved the monasteries and the *deyes*, *caseators* and lay brothers went out looking for work.

Having staked a claim for the *deyes*, *caseators* and lay brothers having been the principal cheesemakers of the monasteries, I still think that it's likely that monks had some role – possibly in a later stage of the process, as affineurs – and that their involvement was a result of the way that the houses were organised.

In each house, a team of monks held offices connected with the smooth running of the monastery. After the abbot, the most important and powerful monk was the cellarer, who was ultimately responsible for the production, storage and provision of food for the house. He was one of the few monks who could leave the precincts of the monastery, for it was part of his role to oversee the granges, mills and storehouses and to manage the lay brothers who worked on them. At mealtimes, the cellarer stood by the serving hatch checking the quality of the food and the fairness of its distribution.

CHAPTER THREE 🐭 THE BENEFIT OF MONKS

There was a spiritual value to this work, as Benedict himself had made clear: 'let him look upon all the utensils of the monastery and its whole property as upon the sacred vessels of the altar'. And under the cellarer was another invaluable staff member, the refectorian. Among his duties was sampling the cheese intended for the community on its arrival at the monastery. I imagine him armed (like modern-day cheesemongers) with a cheese iron, a half-cylinder of iron or steel with a T-bar handle, which you use to take a core sample from a cheese.

Another obedientiary was even more like an affineur. This was the kitchener, who, alongside running the kitchens, oversaw the storage of food. I know I've mentioned this before, but cheese needs a lot of looking after. You can't just leave it on a shelf and forget about it until you're ready to eat it. Cheeses need to be turned to stop their bottoms getting sticky, and rubbed and patted and even washed to control mould and mite growth. Cheese can be a wilful and stubborn beast and you have to be flexible and creative in your dealings with it.

This might be how and where washed-rinds came into being: perhaps a kitchener and his staff were washing young cheese to keep the mites or mould in check and discovered that some of them turned into pink and excitingly pungent cheeses, particularly (as we saw earlier) if they had been made from the sweet milk produced by those colossal flocks. A crucial quality of an affineur is a sort of courageous inquisitiveness, so once they'd discovered this interesting effect I'm sure it wouldn't be long before they developed a method to reproduce washed-rinds of a consistent quality.

Perhaps the kitchener recruited his staff of affineurs from the body of choir monks who, under Benedict's rule, were encouraged to do some physical work to keep them too busy to descend into 'murmuring'. One example would be weeding the abbey's herb garden. Like that job, looking after some cheese in the abbey's cellar would be an appropriate thing for a choir monk to do, since it was carried out within the precincts of the monastery.

A dairymaid or deye *handpressing cheese, with a dog snaffling whey before it gets to the pigs. The* deyes *gave their name to their workplace.*

At Jervaulx, the cellar where the abbey's cheese would have been stored and cared for by the kitchener and his team was underneath the abbot's rooms. As I stood in what remained of these rooms on what would have been the cellar floor – now carpeted with turf and a sprinkling of daisies – I thought about them at their work. Washing cheese is a rhythmical, meditative business and very satisfying. As you wash the younger cheese you can look at the older batches, the fruits of your labours, developing their deep, pinkish-orange colour and rich barnyardy flavour. I wonder if they sang as they worked? In the cellars in Covent Garden, my colleague Bill Oglethorpe used to play his saxophone. He told me it was because he didn't want to annoy his neighbours, but I know that really he was playing for the cheeses.

🧀 🧀 🧀

The centuries following the Norman Conquest were a boom time for the monasteries and, as their populations grew, so did their cheesemaking. Accounts of the Kentish manor farms owned by Canterbury Priory show how the industry took off. In 1285 Orgarswick, a manor in Romney Marsh in Kent, produced seven weys of cheese, which is almost eighteen hundred pounds or about eight hundred kilos. A wey was a measure of cheese that differed from county to county; in Kent it was two hundred and fifty-six pounds. By 1291, just six years later, they'd increased production to ten weys – two thousand five hundred pounds of cheese. And forty years later, in 1323, they were producing a staggering thirty-three weys, or eight thousand five hundred pounds!

Canterbury was a Benedictine priory and the cheeses they were producing were mostly cow's milk, since, in the clement climate and flatter lands of southern England, cows were the mainstay of monastic dairying, as opposed to the harsher weather and hilly territory of the Cistercian north, where the hardy sheep held sway. The Benedictines tended to delegate the management of their farms, rather than running them directly like the Cistercians, but the monks still kept a very close eye on things, requiring detailed accounts to be kept by the serjeants or reeves who ran the farms.

We know the name of the serjeant who ran the Kentish manor of Ebony, another possession of Canterbury Priory: he was called Stephen atte Broke. I feel for Stephen, since his manor farm at Ebony produced less cheese than the one at Orgarswick. It may just have been that it was smaller, but I imagine him having to explain to his monastic manager at the Priory why he was producing less cheese than the neighbouring manor. It is possible that a cloud of suspicion hung over Stephen, that he was (literally) skimming off profits from dairying for himself. The fat skimmed from milk was used to make butter, a high-value product, and, judging from the dire warnings in various agricultural treatises of the time, illicit skimming was a common threat to monastic profits.

Thanks to their agricultural treatises, the monastic manager of the Priory's dairying operation would have had a clear idea of how much cheese and other dairy products, largely butter, ought to have been coming out of each manor. The best known of these treatises was Walter of Henley's *Husbandry*, written in 1280, which is written as a sermon delivered from father to son. Walter clearly knew his stuff and his book was still highly regarded in the sixteenth century. *Husbandry* gave very detailed numbers for how much milk you could expect to get from a cow or a sheep, including, crucially, the ratio of cheese to butter. Impressively, Walter also gave figures for the changing average yield over the changing seasons – essential information for financial planning, as you could then predict how many cheeses you would be making over the year. It was also a useful way to check if your *deyes* or lay brothers were helping themselves to some extra butter or cheese.

After 1306, the cheeses in the Kent Manors were standardised into three sizes: *majoris forme* (twelve kilos – about half the size of a modern Cheddar), *medie forme* (nine kilos) and *minoris forme* (seven kilos). Having accurate and detailed accounts and standardised sizes would help enormously in the planning and management necessary to develop a large-scale cheese industry. And manors and granges run like this could send more cheese to more distant markets than the smaller, less networked secular farms.

The cheeses made for internal trade and export, however, can't have been the unctuous and aromatic washed-rinds that monkish affineurs might have been creating in their cellars. Those cheeses are too soft and delicate to withstand the rigours of medieval travel on rutted roads and the damp holds of cross-channel cogs, the cargo ships of the day. Nor would their high-maintenance maturing regime suit an economy of scale. In fact, you can tell that these would have been hard cheeses just by the sizes recorded. Sadly, there seems to be a marked lack of interest as to what the cheeses actually looked or tasted like among the scribes or modern scholars of medieval monasticism. Or so I had thought, until one day in the Rare Books Reading Room at the British Library, I opened R.A.L. Smith's *Canterbury Cathedral Priory – A Study in Monastic Administration*. The somewhat dry title of this volume concealed a treasure. It was published in 1943, with the war raging and prospects for the Allies not looking too good, and must have brought our man Smith much comfort. For it is clear from the detail and insight in his descriptions that he was a keen cheese fancier with an unrivalled understanding of monastic dairies. In the 'simple and uniform' dairies on the Canterbury estates, salt was the most regular expenditure, a commodity vital in cheesemaking for extracting moisture, slowing the bacterial activity of the starter culture and adding taste. Other purchases that show up regularly are wooden 'presses' (by which Smith means cheese moulds) and *canvenacium ad caseum imprimendum* (canvas to wrap the cheeses in the press). The priory produced cow's milk cheeses, ranging from fourteen to twenty-four pounds in size. Salted and pressed in wooden moulds, they wouldn't have had the hardness or density of a modern Cheshire or Cheddar, which have benefited from advances in cheesemaking technology such as cast iron presses and curd milling. Perhaps they were more like a hardish Caerphilly, with a protective rind created by dry-salting or brining (rather than traditional Caerphilly's mould rind). Cheeses that could survive a trip in an unsprung cart from Orgarswick manor to the Kentish port of New Romney, or farther afield to Rye after Romney silted up in 1387.

Smith goes on to explain that, of the cheese eaten in the monastery (rather than sold), the largest went to the prior's table and the smaller ones to the monks' refectories, which suggests that larger cheeses were considered to be of higher quality. This makes sense to me. A larger cheese loses moisture more slowly and can be matured for longer to develop more flavour. A smaller cheese will dry out faster, offering you the option of eating a less complex young cheese or an old dry one. So – top tip here – if you want to buy a cheese as a present for someone, don't buy one of those mini cheeses, like a small truckle of Cheddar or Stilton. Sure, they look cute, but they will not have the richness, the depth and complexity of a larger cheese. Better to buy your friend a heroic piece from a full-size wheel. And then wait around while they unwrap it, looking at them in a meaningful, expectant and frankly hungry way. That is how I do present-giving.

Though cheese was obviously a staple food for choir monks and lay brothers alike, it was also a food fit for royalty. Edward I (1239–1307) had special coffers made to carry his cheeses so that he could take them with him when he was hammering the Scots or the Welsh.

While some of Edward's cheese might have come to him as manorial rents from farms, monastic cheesemakers also supplied the royals. And it seems that cheeses from certain houses were much prized. In 1502, Elizabeth of York, wife of Henry VII and mother of Henry VIII, was gifted a cheese by the Archbishop of Canterbury, from the Priory of Llanthony in Gloucestershire. A week later Elizabeth received more of this cheese, this time directly from the Priory and delivered by a servant of the Prior. For the next three months she got a delivery of cheese from Llanthony each month, with the long-suffering servant of the Prior having to find a new address for each delivery as the Queen travelled between her palaces at Woodstock in Oxfordshire, Langley in Berkshire and finally Berkeley in Gloucestershire.

It's telling that the Archbishop of Canterbury felt that cheese was a fitting gift for a queen, and that he chose the produce of

Llanthony Priory in Gloucestershire – a medieval cheese centre to be reckoned with.

a distant priory over the cheese made in such great bulk at his Kentish manors. That Llanthony cheese must have been quite something.

Though exporting cheese to the continent wasn't a Norman or monastic innovation (tolls on English cheese are recorded at Arras in northern France as early as 1036), the cheese business boomed with monastic involvement. The conditions were perfect: there was a high volume of a consistent and standardised product, and the international network of monasteries facilitated exchange and transport. For example, the Priory of Ogbourne in Wiltshire administered lands owned by the Abbey of Bec in Normandy and part of its obligation was a food rent of thirty-two weys of cheese – that's around four thousand kilos of cheese a year. The monks of Bec must have liked Wiltshire cheese.

Monasteries, just like temporal lords, also demanded services from their tenants as part of their rents, and these services could be in the cheese export industry. As one of their obligations to their monastic landlord, the virgaters (landowning peasants) of Minchinhampton in Gloucestershire had to carry cheeses to Southampton to ship to the Abbey of the Holy Trinity at Caen; this was documented from 1170 to 1320. Not only was this export business providing a nice big market for the cheeses of Britain and Ireland, it was also spreading their reputation far and wide. And these cheeses must have been good, to compete in the markets of Caen and Arras, given the high cost of transport.

Cheese was also imported to the British Isles from the continent. We know this because of an instance of cheese piracy. In 1242, an East Anglian pirate called Ranulph de Oreford took a ship carrying goods from Rouen whose manifest included four cheeses. Just that bare fact tells you two things – first, they must have been large cheeses, and second they must have been pretty damn good to be worth the bother of pirating. Sadly the account fails to tell us whether Ranulph was a specialist cheese pirate or more of an opportunistic plunderer.

In addition to the physical trade in cheese between the British Isles and the continent, there must also have been a movement of ideas about cheese, as monks from abbeys in mainland Europe came over to run monasteries in Britain and Ireland, bringing their tastes in cheese with them. This traffic in cheesemaking theory can't have just been one way. I like to think of Peter de Quinciaco, the first cellarer of Jervaulx, returning to his parent house in Savigny with some of the fruits of Jervaulx's dairying operation. If these truly were inspired by the cheeses of Roquefort, they would have been lusciously textured, spicy-blue sheep's cheeses – though perhaps with the mould rind characteristic of northern Dales- style cheeses rather than the unblemished skin of a modern Roquefort.

🐷 🐷 🐷

The to and fro of monastic cheesemaking means we'll never know for sure where exactly the monks developed a taste for washed-rind cheeses and the skill to produce them. I personally love the idea that washed-rinds evolved in the briny Irish climate of the earliest Irish monastic communities in places like Glendalough in County Wicklow.

I heard this idea from Quinlan Steele, the current maker of Milleens. I first met Quinlan at Borough Market in 2003. He had come to stand outside the Dairy and hand out Milleens to passers-by. As he explained to all comers, the cheese had been developed by his mother Veronica, one of the first of the new wave of artisan cheesemakers in the British Isles. There followed a rather boisterous night at the Wheatsheaf, the cheesemongers' pub of choice at Borough, with the result that, while I remembered what a great storyteller and conversationalist Quinlan was, I had only the haziest memories of the stories and conversations themselves. So, researching this book, it seemed sensible to head off to Cork to talk to him again. Also, Milleens was the first washed-rind I had ever tried, and I wanted to make a pilgrimage to its place of birth.

I took a bus from Cork to Castletownbere, the nearest town Quinlan's place, which stands at the remote end of a peninsula in the very westernmost bit of County Cork. The landscape immediately outside Cork City is rumpled, hilly and of a dizzying greenness that comes from lots of rain. As I sat open-mouthed, staring at the view of Bantry Bay, a nice chap struck up conversation. He began with so little preamble that at first I looked around to see who he was really talking to, but in minutes I was having a lively conversation with him and a woman sitting behind me, who turned out to be my new friend's sister.

We spoke about the nice weather (for by now the cloud had lifted and it was becoming a glorious day) and the relative merits of Guinness and Murphy's, and then the most forbidding mountain range I have ever seen – massive vertical shards of granite that put me in mind of the more grim bits at the end of the *Lord of the Rings* – appeared outside. This rocky spine, my friends explained, runs along the centre of the Beara Peninsula – in between me and Quinlan. I had been idly thinking that, if there weren't any taxis, I would just walk the five or six miles from Castletownbere to the guesthouse where I'd booked a room. I was beginning to imagine what it would be like to clamber over those unforgiving shards of stone dragging my little wheely suitcase like a latter-day Frodo.

My new friends noticed my disquiet and, after having a couple of goes at calling a taxi for me, pointed out MacCarthy's pub on the other side of the square from the bus stop: 'The lady who runs it, her husband drives a taxi, she can call him for you.' My ride turned up at exactly at the moment I was finishing the last silky drops of my first proper pint of Murphys' Irish stout in a decade, the impeccable timing confirming my belief that magic and benevolent coincidence permeate the business of cheesemaking.

The view from my guesthouse that evening of the sun setting over the Atlantic was pretty special, but there wasn't much to see out of the window at six the next morning. The Atlantic weather had changed as swiftly and thoroughly as it always does and all I could see was a thick bank of low cloud. Fortified by a truly heroic breakfast – black pudding *and* white pudding, thank you very much – I set off for Milleens Farm, whose white buildings I could just make out at the bottom of the cloud layer.

It pays to approach farm gates circumspectly – farm dogs are large, territorial and not always very well secured – but there didn't seem to be anyone about at Milleens, human or canine. I

Milleens' terroir – the Beara Peninsula in County Cork.

walked across the yard to a low stone building with a big shutter
that to a cheesemonger's honed instinct had all the hallmarks
of a cheese-packing operation. I hadn't seen Quinlan for fifteen
years, but the tall figure coming out of the dairy was instantly
recognisable. It wasn't cheesemaking time yet, so we headed off
to the farmhouse where Quinlan lives with his wife Deirdre, the
local vet, and their two children, for coffee and cheese. I'm sorry to
harp on about the beautiful views, but the one from Quinlan and
Deirdre's kitchen and living room is quite something, with small
rugged fields stretching down to the sea, with the rocky islands of
the bay and the coast on the other side on the horizon. 'Dad and
I built this place,' said Quinlan as we sat down at the table. 'And
that?' I asked pointing at one wall made of rough stone in contrast

to the plastered brick of the other walls. 'Oh, that's original,' said Quinlan. 'Pre-Famine.'

Quinlan, a recovering journalist, farmer and cheesemaker, is the son of two philosophers. He also volunteers on the local lifeboat. This makes him a fascinating and free-ranging conversationalist with the result that, when I look at my notes of my visit, they are not in any particular order and cover subjects more connected to my purpose, like Irish hygiene auditors, permaculture and Quinlan's sense of stewardship of the land, or broader issues like moral relativism. When Quinlan's father Norman joined the conversation, Wittgenstein and poetry got a look in too, although to be fair to Norman he was relating both those subjects to cheesemaking. I will try and do justice to this marvellous whirlwind of a visit, cobbled together from the crumpled, slightly muddy, beer- and cheese-stained notes that I brought back.

Over coffee we tried a pink, sticky, yet surprisingly gentle Milleens. Usually with washed-rinds, a brighter colour and glistening surface promise a pretty wild ride, and novices may prefer to start with something a little drier and less highly coloured.

Quinlan immediately began to talk about how the cheesemaking was going. It had been a disastrously long winter and my arrival coincided with the end of nine months of rain. This had meant the cows on the nearby dairy farms that supply Quinlan with milk had had to be kept in the barns for far longer than was ideal. When the ground is very wet, the cows' hooves will break up the ground and ruin the pasture. What this meant was that they were still being fed on silage, which this late in the year was causing mould problems with the cheese. The farmers were going to heroic lengths to remedy this problem, harvesting grass from the fields and bringing it into the barns for the cattle, so as to maintain Quinlan's need for high-quality milk.

Quinlan told me that there used to be seven hundred small dairy farms on the Beara Peninsula, but now there were only three. This might be partly to do with the trend towards consolidation that has characterised the farming industry throughout Ireland and Britain, although perhaps 'beset' or 'plagued' might be better verbs. It is also a function of the low price of liquid milk, driven in part by supermarkets selling it as a loss-leader. Thankfully cheesemakers tend to pay a higher price for milk. In fact, Quinlan, like many cheesemakers, offers a bonus for good-quality milk, which helps the farmers carry on.

Coffee time over, we went to visit Quinlan's small herd of cows on a field just above the hill from the farmhouse. Whenever I visit a cheesemaker who is also a farmer, we always at some point go for a walk around the farm. I don't think this is just for my benefit, but a practical need, to keep a regular eye on what's going on, and in a wider sense of stewardship, a sort of walking of the bounds. I saw immediately how serious the problem of the waterlogged land was as it tried its best to pull my walking boots off – I'd foolishly left my wellies at home to make room for gifts of cheese and wine.

Quinlan's own cows, which are smaller than most of the dairy cows round about, could come out while the land was still wet. He raises his animal for meat, their original dairy herd having been lost to the cull enforced on them during the BSE outbreak in 2001, which Quinlan told me nearly broke his father's heart. Farmers on this scale have a close relationship with their animals, as we saw with Mary Holbrook and her 'girls'. This was obvious here, too, as Quinlan introduced me to Dora and Spot, who he recalled carrying down to the barn just after she was born.

After our stroll – or in my case ungainly stumble with the threat of bootlessness – it was time to fetch the milk from the nearby farm, ten minutes' drive through twisty, hedgerowed lanes. Milleens has been made with pasteurised milk since 1996, when Irish law became much stricter about raw milk cheeses. This was a major blow for the Steeles' cheesemaking business at the time. Quinlan's mother, Veronica, had always made her cheese with raw milk, believing that this method best expressed its local character. Veronica also celebrated the variation that comes with raw milk cheesemaking, as the milk changes not only across the season but from day to day with shifts in the bacterial population of the milk.

Quinlan recalled that the move to pasteurisation knocked back the business for a while as Milleens lost its glamour as 'raw cheese'. But this distinction is, to my mind, a bit overblown. One needs to understand that there are different kinds of pasteurising. The most common method heats the milk to 70° C for fourteen seconds. This is done by running the milk through narrow pipes at a high velocity in a sort of heat exchanger, and this rather brutal treatment can affect the final texture of the cheese. At Milleens, the milk is treated in a much gentler way, sitting still and quiet in a tank, where it is heated at a lower temperature for a longer time. The milk I saw in Quinlan's vat had that deep ivory colour and heaviness of texture that I associate with milk that has been left to rest unbothered. It looked like happy milk. And I am delighted to report that Milleens' sales have long since bounced back from the pasteurisation crisis.

Every time I go off to make cheese with someone, I find myself surprised by their processes. With Quinlan it was the speed of his make. With soft cheese, you expect the process to be slow, and indeed many makers allow twenty-four hours for the milk to set into curd. But Milleens curd sets in just two hours, as the coagulation is driven more by the rennet than the starter culture. This leads to a much less acidic cheese – providing that sweet milk that we spoke about before. Not allowing the milk to reach so high an acidity also adds urgency to the process. Once the curd has set to the right consistency, it has to come out of the whey and go into the moulds sharpish, so that it doesn't set too hard.

Another surprise was that the curd is cut into very small bits – the size of basmati rice grains, Veronica used to say. This was counterintuitive for me, as until this point I had thought that

Quinlan steps out with a perfectly formed Milleens.

smaller curd particles would make harder cheeses. But that is how it is with cheesemaking. Your certainties are constantly challenged or even overturned. Cheesemaking is such a complex system that actions in the early stages of a make can have quite counter-intuitive outcomes. I still haven't worked out how small particles lead to softer cheeses.

When cutting the curd, Quinlan uses a harp, a many-bladed knife on the end of a long pole, which he moves with a practised and elegant sweep, changing direction as he goes. Like so many cheesemakers (even the technical ones with their laboratory instruments), he uses his sense of touch to decide when it's time to run the whey off the curd. Quinlan recalled that his mother said using an acidometer would take the fun and the art out of cheesemaking, but these days he has to test for and record the acidity of the curd as part of the hygiene regulations, and so the acidometer has its place in his dairy.

When Veronica started selling their cheese, she and Norman wrote to the Irish Minister for Food and Agriculture asking what the regulations were for making farmhouse cheese. The minister wrote back personally, as that was how things were done in the 1970s, saying 'There aren't any, but could you help us to design some?' So as well as setting up classes to teach cheesemaking, Veronica helped to set up the Association of Irish Farmhouse Cheesemakers – known by its acronym of CAIS, the Irish for 'cheese'. Other founder members included the Willems family, originally from Holland, who make the startlingly sweet and toffeeish Gouda-style Coolea, and two of Veronica's contemporaries, Giana Ferguson, who makes the springy-textured delicate Gubbeen, and Jeffa Gill, who makes rich creamy Durrus. All of them are based in County Cork.

But, back to the making of Milleens. When the cut has been done, the curd is placed into moulds made from sections of plastic piping, with drainage holes poked through the sides. Within minutes it was time to flip the nascent cheeses in their pipe-moulds. The moulds have no bottoms and the curd stuck a bit to the racks they sat on. To detach it cleanly involved a practised flick that was beyond my skill set.

With Quinlan off to the less glamorous but equally vital task of assembling paperwork, it was my chance to have a chat with his father about the origins of Milleens. We met in the old stone farmhouse, in the very kitchen where Veronica started making cheese. Norman pointed to the range, saying, 'That's where we used to heat the milk,' and to the battered wooden schoolroom table, saying 'that's where we ladled,' then turning to the sink, 'and that's where the cheeses drained in their moulds.' I love Milleens and was aware of Veronica's importance to the artisan cheese movement both in Ireland and Britain so that at this point I was wiping a reverent tear from my eye. I was later to discover a film, *The Cheesemakers of Beara*, made in 1986 by David and Sally Shaw-Smith, that showed Veronica making cheese in this very kitchen, with the milk heating in five-gallon metal pans on the stove. It opened with the narrator saying that people have been making cheese in Ireland since the seventh century, and that the craft was preserved in the monasteries throughout the Dark Ages, which pleased me no end.

Norman and Veronica met when he came down from Queen's College Dublin to give a lecture on Wittgenstein at University College Cork, where Veronica was studying Philosophy. Norman said that she stood out, as she was the only person in the room not

Veronica Steele — mover and shaker in the revival of farmhouse cheeses, not just in Ireland but across Britain, too, at work in her kitchen dairy.

wearing a dog collar or a wimple. They bought the farm in 1975 and soon gave up the philosophy business to farm full-time. In time-honoured tradition, Veronica started making cheese to use up surplus milk in the summer and to provide a store of food that would keep over the winter. The milk originally came from a one-horned cow called Brisket (her one-hornedness came from a too-hasty descent of a hilly field).

Norman told me that when they started they weren't doing it for anyone but themselves and so there wasn't a need to fit into a market. In fact, the way he characterised this to me was, 'the poem is the poem,' paraphrasing a remark of Wittgenstein's, which I took to mean that the poem, or the cheese, stands on its own and needs no other use value to justify it. Cheesemaking, you see, is well served by philosophy.

Veronica started out making a hard cheese but at some point began experimenting with soft-cheesemaking. In the wet and salty air, these cheeses would have tended to develop pink bacterial rinds rather than white-mould ones, so it would have made more sense to go with that current and make a washed-rind rather than swim against it. As Veronica used to say, 'You have to make the cheese the land wants you to make.' Quinlan told me that the very air around them on the farm is part of their terroir and that, if the cheeses start to grow unwanted moulds, all he needs to do is open the door and let the air in.

On my way back home, I had time to have a look round Cork itself, which is shorthand, if you're a cheesemonger, for a visit to the local cheese shops. In Cork City, this means Iago's, a lovely shop near the covered English Market. I asked Sean, the manager, what he thought traditional Irish cheese might have been. In answer, he reached for a semi-hard cow's milk cheese called Dunmanus, also made in County Cork by Jeffa Gill.

Dunmanus looks a bit like Tomme de Savoie from the French Alps, and I get why Sean picked this as a candidate for traditional peasant Irish cheese. It's low-tech in that you don't need to heat the milk and the cheese doesn't need to be pressed in a cheese press – just the weight of other cheeses stacked on top of it or a bit of hand pressure will do the job. Weighing about three kilos, a Dunmanus is not a huge cheese, another aspect that makes it sound like a peasant cheese to me, in that peasants, unlike feudal lords or monastic farm bosses, don't tend to have many animals and thus make smaller cheeses. Of course, I bought some, and I can tell you that it also tastes like a Tomme, fresh and slightly acidic with a hint of earthy cellariness.

After my visit with Sean, I had just enough time for another pint of Murphy's, after which I felt that my work here was done and tottered off to catch a plane. After clearing the Irish coast, I was treated to a perfect view of the Bristol Channel. Oddly, on such a beautiful day, my thoughts turned to the dark cargo that arrived in Bristol in the early summer of 1348 – a cargo that would change everything in the British Isles, including the cheese. That cargo, having travelled overland from the port of Weymouth in the bloodstream of a flea, was the Black Death.

🧀 🧀 🧀

CHAPTER FOUR

Gorwydd Caerphilly

Market forces

1348–1547

I DO LOVE A NICE OLD COUNTRY CHURCH, and St Edmund the Martyr, in the Norfolk village of Acle, is, as we parish church fanciers say, a banger. Its round thirteenth-century tower (a bit of a rarity, as Pevsner points out) is a sign of treats to come, as is the massive wooden door studded with ancient iron nails. And inside, it has a quiet, cool atmosphere and the smell of moist stone. It has a fifteenth-century font with traces of medieval colour and a painted rood screen that somehow didn't get smashed in the iconoclastic frenzy of the Reformation. But what caught my eye, most of all, was a Latin inscription in charcoal on the wall of the chancery, which reads (according to the Parish Notes):

> Oh lamentable death, how many dost thou cast into the pit!
>
> Anon the infants fade away, and of the aged, death makes an end.
>
> Now these, now those, thou ravagest, O death on every side;
>
> Those that wear horns or veils, fate spareth not.
>
> Therefore, while in the world the brute beast plague rages hour by hour

As the Parish Notes went on to explain, the inscription being in Latin dates it as pre-Reformation and the 'horns or veils' likely refer to the headdresses popular in the middle of the fourteenth century. So this anguished cry could well have been written during the Great Mortality – the plague of 1348 – which carried off as much as half the population of Britain and Ireland.

This chapter of cheese history thus covers a momentous period, when plague, war, peasant revolt and the dissolution of the monasteries shook the land. Happily, though, it was a time when many peasants threw off their shackles and started to make cheese in a big way, to supply the towns springing up all over Britain. And, even more happily, to characterise this period, I will present one of my favourite cheeses of all time, Trethowan's Gorwydd Caerphilly, which I believe is the sort of cheese those peasants who survived plague, war and revolt would have made.

Now, if your only experience of Caerphilly is the white plastic-wrapped blocks of dry, tasteless cheese you find in supermarkets, you may wonder what it can have to do with the flowering of medieval cheesemaking, or why I might be so fond of it. All will become clear.

🧀 🧀 🧀

Since 1100, the population of the British Isles had been booming, and even with the oppressive and restrictive feudal system imposed by the Normans it was a relatively good time to be a peasant. Food was plentiful and the growth of the economy meant there was an opportunity for peasants to sell their surplus in the markets of the many new towns.

We can see the changing fortunes of the peasants in the manorial records of the time. For example, in his tax assessment of 1293, David Fychan of Marchros in North Wales had, among other assets, six cows. They would have produced five hundred pounds (250 kilos) of cheese and butter a year – far more than his family would have needed – and he'd have likely got ten shillings if he sold only half of it. Ten shillings back then would have had the purchasing power of more than £17,000 today.

All this bounty was too good to last, as no doubt the old men were muttering into their beards. And, indeed, towards the end of the thirteenth century the population boom was slowing, as the ability of the land to feed all these mouths reached its limit. A run of livestock plagues and poor harvests then culminated in the Great Famine of 1315, which lasted for two years. The death rate in the famine reached fifteen per cent of the population, low compared to the horrendous rates of the coming plague, but horrific nonetheless. Also, the run of poor harvests made society in the British Isles more 'catastrophe prone', in the words of one historian. And catastrophe was on its way.

When the Black Death arrived in May 1348 at the port of Weymouth, on a trading ship from Gascony, some of the sailors were already showing symptoms – large lumps in the armpits and groin, known as buboes. These growths gave the name to the form of the sickness that is most familiar to us now, bubonic plague. By August, the plague had reached Bristol and in that tightly packed city it spread like wildfire. 'Almost the whole population of the town perished', according to Henry Knighton, a monastic chronicler writing thirty years later.

As Bristol was a major trading hub, the infection was soon countrywide, in November reaching London, where people began dying in their thousands. By March 1349, every town south of Nottingham was infected, and plague had spread into Wales; in 1350, plague reached central Scotland.

The losses were almost beyond comprehension. Knighton wrote: 'Buildings of all sizes in every city fell into total ruin for want of inhabitants. Villages and hamlets were deserted with no house remaining in them, because everyone who had lived there was dead.'

The sickness had arrived in Ireland at Dublin Bay in July 1348, also by sea. According to one Geoffrey le Baker, this first wave of plague was confined to the area of English settlement, the Pale, and did not spread among the relatively scattered rural Irish population. Their turn would come in 1357, when a second wave of plague decimated Ireland.

For the survivors, the plague heralded great changes for peasants and lords alike, and you can see these unfolding in the manorial records of the time, which tell the story of loss and reconstruction in reports of land bought and sold. A perfect example of that can be found in the records of the Hundred of Farnham, a manor in Surrey owned by the Bishop of Winchester.

In autumn 1348, the old reeve of Farnham died, one of the first local victims of the plague, and John Runwick took up the vacant post. In the manorial records, the lists of feudal dues paid, bushels of wheat harvested and cheeses made, something of John's professionalism and sheer doggedness during this disastrous time speak to us across the centuries. In 1349, around seven hundred and fifty people died, a third of the population of the manor. Strangely, the first effect was that the income of the manor increased because surviving relatives had to pay a feudal fee to enter the tenancy they had inherited. At the same time the manor's livestock holdings grew as the families of the dead also paid their heriots – the payment to the manorial lord of the best animal from the deceased head of household's stock. The church took their cut too: after you'd given your dead father's best sheep to the lord of the manor, the priest turned up and took the second best one as a 'mortuary' tithe. In a normal year the manor of Farnham might get two or three heriots. In 1348, it received two hundred animals, a foal, a bull, nine wethers, twenty-six sheep, twenty-six bullocks, fifty-four cows, twenty-six horses and fifty-seven oxen.

John's first action would have been to sell the surplus livestock, but here he had a problem. All the other manors were facing the same issue and, with a massive glut on the livestock market, prices fell precipitously. So he sold what he could and did what was needed to keep the rest, enlarging stables, turning meadowland over to pasture and hiring boys to look after the extra animals.

There was also a glut of vacant land. In September 1349, the Farnham manorial record shows fifty-two tenancies lying vacant, and behind this number hides a terrible truth. Where a tenancy lay vacant, it meant that there was no relative surviving – the whole extended family had been wiped out. John's problem was twofold. In the short term, the rental income for the manor had fallen and his boss, the bishop, would be on at him to get this back up. In the long term, the vacant land left uncultivated would quickly deteriorate. John had to get these tenancies filled, and he did.

The Dance of Death, memento of the Great Mortality.

Sometimes this was a touch coercive, as neighbours were forced to take on derelict tenancies. But he probably managed to get new blood in from outside the manor by offering lower rents. John himself took over his deceased neighbour Richard atte Ford's five acres for eighteen pence.

In a reversal of the situation before the plague, where land shortages meant high prices, there was now more and more land available at rock-bottom prices. People were not slow to take advantage of this and moved to enlarge their holdings, often by marriage as well as by purchase. As early as November 1348, one John Fish, a freeman of the manor of Thornbury on the banks of the River Severn bought the land of Isabel Lynch for a very reduced price, then in April married Agnes Gibbs whose husband John had died in November, getting her land too. In five months he had put together a holding of over ten acres. Between December 1348 and March 1349, in the same manor, John Cole, a fisherman, by marrying another widow and taking over his father's land, had taken control of twenty-four acres. By the way, if you are having a bit of trouble keeping track of all the Johns, first names being in short supply among the peasants of the fourteenth century, that's John the Reeve, John Cole the fisherman, John Fish the freeman and old John Gibbs the dead one. Okay?

Back in Farnham, John the Reeve showed that the confidence of his fellow tenants who had voted him in was not misplaced and by the autumn of 1350, thirty-six of the vacant tenancies had been filled. But his troubles were not over. John faced another barrier to balancing Farnham's books: a hike in labour costs, as the few workers left used their scarcity to leverage higher pay. By 1350, the carpenters and tilers he hired to make repairs were charging between six and ten pence a day, three times their old wages.

It's testament to John's leadership skills and to the graft and sheer grit of his much-reduced workforce that the harvest of 1349–50 at the demesne farm of Farnham was only slightly down on the previous year's and the acreage sown for the next year was also only slightly reduced. And the manor's dairymaid, who sadly remains nameless, made the usual amount of cheese – one hundred and forty-two cheeses across the summer and twenty-six in winter. Cheesemakers are tough.

After 1350, the plague began to abate and by the next winter it seems to have disappeared from most parts of Britain – at least, until the next round. John Runwick's name appears for the last time in this record in 1351 but, happily, he doesn't appear in the lists of plague deaths. I like to think that, having shepherded his community through the Great Mortality, he retired to look after his own land and that of his deceased neighbour, and that the survivors gathered together at one table to mourn and to celebrate with plenty of ale and one of the Farnham dairymaid's most excellent cheeses.

While everyone in the villages and towns where the Black Death seemed to have burnt itself out were heaving sighs of relief and getting back to normal life, there was one group of people who weren't feeling quite as relaxed – the landowners. As John Runwick had found in Farnham, the scarcity of labour was driving wages up, and workers were also becoming more mobile, as they could shop around for better pay and conditions. The lords complained to their king and in 1351 Edward III issued the Statutes of Labour. These statues attempted to limit wages to pre-plague levels and, by enforcing longer contracts on unfree workers, limited them to their original manor. The statues also levied penalties against landowners who enticed workers away from other estates. For workers who refused to swear to abide by the statutes, it was the stocks and jail. As a measure of how widely these labour laws were to be enforced, the statues stipulated that stocks be built in every village.

As you can imagine, these laws weren't very popular, nor were they observed all that consistently, and the rise in wages turned out to be an economic trend as inexorable as the the rising of the tide. Eventually even the most reactionary landlords had to accept the new reality and change their practices. This meant the disappearance of demesne farming. It had become uneconomic to directly manage the demesne farms of the manors and it now made more sense to rent the land out and take profits in cash. Peasants who had already expanded their property portfolio during the first outbreak of the plague were well placed to rent or even buy land from their old masters, who then (as landlords tend to) raised the rents. So the new farmers needed to to generate more cash, and the best way to do that was to produce high-value, low-bulk goods to sell in the new markets. It was time to make cheese. Lots of cheese.

The new markets, in turn, led to new technology. If you want an example of the 'for the want of a nail' theory of historical change, the invention and adoption of the horse collar, which allowed horses, with their greater speed and endurance, to replace slower-moving oxen as a means of transport, is a great one. Invented in China, the horse collar seems to have spread to Europe in the tenth century and by the time of the Black Death horses were replacing oxen across Britain. Suffolk led the shift, and it was the peasant farmers of that county who were piling on the horsepower; by the end of the thirteenth century, seventy-five per cent of their draught animals were horses. The early adopter peasant cheesemakers of Suffolk could shift larger loads more quickly than their more hidebound contemporaries in other counties. Horses also eat less than oxen, and so the change made much more fodder available to feed the growing dairy herds.

Suffolk also had its own breed of dairy cow, dun-coloured with a large head and pot belly. Suffolk dairy cows gave a large yield of milk for comparatively little food and their milk was full of butterfat – good milk for making nice rich cheese, and good for skimming off to make butter, which was highly prized in city markets. The cheesemakers of Suffolk were nicely positioned for shipping cheese to London, while East Anglian ports such as Ipswich gave access to the English army, which once again was active in France. In 1386,

This thirteenth-century manuscript illustration shows a peasant woman milking a dun-coloured cow much like the popular Suffolk breed.

King Richard II, Edward's grandson, is recorded as commanding a serjeant-at-arms and an Ipswich merchant to buy sixty weys of cheese for the English garrison in Calais. A Suffolk wey weighed more than a Kentish wey, three hundred and fifty six pounds to be exact. So that meant the hungry soldiers would be getting almost ten thousand kilos of good Suffolk cheese.

Now might be the time to talk about what the English army was doing in France. For, all the while John Runwick and his cheesemakers had been struggling to keep things going through the Great Mortality, there had also been a war on – the Hundred Years 'War, which actually lasted a hundred and sixteen years. The war kicked off in 1336 and was fought in the main by the French and English, although Castilians, Basques, Portuguese, the Holy Roman Empire and even Danes also got involved at various times. Fighting took place mainly in the English possessions in France and eventually ended at the Battle of Castillion on 17 July 1453. The French won and the English ended up losing all of their French possessions except for Calais.

Though the war was fought on the other side of the English Channel, the effects of the conflict were almost as profound as those of the plague. One of the groups of people who benefited, however, were the cheesemakers, since – as we noted with the Romans – cheese makes great food for soldiers, being compact, portable and nutritious. At the end of the thirteenth century, during Edward I's campaigns in Wales, the army had become much more organised; not only did troops get paid an actual wage, but the government took on some of the responsibility of feeding them, rather than relying on foraging. Hence the big contract to supply cheese to those troops at Calais. This marked the onset of East Anglian domination of the cheese industry, which would persist for the next few hundred years. And, as these cheesemakers had already made the shift from sheep to cattle dairying, this period established the domination of the cow as the main provider of milk for cheesemaking. Indeed, the cow takeover was so complete in Britain and Ireland that even today many people are surprised to discover that sheep's milk cheeses exist, let alone that anyone is making them in the British Isles.

Perhaps not quite as momentously, French cheesemongers will have you believe that the Hundred Years' War changed the shape of one of their cheeses. Their exhibit is the white, mould-ripened Neufchâtel, a creamy cheese from Normandy with an impressive pedigree, having been mentioned in a charter of 1037. According to legend, Neufchâtel cheeses got their characteristic heart shape when the English army went home and lovesick peasant dairymaids sent their army boyfriends cheese valentines. This is a sweet story, but almost certainly fiction, given first the misery handed out to the French peasantry by the English army, and second the cost of transport at the time. It wouldn't have been cheap or easy to send a single heart-shaped cheese to your English soldier boyfriend.

Whether cheeses changed their shape or not, though, the war changed the people who fought in it. While it can't have been fun getting bludgeoned in battle or experiencing dysentry in an army camp, many of the soldiers that survived came back richer, with plunder that would enable them to buy some of that newly available land. Such peasant soldiers may also have felt greater confidence in conflicts with their feudal overlords, not to mention the use of the weapons they had brought home.

🧀   🧀   🧀

Another significant effect of the Hundred Years' War is that it cost an awful lot of money, money that was raised in part from some singularly unpopular taxes, which were to cause all sorts of trouble and social change.

The Peasants' Revolt, which ran from May to August of 1381, was led by Wat Tyler, probably a veteran of the war in France, alongside the charismatic preacher John Ball – author of the couplet that characterised the uprising, 'When Adam delved, and Eve span, who was then the gentleman?' Resentment had been building over the failing and costly war in France, and the efforts of the landed classes to maintain their feudal domination. The spark for revolt was a massive poll tax of £160,000, raised in the spring of 1381. In Brentwood, in June, representatives of various local villages, probably armed with 'souvenirs' from the war, refused to pay the tax and sent the collector and his guards packing. Word spread through Essex and Kent and well-armed and organised bands of rebels coalesced and headed for London, the Kent rebels stopping on the way for a bit of a practice ravage of the city of Canterbury.

Rebels from Essex arrived at Aldgate, where they were let in by fellow London rebels, and the bands from Kent turned up at Borough, on the south side of London Bridge. They joined forces in the City and set about Savoy Palace, the opulent town residence of the hated John of Gaunt, whom many saw as the architect of their misfortunes. There followed a massacre of Flemish merchants who lived and ran their business in the city. Horribly, they were challenged to say 'bread and cheese', and if what they said sounded too much like 'brote and kase' they were killed. Meantime, a group of Crown officials were taken from their refuge in the Tower of London and beheaded, among them Simon of Sudbury, archbishop, lord chancellor and partisan of Gaunt, which in the rebels' eyes counted as three strikes against him. You can if you wish visit St George's Church in Sudbury, Suffolk, and see his mummified head there.

The revolt in London lost much of its momentum when the young King Richard II rode out to Mile End to meet with the rebels and at first appeared to acquiesce to many of their demands. This was a brave move and a bit of a masterstroke. Soon after, in a confused melee at Smithfield's, Mayor William Walworth, who had let the rebels cross London Bridge, stabbed Wat Tyler, who was then finished off by a royal squire. Confused and leaderless, the rebels were commanded to disperse and go back to their villages, which, perhaps rather sheepishly, they did.

The Peasants' Revolt included not just rural workers but the urban poor, tradespeople, burgesses, and the newly powerful townspeople, who hated the feudal restrictions that held back their development. This was particularly the case in riots that broke out in towns and cities outside London, such as the East Anglian town of Bury St Edmunds, with its growing bourgeoisie.

From 1100 to 1300, the total number of towns in Britain had grown from a hundred to eight hundred and thirty. In England, the proportion of population living in towns doubled, and in rural Wales and Scotland it increased by ten times. Ireland saw less change, as the urban population were confined to the Pale around Dublin, while in the rest of the country people still tended to live in small, widely distributed villages.

The growth of the towns was particularly good news for people with cheese to sell. The thing about towns is that the people who live in them are too busy, and have too little land, to grow or make their food. They were ripe for the cheesemakers, and for their salesmen, the cheesemongers. Like other mongers, they found that running a market stall could be a lucrative business, as is shown by records of the rents. A stall of one hundred square feet at a good location might cost ten shillings a year, which outside a town would get you twenty acres of good agricultural land.

The network of markets was, by law, widely distributed, in order to reduce the possibility of competition and conflict between the towns that ran them – a major issue in the days when everyone carried a sword, or a knife or some sort of terrifying agricultural implement like a billy hook or a flail. The optimal distance between markets was, as a thirteenth-century lawyer Henry Bracton recommended, 'no closer together than six and two thirds miles'. And they really weren't kidding about this. In the twelfth century, Abbot Samson of Bury St Edmunds sent six hundred armed men to break up the nearby market at Lakenheath, which he reckoned was drawing profit away from his market in Bury town square. His men smashed up stalls and took produce and livestock from the stallholders.

Timing was another factor that could cause trouble, so markets near each other were set up on different days. But, despite all such efforts, there was sporadic conflict between market towns. In 1274, the people of Salisbury complained that the bailiffs and men of nearby Wilton had been waylaying travellers on their way to Salisbury market and forcing them to sell their goods in their market. In their defence, the people of Wilton claimed that the Salisbury market was open every day instead of just on Tuesdays, as its royal charter stipulated. Since Wiltshire was and is a county famous for its cheese, this raises the engaging possibility of medieval cheese highway robbery.

This distributed network of smaller markets, leading up to a large one at the end of the week, was perfect for the small-scale cheesemaker who couldn't leave their farm for more than a day or so. They could take their cheese to a small market a day's travel away, at most, and sell it to traders who would shift it up the network. And, to make it easier for buyers, markets had specific goods areas. In 1416, in Salisbury market, a sheltered area known as the Cheese Cross was built (along with a Poultry Cross and Crosses for livestock and wool), and cheesemongers ordered to stick to the area around it. Chippenham market, established by King John in 1205, still has a Butter Cross – a pitched roof supported by stone pillars, under which the cheesemongers could shelter from the elements to sell their cheese. I very much like the sound of these medieval markets with their covered purpose-built stalls. At Borough Market, where I began my trade, there was no more covering than a large umbrella, and in the winter the icy wind fairly whistled up off the Thames.

Of course, if you really wanted to cash in, London was the place. The cheese trade had been going on in the capital ever since the city's early medieval revival (remember those women paying King Aethelred a premium toll for their Christmas cheese stalls?) and by the thirteenth century cheese was big business. Parish records recall that on 7 July 1227 the unfortunate Elias the Porter fell dead in Bread Street under a load of cheese. Whether his overworked heart gave out under the weight of the load or he was killed by a falling cheese, the record does not relate. Fatalities aside, by the mid-fourteenth century cheese was important enough for the City authorities to regulate the trade. In 1377, the last year of Edward III's long reign, the Ordinances of the Cheesemongers were presented to the aldermen of London at the Guildhall.

The Ordinances of the Cheesemongers give us an idea of the scale of cheese trade in London and, by their prohibitions, the sharp practices cheesemongers were prone to. There were two official markets for cheese in London at the time. One was at Leadenhall, where there is to this day a cheese shop; the other was between St Nicolas Shambles and Newgate, near St Paul's Cathedral. The Ordinances specify that 'foreigners' (i.e. not Londoners) bringing their cheese in by horse and cart must sell their cheese at the official markets and not 'put away in houses or in rooms...any cheese or butter', on pain of confiscation of their product. The nefarious 'bersters' of Ham and Hackney had, it seems, been intercepting cheese on its way into the city and adding their mark-up before selling it 'to the great damage of the commonality', a practice known as forestalling. They would tell unsuspecting customers

Chippenham's Butter Cross. A reconstruction of the original, this would still provide some shelter for a chilly cheesemonger.

that they were the producers of the cheese and that it was made on their very own farms. Particularly egregious, apparently, were the Welsh 'strangers' bringing in cheese from Talgarth. These wily mongers stored their cheese in Fleet Street and Holborn and sold it it in secret 'against the old custom'. The hours of trading were regulated, too. Selling cheese before 7 a.m. earned you a stretch in the notorious Newgate Prison, where your cheese would be seized and handed out to the inmates.

The aldermen required that the 'good folk of said trade' pick two from their number each year on the feast of St Michaelmas to oversee the cheesemongers, and heavy fines awaited the cheesemonger who abused the powers of such office. It is thanks to that last ordinance the we know the names of two of the cheesemongers of medieval London: 'On the seventeenth of June, in the fifty-first year etc. [this means the fifty-first year of Edward's reign, 1377] William Sparke and Robert Whyte were here sworn well and trustily to oversee the articles above written.'

The presentation of ordinances was normally followed by the establishment of a guild, which might have led to the marvellous occurrence of a cheesemonger as Lord Mayor of London, but sadly this was not to be. While many, if not all, of the medieval trade guilds still exist, a Worshipful Company of Cheesemongers was never formed.

But what cheeses did Messrs Sparke and Whyte sell at Leadenhall Market? George and Kathleen Fussell's authoritative book, *The English Dairy Farmer 1500–1900*, suggests the following varieties were known: one-meal cheeses; two-meal cheeses; morning milk cheese; nettle cheese; skim or flett milk cheese; cheese made from the stroakings (the last and creamiest milk from a cow's udder), like Angelot cheese; and cream cheese like that of Padua. Most of these styles are familiar to us. Here are some modern examples in the same order: Single Gloucester (made from lower-fat milk from the morning milking session); Double Gloucester (made from both morning and evening milk for a richer cheese); Cornish Yarg (wrapped in nettles);

Parmesan (made from skimmed milk); and Reblochon (from the French *reblocher*, to hold back milk from the first milking, ending up with creamier milk for cheesemaking); Philadelphia (cream cheese – well, everything's got to start somewhere).

It's interesting that the only named cheese in this list, Angelot, is foreign – Norman in fact. It's almost as if the cheese fanciers of medieval London prized foreign cheeses over their own. Angelot, a small, square, washed-rind cheese, seems to have been around for almost as long as Neufchâtel. Ancient lore has it that it was developed in the monasteries of Normandy in the twelfth century. You can very easily try a descendant of Angelot if you want to explore medieval tastes. It's called Pont l'Evêque and comes from the eponymous Normandy town.

When you think about it, if foreign cheeses were going to find their way to the London markets, Norman cheeses would have a pretty good shot, given the background of the English ruling class, their tastes and their connections with their homeland. Of course, the most famous Norman cheese is Camembert, and although cheese legend only traces this signature French cheese back to the eighteenth century, and a meeting between a cheesemaker and a clergyman from Brie fleeing the persecution of the Revolution, I think it's fair enough to say that peasant cheesemakers were making small mould-ripened cheeses a long time before then. In fact, I'm picturing quite the selection of fancy 'fromages Normandes' at Sparke and Whyte's of Leadenhall, what with a funky little washed-rind Angelot, a super-creamy heart-shaped Neufchâtel and a wrinkly orange-flecked Camembert.

Norman cheeses also come highly commended in sixteenth-century writer Barnabe Googe's list of the best cheeses 'in our daies.' He ranks them third – and places English cheeses, rather gallingly, last. The number two spot, according to Barnabe, is occupied by 'the Hollande cheese', which might come as a surprise if the first thing that springs to mind is a rubbery factory-made Edam from the corner shop. In fact, the ubiquity of Edam today is a testament

A medieval cheesemonger having a nice chat with a customer. That cat probably shouldn't be sitting on the maturing shelves.

to the cheese-marketing skills of medieval Dutch farmers, who after too-aggressive draining of wheatfields had switched en masse to dairying. Mindful of the need to develop an export business to pay for wheat imports, these canny cheesemakers designed their cheeses for ease of shipping, durability and distinctiveness. The round shape of Edam and Gouda, named after famous regional cheese markets, meant their edges wouldn't get damaged in transit, and their bright red and yellow rinds were a result of coatings that protected the cheeses from insect damage and made them stand out nicely on a cheese stall as 'Hollande cheese'.

And Barnabe Googe's top cheese? This, he says, was 'counted the Parmasines', whose origin he correctly locates 'about the River of Po' in Northern Italy, where they are still made. Googe records that these cheeses are 'much stemmed for their greatnesse and daintinesse' and weigh 'above threescore pound,' pretty much the same as they do now. We have other authorities for its status, too. In 1532, a courtier called Antony Cassydony gave King Henry VIII a whole Parmesan for New Year's Eve. And, not to be outdone, in 1533, Edward Bonner sent his boss Thomas Cromwell four whole Parmesan cheeses which he had brought back himself from Parma, on the way back from a meeting with the Pope over the King's desire to divorce Catherine of Aragon. Two hundred and eighty pounds of top quality Italian cheese was quite a gift. And it paid off, for in 1539 Bonner would be ordained Bishop of London.

Parmesan cheese is thought to have a monastic origin, as the usual suspects, Cistercian monks, moved into the Po valley in the twelfth century and developed irrigation systems of such colossal scale that they were able to farm enough cattle to produce such large cheeses. Paul Kindstedt, author of the estimable *Cheese and Culture*, believes that these monastic producers borrowed from the techniques of Alpine cheesemakers to make their large hard cheeses, cutting the curd into small particles and heating it in its whey to very high temperatures in great copper vats, as their secular descendants still do today. He suggests that this knowledge was transferred from Alpine monasteries like St Gall through the continent-spanning network of monastic houses.

The international cheese trade of the period wasn't just one way. Cheeses from Britain also made their way to foreign markets on the back of the wool trade, as wool buyers bought up consignments of cheese to sell in the Flanders markets.

We have an enthusiastic description of these cheeses from an Italian writer, which also gives us a rare account of what they looked like. Pantaleone da Confienza, physician to the Duke of Savoy, published his *Summa Lacticiniorum* (*Compendium of Milk Products*) in 1477, the first significant literary work on cheese and cheesemaking since the agricultural writers of classical Rome. It is a comprehensive account of regional and local cheeses, beginning with those of Pantaleone's home region of Northern Italy and moving on to French cheeses (notably Brie and the goat's cheeses of Poitou), before dismissing German cheese out of hand. But then a surprise. According to Pantaleone, British cheeses are terrific – and comparable to the best Italian produce. He celebrates the pastures of Britain, which ensure a plentiful supply of excellent wool and make for cheese of excellent quality and abundance. Pantaleone says that, had he not seen the amount and excellence of British cheese with his own eyes, he would not have believed this – which suggests that even five hundred years ago, British gastronomy had a poor reputation on the continent.

In particular, Pantaleone compares British cheeses with those of Piacenza in colour and flavour, although not in size, being 'not as massive'. Piacenza is still famous for its Grana Padano, a close cousin to Parmesan whose wheels weigh in at a respectable thirty-five kilos. It's tempting to think, then, that British cheese might have had the dense but moist texture and lovely golden colour of these massive, noble cheeses. Pantaleone also gives us a wonderful description of how beautiful these cheeses were – 'stamped with figures of animals, letters, flowers and similar things'.

Confirming the transition from sheep's to cow's milk at this time, he notes that English cheeses are mostly made of cow's milk, but with some sheep's milk still mixed in. His only mild criticism of the cheese is that, being quite hard, it is difficult to digest, and that if makers used less sheep's milk in the mix these cheeses might be a bit softer. He may have had a point. Sheep's milk has a higher proportion of solids to liquid than cow's milk and tends to need less rennet to coagulate. That means if you're using the amount of rennet needed to coagulate cow's milk, a mixed-milk cheese might turn out much harder. On the other hand, sheep's milk is higher in nutritious mineral content than cow's milk and may be easier to digest, as the fat particles are smaller. Cheesemaking is complex.

As to the size of the beautiful English, or British cheeses, while 'not as massive as the cheese of Piacenza' isn't a very accurate guide to size, Kindstedt, another foreigner, writing five hundred years later, believes that the British cheese of this period were wheels of around eight pounds, twelve inches across and four deep. Which is exactly the size and shape of a Gorwydd Caerphilly.

I wonder if something like this is what those wily Welsh 'strangers' brought into London with them.

Caerphilly is to the Welsh what Cheddar is to the English. It first appears in the historical record in the 1830s, when cheeses coming in for Caerphilly market started to get an official grading. The best cheeses, according to the world's first Caerphilly grader, Edward Lewis, would get a circular stamp saying 'Genuine Caerphilly Cheese'. But the native cheeses of a region don't just come into being when a bloke turns up with a stamp. They grow out of a local

*Fourteenth-century cheesemaking. Note the mould and ladle on the table,
and the woman stirring curds as they heat.*

tradition of cheesemaking and I am confident that was the case
with Caerphilly. What got stamped in the market-place had been
made locally since medieval times.

The Great Mortality had killed at least a quarter of the population
of Wales and, as in England, speeded up the change in how land was
owned and managed. Norman English rule had been even more
despotic in Wales than in England and the burgeoning resentment
culminated in Owain Glyndwr's rising in 1400. As much as this
was a nationalist rebellion against a foreign ruler – Henry IV, who
deposed Richard II in 1399 – it was also a people's rising against

oppressive overlords, in line with the Peasants' Revolt twenty years earlier in England. The Welsh recovery from the plague had also been cruelly retarded by financial demands made upon them from the English exchequer to fight the Hundred Years' War.

Henry V learnt his soldiering in Wales, and carried on the war against the Welsh after his father, Henry IV, died, although he seemed to have a more conciliatory attitude. Henry even offered Glyndwr a pardon, although the doughty old warrior refused it. Glyndwr seems to have died around 1415, whereupon the revolt ended.

The immediate aftermath of the Revolt was a hard time for the Welsh, who had to contend with the devastation wrought by the conflict and a harsh penal code. Under these new laws, the Welsh had no right of public assembly, nor could they hold senior public office, bear arms, or live in a fortified town, which for some decades barred them from the benefits of urbanisation their English counterparts were enjoying.

But, in the decades after 1420, things improved. Port records show the import of luxury goods from Europe as well as necessaries, implying an upward trend in the economy. From Welsh ports, goods and people were shipped across to Ireland, up and down the coast of Wales and to south and northwest England. Goods included iron, ginger, salt, figs, resin, wool and cheese. Frustratingly, no one bothered to tell us what these Welsh cheeses looked like or how they tasted, but I'd assume that the carters and merchant seamen weren't bothering with little soft cheeses but were shipping firmer cheeses of a decent size, perhaps something around four kilos in weight, and twelve inches across, like a Caerphilly. Wales is famous for its sheep farming and, as the economy bounced back after the revolt, the wool trade boomed, particularly around the border towns. Also, by the 1470s, Welsh cattle had become big business, with drovers taking stock to cities as distant as London. So perhaps these proto-Caerphilly cheeses were made from either sheep's or cow's milk, or a mixture of both.

A remnant of Welsh cattle droving into London still exists in Columbia Road Market in the East End of London. It's a Victorian shopfront, with its original shop sign, 'S. Jones', that dates from the time before refrigeration, when herds of cattle would be taken to the city to provide fresh milk. The dairy (now a cafe) had been through various Welsh family owners – Jones's, Morgans and the like. Funnily enough, Todd and I used to have a little stall set up in there to sell the good people of Hackney his lovely Caerphilly.

But, to return to the 1430s. The fortunes of the Welsh shifted when a courtier from Anglesey, Owain ap Maredudd, married Catherine, the widow of Henry V. He took the name Tudwr, or Tudor, and, although he himself lost his head in the Wars of the Roses, his grandson was to become Henry VII, the first Tudor king. Under the new dynasty, the Welsh were widely recruited for the English army – valued particularly as longbowmen, they were thus the heroes of the victories over the French at Crécy and Agincourt. And, as well as their longbows, the Welsh were famed for their love of cheese, particularly of the toasted variety. A Tudor joke book called *A Hundred Merry Tales*, published in

Jones's Dairy in Ezra Street, just off Columbia Road.

1526, has a story about this. God, displeased with the many chattering Welshmen in Heaven, tasks Saint Peter with their removal. Peter opens the gates of Heaven, stands outside, and shouts 'Toasted cheese!' at which all the Welsh rush out to get their hands on their favourite delicacy.

It is thus no accident that the most famous Welsh dish is Welsh Rarebit, in which (if made properly) cheese is melted with beer, salt and pepper to make a luxurious sauce that is spread on bread and grilled. If you haven't tried it, I suggest you put down this book now and go and make it. Fergus Henderson, founder of the St John restaurant, has a great recipe in his book, *The Whole Beast*, which calls for Cheddar (450g), a knob of butter, Guinness (200ml), cayenne pepper (1/2 tsp), English mustard powder (1 tsp) and Worcestershire sauce ('a very long splash'). But, for a more Welsh flavour, you could use Gorwydd Caerphilly. And don't cut the rind off when you grate it, by the way; the rind goes lovely and peppery when you grill it. For the beer, to maintain the Welsh theme, I recommend Cwtch Red Ale from Tiny Rebel Brewery in Newport. You don't need much beer for the sauce, so you can drink the rest of the can while your rarebit grills. As to where I stand on the whole rarebit/rabbit debate (it is said that 'rarebit' is an eighteenth-century attempt to give the dish ethnic authenticity), Fergus calls it rarebit, and that's good enough for me.

Further evidence of a longstanding Welsh enthusiasm for cheese can be found in the country's fairy tales. According to Wirt Sykes, journalist, folklorist and US consul in Cardiff in the 1880s: 'Bread is found in the folklore of every country; but cheese is thus honoured only in Wales.' I don't agree with Sykes about the exclusivity of Welsh cheese folklore, but cheese certainly turns up a lot in the Welsh tales. One story tells of a farmer besotted with a lake spirit. A soothsayer advises him to tempt her with an offering of bread and cheese. but it is only when he throws his largest and finest cheese into the lake that she consents to be his wife. In another tale, the cows of Corwrion are feted for the excellence of the cheese they

Welsh rarebit, St John style. Don't forget the Lee & Perrins. *Nor the pint of Pale Ale.*

produce because they have been crossbred with a fairy herd. If this Corwrion is modern Corwen in Denbighshire, famous for its dairy farming, this might have been an astute bit of marketing on the part of the locals. Mischievous fairies, or Tylwyth Teg, seemed to have a particular fondness for dairy products, milking cows and goats dry in the night and breaking into dairies.

Far and away the nicest bit of Welsh cheese folklore, though, is the old custom of making a large creamy cheese for the birth of someone's first child. The cheese is made, as always, by the women, who must tell no man what they are doing. At the birth celebration the women refuse all offers of food from the new father, but as soon as his back is turned they feast gleefully on this lovely rich cheese, accompanied with some nice beer. And at the end of the party all the women take a piece of the cheese home with them, thus ensuring health and prosperity for mother and child.

☞ ☞ ☞

In my search for the origins of Caerphilly, I sought out a woman called Eurwen Richards, who, I was told, had been making, grading and teaching cheese since the 1950s.

Eurwen began making Caerphilly cheese with her mum in the 1940s, in the kitchen of their farmhouse in the valleys north of Cardiff. They used milk from their herd of fifteen dairy cows, which was quite a decent size for a family farm in those days. She still remembers her mum's method clearly. The milk was curdled in great conical earthenware bowls and they didn't need to use starter, since the raw milk, straight from the cow, was already beginning to sour. Her mum used rennet from a little bottle, but their neighbour still did it the ancient way, with a piece of dried calf stomach which she just put in the milk. There was none of your fancy measuring of acidity; Eurwen's mum simply felt the curd with her hand, knowing by experience when it would be ready to cut, which she did with an ordinary kitchen knife. After the cutting, the curd would be heated ('scalded', in proper cheesemaker talk), the whey drained off and the resulting curd – 'moist, soft and velvety', in Eurwen's words – packed into cheese moulds and pressed.

That was her family's Caerphilly, but there was plenty of variation. Eurwen's father once interviewed an elderly cheesemaker, who must have learnt her craft in the nineteenth century. Her house was on the side of a hill, and its cellar, dug into the hill, was quite damp. Her Caerphillies tended to be blue, which didn't seem to bother anyone. This lady sold her cheese straight from the window of her farmhouse with a cut cheese resting on the windowsill to tempt passers-by. Eurwen's cousins made cheese in the Vale of

Glamorgan, on lush farmland now covered by a car factory. Their cheese was made from cow's and sheep's milk mixed together (like the cheese our man Pantaleone da Confienza tried), but they also called it Caerphilly.

I asked Eurwen if people ever made skimmed-milk Caerphilly, taking off the cream, like the medieval cheesemakers of East Anglia. She thought that medieval Caerphilly would usually have been skimmed, since the cream was so valuable, and that people would have eaten the skimmed-milk cheese young, before it got too hard. Eurwen and her mum made skimmed-milk cheese seventy years ago in the farmhouse kitchen, which they ate at a few weeks old before it had 'turned to stone'. To give the young cheese flavour, Eurwen's mum would send her out to the garden to pick sage to add to the curd. As the sage tends to look a bit black and unappetising, they added the juice from spinach leaves to give it a nice green colour. Eurwen sniffed dismissively as she told me this. 'Nowadays, they just get green colouring from a bottle.' I was oddly excited when Eurwen told me all this, because I had made cheese flavoured with sage and coloured with spinach juice in a real Tudor kitchen as part of a medieval cheesemaking course held at the Weald & Downland Living Museum in West Sussex. This cheese didn't have time to turn into stone, because my wife and I ate it that night. It was very nice.

Eurwen told me that all the local farmers' wives would have had their own cheese recipes. The cheese we now think of as Caerphilly was simply the best cheesemaker's recipe – the most popular at Caerphilly market, or wherever else it was being sold – which other cheesemakers would have tried to match. Eurwen believes that all the traditional cheeses around today have come down to us through this process, a sort of survival-of-the-fittest cheese, and her idea makes much sense.

Even today, there is still some argument about the definition of Caerphilly. Once, in preparation for doing a tasting, I rang up a woman called Jemima who had taken over making Duckett's

Caerphilly from cheesemaking legend Chris Duckett, and asked her how she would define it. Jemima had a very clear idea of what the cheese should be, down to the correct pH level of the final cheese and the depth of breakdown – the creamy line between rind and paste. Todd Trethowan had a less precise definition of Caerphilly, more in keeping with what I heard from Eurwen. His actual words were, 'I don't know fella, it's just the cheese I make on my farm.' He also speculated that in its early days people didn't deliberately mature the cheeses and grow their velvety rinds, they just ate it when they thought it was ready. If they had made enough for some of it to sit around for longer in a cellar or barn waiting for market day, then it would have developed more of a rind and a deeper flavour.

❧ ❧ ❧

For those unlucky readers who have not yet encountered a handmade rinded Trethowan's Gorwydd Caerphilly, in all its velvet-robed glory, now is the time for a bit of explaining. The Caerphilly you may have seen or even bought in a supermarket – square, plastic-wrapped, bone white and crumbly all the way through – is essentially the young 'Caerphilly' that Somerset Cheddar makers used to sell for a quick return. Top-of-the- range Caerphilly is today a very different beast – soft and creamy on the outside and with a firmer, whiter centre. Here's how it came about.

By the time I got to Neal's Yard Dairy in 2002, all the Caerphilly – we stocked both Duckett's and Gorwydd – was matured until it had grown a mould rind about five millimetres thick. This habit, according to Todd, was an accident. In the early days Caerphilly had been sold young and rindless. The story goes that one day a Dairy monger happened upon a batch of slow-selling Caerphillies waiting on shelf in a nearby Soho deli. Sitting in their cardboard boxes in a cool cellar, these cheeses had grown an attractive grey rind. The cheeses were tasted and found to be good, and experimentation began. Years later, when I was looking after Caerphillies, we still kept them in their cardboard boxes, three to a box, in their first blush of youth. The cheeses, all hugger-mugger, keep each other warm and the mould gets a good start.

I believe that this practice of maturing Caerphilly so that they develop a rind isn't so much of an invention by Neal's Yard Dairy as a rediscovery of an old practice. One reason I have for saying this is that back in 2000 there were still older customers around who, on

A very big cheese or a very small cheese shop? Trethowan's Caerphilly, with extensive breakdown.

tasting the Gorwydd's, would exclaim with happy nostalgia, 'that's what it used to taste like when I was young!' Which suggests that in the early decades of the twentieth century at least some Caerphilly was being matured to this point.

Whether rinded Caerphilly is true Caerphilly is a bit contentious. I know of at least one Welsh cheese expert who believes the rind to be a fault and marks cheeses like that down in agricultural shows. Todd reckons that, in the old days of farmhouse cheesemaking, people didn't have such fixed ideas of what a cheese should be. They would enjoy eating cheeses fresh at a few days or a week old and, if there was enough of a surplus for some to be left to mature, these were eaten with equal enthusiasm. I'm with Todd on this.

Caerphilly rind, like that of Camembert, ripens the cheese from the outside in, breaking its firm dry texture down into something almost liquid and softening the bright citric acidity of the young cheese into a rich, cabbagey creaminess. We call that creamy layer between rind and centre the 'breakdown', and in maturing a Caerphilly it's all about the proportion of centre to breakdown. I like my Gorwydd to be balanced, with only about a centimetre of creamy breakdown, in exciting contrast to the firmer citric middle, and in this I follow its makers, who prefer their cheese on the younger side. Todd once found one of his cheeses in a French cheese shop, where they had matured it until completely broken down and creamy all the way through, with a cracked and gnarled rind. Todd picked it up and, aggrieved, accosted the unsuspecting cheesemonger on duty who had no idea who he was, saying, 'What have you done with my baby?!' Feelings run high in the world of affinage.

Eurwen also said that describing Caerphilly as a 'Welsh cheese' is not telling the whole story. She pointed out that it is traditionally a cheese of South Wales. On the salty soil of North Wales, cheesemakers made Cheshire, or more properly a Cheshire-style cheese, like their sister cheesemakers over the border in Cheshire and Shropshire. She told me that in the nineteenth century the

Cheddar makers in Somerset made Caerphilly when they needed some ready cash, since Cheddar needs to mature for a year or more, so you can be waiting a while to see the profit on it. By contrast, they could make Caerphilly ready to eat in two or three weeks. Todd believes that this appropriation of Caerphilly by Cheddar makers might be one reason why the perception of Caerphilly changed from a mould-rinded cheese with moist and creamy layer to a drier, unrinded more crumbly cheese. Cheddar makers are big chaps, as they need to be, for in their mature state traditional Cheddars weigh about twenty-four kilos. The curd for Cheddar is also resilient and can stand a bit of bashing about. Caerphilly curd, on the other hand, is delicate and requires gentle treatment to retain its moisture and structure. Used to a more resilient curd, these hefty West Country cheesemakers ended up making a firmer, drier cheese.

Todd Trethowan, like almost every single cheesemonger I know, didn't really plan a career in cheese. In the early 1990s, he was about to begin a degree in archaeology when he happened to wander past Neal's Yard Dairy. Enticed by the intriguing and heady aroma, he tried some cheese and had a similar experience to the one I would have years later on his stall – a cheese epiphany. Luckily for him, me and the fortunes of Caerphilly cheese, the Dairy happened to be advertising vacancies and so Todd went for what he thought would be a summer job (as many of us did when we went for that fateful interview). He soon demonstrated his selfless commitment to cheese when he fell down some steps while carrying a twenty-four-kilo Lancashire, saving the cheese rather than himself as he bounced on his behind from step to step, earning a bruised coccyx and a permanent place in Dairy legend. Having demonstrated his love of cheese to himself as much as his new colleagues, Todd was

The Trethowan brothers – Todd (left) and Maugan (right). Stirring by hand for extra creaminess.

soon spending every holiday selling cheese and looking after it in the cellar.

In the battle between cheese and academia, cheese won, although it was a close-run thing. On the day he was supposed to be turning up at Sheffield University to begin his PhD (on the evolution of modern humans), Todd set off for Dougal Campbell's farm in the hills above Lampeter to start making a cheese called Tyn Grug. Unbothered by the mental and physical demands of cheesemaking, and boldly if politely declining to go into business with Campbell, a leading light of the artisan cheese renaissance, Todd decided to become a cheesemaker in his own right.

Victorian cheese press still in use to make Trethowan's Caerphilly.

Luckily, his family owned Gorwydd farm, just outside the village of Llanddewi Brefi. Gorwydd is a sheep farm, and at the time Todd thought he would make a sheep's cheese. But fate intervened in the person of Jane Scotter, part owner of Neal's Yard Dairy, who suggested he make Caerphilly, since there was no one else making traditional Caerphilly in Wales at the time, which seemed a shame.

There being no one to learn from in Wales, Todd travelled to Somerset to learn the art with Chris Duckett, whose family had been making the cheese on their farm at Wedmore in the Somerset Levels since the 1920s. For the next six months, Todd lived alone in a caravan, in a field next to the dairy. He had no car, and no way to get into the village and so, for seven days a week, he made cheese in the mornings and then spent the afternoons in his caravan writing notes on what he had learnt that day.

Chris Duckett himself was a man of few words; in fact, to describe him as taciturn would be like saying that Everest is quite high. On Todd's first day he engaged a new colleague in friendly conversation over the cheese vat, only to be told, 'Chris doesn't like us to talk.' 'You mean, about non-work stuff?' asked Todd. 'At all,' came the reply. 'I figured out I had three questions a day before he'd get fed up,' Todd told me years later, 'so I had to make them count.'

Todd also recalled that Chris Duckett had three fused vertebrae in his back, from a lifetime of bending over a vat. I had always thought that big hard cheeses like Cheddar, weighing in at more than thirty kilos when young and full of moisture, must be the most physically debilitating cheeses to make, but Todd put me right, having recently added Cheddar making to his portfolio of cheeses. 'Caerphilly's much worse: all that leaning over the vat to texture the curds with a knife, then still bent over it to pack the curd into the moulds. Cheddar curd goes onto the draining table where you can work at a civilised height. Cheddar's easy.'

Having completed his apprenticeship, Todd went back to the farm at Llanddewi, where in 1996 he began to make cheese with his brother Maugan, who had also begun a career as an archaeologist before he too succumbed to the lure of cheese. The brothers set up their new dairy in a small stone outbuilding on the farm. Stone is a perfect material for a dairy, keeping a constant temperature in the building across the seasons and providing a happy home on its rough porous surface for the mould spores that give Gorwydd its unique flavour. The brothers then set about experimenting, in order to make the ultimate Caerphilly. They way they did so speaks to the painstaking, one might say obsessive, attention to detail that characterises great cheesemakers.

Their approach was to take one step of the process at a time and vary it massively – for example, if the ideal temperature of the milk is 22° C, they might take it up to 50° C. They did this to see what role each step had in the final outcome, so that they could really understand their process. When he told me about this, I was surprised, since I'd always thought of Todd as an instinctive cheesemaker, doing things by feel and taste rather than instrumentation. 'Maugs is the scientific one,' he explained. During that early phase of mad scientist experimentation, Maugan 'martialled the data, looked for the patterns and worked out what experiment to do next'. The very definition of a cheesemaker.

Combining Todd's instinct and Maugan's brain, plenty of hard graft and probably a bit of luck, things paid off. Just taking the last four years' crop of awards, Gorwydd Caerphilly has won eleven gold medals and two super gold medals in a variety of competitions both national and global. Nigel Slater has pronounced it 'one of the best cheeses in the world'. It's seriously good cheese.

Graft aside, I think one reason that Gorwydd Caerphilly is so wonderful is that it was born in a lovely place, the little village of Llanddewi Brefi, nesting in the green hills of Ceredigion in west Wales. Gorwydd Farm is on a hill just outside the village and, with its stone buildings, if you squint a bit with your back to the tractor, it look likes like nothing has changed there for hundreds of years. I remember on my first visit marvelling at the light and airy cheese room with its white walls and red floor, and the vat in the centre with more milk than I'd ever seen in one place before. Also the considered movement and soft voices of people making a cheese with a delicate curd like Caerphilly, where impatience and un-gentleness could ruin the texture. And then the maturing room, whose three-foot-thick stone walls keep it dark, cool and quiet. Ranks of cheeses on their wooden boards filled the room from floor to ceiling, shading in colour from young to old, the young ones a pale ivory, darkening and turning grey-green as they grew their coats of mould.

Later that day, we went to the New Inn, the village pub. As befits a village of just five hundred people, it felt like you were sitting in the landlord's living room with some nice new friends (who kindly switched from speaking Welsh to English so that I didn't feel too left out). There wasn't a large range of beer, since there wasn't much room, and the casks of real ale were kept outside. To order one, you asked for a pint of 'Out the Back'. Funnily enough, it was just the sort of beer that went perfectly with a delicate and restrained cheese like Gorwydd, its lemony centre and earthy rind working together with those hoppy flavours.

Gorwydd Caerphilly is now made in Somerset – Cowslip Lane, near Weston-Super-Mare, to be exact. The Trethowans moved their operation there in 2014, partly because of a very-wel-looked-after pedigree herd of Holsteins and Jerseys, who give lovely milk, partly because Llanddewi is small and remote and, after twenty years of the quiet rural life, everyone fancied a bit more excitement. When they moved, they took a lot of unwashed cheese boards with them, from the old maturing room, and left them stacked in the new one so that the mould could get used to its new home and keep on making those lovely rinds that give Gorwydd its distinctive and addictive character.

🧀 🧀 🧀

CHAPTER FIVE

Appleby's Cheshire

Big cheese

1547–1688

MY FAVOURITE CHESHIRE, and in fact one of my very favourite cheeses, is Appleby's, produced by Paul and Sarah Appleby and their head cheesemaker Garry Gray on Hawkstone Abbey Farm in Shropshire, not far from the medieval town of Shrewsbury. If you think of Cheshire as a pale, white, rather dry, crumbly cheese with a simple acidic flavour, Appleby's might be a bit of a surprise. The cheese, which comes in eight-kilo cylinders, is a sunset orange colour. The texture is crumbly but moist, a bit like firm fudge, and the flavour is complex yet perfectly balanced: a flinty minerality, butteriness, earth, all knitted together with a gentle acidity. When I went up there to visit the farm and see the cheese being made, Sarah described a particularly excellent batch as 'juicy'. It is a word I had never heard used to describe cheese before, and yet, juicy it is. Handmade with unpasteurised milk from the Applebys' own herd, set with animal rennet, bound in cloth and matured to between two and three months, this is a truly traditional Cheshire cheese.

And, if it seems a little confusing that this archetypal Cheshire is made in Shropshire, fear not: it is all part of this cheese's story.

To see what forces and currents shaped the development of this noble food we must go back to 1547 and the death of Henry VIII. Henry's reign had seen momentous changes sweeping the British Isles, changes driven by his desire for a male heir, religious reform and a massive increase in the state's administrative reach. Let's have a look at the score sheet. Henry married six women and executed two of them. He declared himself head of the English Church and had bibles printed in English placed in every church. But, for the world of cheese, it was his decision to close down the monasteries that had most impact. The Dissolution, as it became known, was effected with great thoroughness and brutality in the last decade of Henry's rule. Here, by way of example, is a letter from Henry to the last abbot of Glastonbury:

> My Good Lord Abbot —
> I hear you will not surrender to my commission. If you do not surrender on Monday, by God I will hang you on Wednesday on the high oak above ye Abbey of Glastonbury.
> Your poor friend, H.R.

And he did. Hang the abbot, I mean. On Glastonbury Tor.

If, as I contended earlier, the monastic affineurs of Britain and Ireland were responsible for washed-rind cheeses, then the Dissolution might explain why these disappear from the British Isles at this point, not to return until the cheese renaissance of the 1970s. A more positive effect of the closure of the monasteries was that their cheesemakers needed to find work on secular farms, and the monastic herds, flocks and the lands became available for purchase by those entrepreneurial peasants who had survived plague and war. These cheesemakers and their new employers were to become the yeomen and women who would be the backbone of British cheesemaking for the next two hundred years.

But first a quick historical review. Henry's son Edward VI established Protestantism throughout Britain, enforcing services in English and allowing priests to marry. Then came the five-year interlude of 'Bloody' Mary, notorious for her execution of Protestants, before the accession of the last of Henry's children, Elizabeth, in 1558. In her forty-four-year reign, Elizabeth ushered in a Church of England that was acceptable to the moderate majority of her subjects, repulsed the Spanish Armada, and presided over a golden age of English drama and global exploration. She was also, it must be recorded, very fond of cheese, declaring that 'a meal of bread, cheese and beer constitutes the perfect food'. It's nice to think that this came from a person who could eat pretty much anything she wanted, and at a time when the British economy was at a level unseen since the Romans.

Elizabeth died heirless in 1603 and the crown went to her nephew James VI of Scotland, the son of Mary, Queen of Scots, whom Elizabeth had had executed in 1587. James's accession was swiftly followed by the Gunpowder Plot of 1605, the work of disaffected Catholics. This was not, however, the first attempt on his life. Back in Scotland, James had allegedly been targeted on numerous occasions by witches, who had tried to kill him by enchanting the weather while he was at sea, setting poison traps, and other magical practices.

James's experiences at the sharp end of magical practice left him obsessed the perils of witchcraft, and he wrote a book about it called *Daemonologie*, published in the very first month of his reign in 1603. The monarch was at pains to warn his new subjects of 'the fearful abundance at this time in this country of these detestable slaves of the devil'. New legislation was enacted the next year, in which responsibility for prosecuting witches was taken from the church and given to secular courts.

Few of the detestable slaves, however, went in for political assassination. When witches or alleged witches got into trouble, it was usually for conflict in local communities, and most often something to do with farming – killing animals, for example, or making them ill or unproductive. Another major sphere of activity for the rural witch was dairying and cheesemaking. Witches were said to curse your cheese.

Before we get properly into the business of witchcraft and cheese, and to the rise of Cheshire, allow me a few brief digressions on the role of cheese in religion and magic. These are necessary and integral to our story, for ever since the Foolhardy Herder stumbled across soured and thickened curds eight thousand years ago, cheesemaking has had an air of the supernatural about it. Even today, knowing all we do of microbiological and chemical explanations, there is still something magical about the transformation of milk.

First, then, to Mesopotamia, four and a half thousand years ago, and to the kings of Ur, who performed an annual re-enactment of the marriage of Inanna, Queen of Heaven. In essence this is a myth of descent and emergence from Death and the Underworld, but its central figure, Inanna, after a brief flirtation with Enkimdu (a boring old arable farmer) pursues and marries a shepherd and cheesemaker Dumuzid (aka Tammuz). The myth spawned a cult that survived into the eleventh century, and inspired ancient Greek and Christian beliefs of rebirth.

Next, then, to classical Greece, where Aristotle (in perhaps one of his lesser known philosophical contentions) declared that human conception was analogous to cheesemaking, with the male sperm acting like rennet to coagulate the female blood in the womb and thus form a child. This metaphor inspired early Christian theologians to give an account of Mary's immaculate conception that drew on the observation that sometimes milk seems to coagulate spontaneously without rennet. (We know now that that is just the action of lactic bacteria, right?)

A further association of cheese with Christianity came in the second century, when a schismatic Christian sect called the

Artotyrites replaced the bread used during Mass with cheese. The Artotyrites (from *artos*, barley-bread, and *tyros*, cheese) were prone to ecstatic trances and speaking in tongues, a fact which conjures up pleasing images of frenzied religious ceremonies fuelled with sacramental cheese. Sadly the sect was declared heretical and disappeared from the mainstream history of the Christian Church.

There is, of course, a full and long association between the mother goddess in all her aspects and the production and processing of milk. You can trace the persistence of this association of women, dairying and the supernatural from pagan to Christian culture in the person of Brigid, who was a Celtic goddess before being transmogrified into a Christian saint. Pre-Christian images of a Brigid figure involved in dairy-related activities have been found carved into stones from one end of Britain to another: from Hadrian's Wall, where she is seen with what looks a lot like a stand churn for buttermaking, to

Carving of Saint Brigid milking a cow on the west face of St Michael's tower, Glastonbury Tor.

Gloucester, where she appears to be pouring cream into a vat, maybe to make some nice cream cheese.

Irish dairy farmers and cheesemakers enlisted Saint Brigid's help in the form of Saint Brigid's mantle, a cloth used to ensure a plentiful milk supply or to heal a sick animal. Brigid's association with milk and the supernatural started an early age. It seems that as a child she couldn't drink normal cow's milk, and so her father had to buy a special cow, white with brown ears, that came from the otherworld. Intriguingly, modern food science might have some light to shed on this story. Some breeds of cow, notably black-and-white Holstein Friesians, the most common dairy cow in Britain and Ireland, produce large amounts of a milk protein called A1, which is thought to cause an allergic reaction in some people. Other breeds, like the pretty brown Jerseys, produce much more of the A2 milk protein, which isn't associated with this allergic reaction.

My favourite cheese folklore tale is again from Ireland and concerns the death of Medb, mythical queen of Connacht. She was killed by one Furbaide, who performed the deed with a well-aimed slingshot to her forehead. The missile was a piece of Tanag, the skimmed-milk cheese of the early Irish, which just shows you how hard that stuff was.

Now let's return to King James and the witches. Cheese magic makes its appearance in the law courts in 1618, when a Welsh Justice of the Peace enlisted the help of a woman called Jane Buckley in a criminal case. Jane was able to identify the guilty person by getting the defendants to eat a piece of cheese that she had enchanted by speaking charms over it before the trial. This was a remnant of a form of trial by ordeal in which the defendant would have to eat a piece of cheese and were declared guilty if they couldn't swallow it. Given that where possible the cheese was the gnarliest, oldest and most dried-up cheese the officer of the court could find – known as choke-dog – if you were dry mouthed from guilt it might be hard to swallow, specially if you'd just seen the local wisewoman 'enchanting' it.

Conversely, if your cheese was really good you might be accused of using dark powers in your dairying practice. In 1690 or thereabouts, one Barbara Gilmour returned to her native Ayrshire from Ireland with a recipe for hard cow's milk cheese. The cheese was so delicious that jealous neighbours accused her of using witchcraft to make it. One explanation for the charge, and the cheese, was that she was making sweet-milk or full-cream cheese, and the locals, used to hard skimmed-milk cheese, couldn't believe that cheese could taste so good. Thankfully the case was quashed and Barbara carried on making her excellent 'Dunlop' cheeses, named after her village. (Production of Ayrshire Dunlop started up again in the 1980s at Dunlop Creamery, using the milk of native breed Ayrshire cows who, by the way, also produce the A2 protein, like Brigid's otherworldly cow.)

Sadly, while it pleases me to imagine witchy cheesemakers making amazing cheese with their special powers, it is more common in the annals of cheese and witchcraft to find accusations of cursing, either of the cheese vat, the butter churn or the animals themselves. Cheese was a vital foodstuff, particularly since it can be preserved and kept as a hedge against seasonal food shortages, and you can imagine that cheesemakers wanted to enlist all the help they could get, supernatural or otherwise, to ensure a good outcome for their work. Plants with power to ward off the evil eye, like four-leaf clovers or rowan twigs bound with a red thread, would often be placed in dairies, and religious symbols were often carved into dairying equipment. To be especially sure, one could make the equipment from a protective wood, like ash. Even in the nineteenth century, if your butter failed in the churn, it was considered a good plan to make a shaft for the churn from mountain ash (another name for rowan).

Often accusations of witchcraft were centred on attacks on cows. In 1628, Katherine Oswald of Niddrie, near Edinburgh, was accused of witchcraft by Mr and Mrs Nisbet, who had refused to sell her a cow. The cow in question passed blood instead of milk for three days after the refusal. In 1653, back in that hotbed of mysticism and magic, Glastonbury, Elizabeth Castle was accused of using witchcraft to kill her neighbour William Fry's cow. When the animal was opened up, a row of pinpricks was seen on the unfortunate creature's heart.

Women were also accused of cursing a dairy so that the cheesemaking failed. In 1666, Elizabeth Kewin of Kirk Arbory on the Isle of Man was accused of cursing a neighbouring dairy farm. The farmer's wife, Catherine Norris, giving evidence, 'saith that for twelve years she could not reare a calfe but all still died; nor make butter or cheese right'. Catherine didn't wait for legal remedy to help lift the curse. She scratched Elizabeth's face and drew blood – it was thought that if you drew blood from the witch that had cursed you, their power would fail. After the scratching incident, Catherine was able to make cheese again, and so Elizabeth was found guilty of 'useing of unlawfull meanes in the nature of sorcery'. But her sentence was more lenient that you might expect. She was required to do penance at three local churches on three consecutive Sundays and to give over a bond of three pounds that she would lose if she performed any more illegal sorcery. Less fortunate was Margaret Harknett of Stanmore, Middlesex, who was also accused of cursing a dairy. In this case, the servants on the farm had refused to give her the buttermilk she had asked for. It looks like poor Margaret had form; she had also been accused of taking action against a brewer who had refused her some barm or yeast. She was executed at Tyburn in 1585.

So who were these witches? In *Select Cases of Conscience touching Witches and Witchcraft*, published in 1646, John Gaule summarises things thus:

> Every old woman with a wrinkled face, a furrowed brow, a
> hairy lip, a gobber tooth, a squint eye, a squeaking voice or a

scolding tongue, having a ragged coat on her back, a skull cap
on her head, a spindle in her hand, and a dog or cat by her
side is not only suspected but pronounced for a witch.

Gaule wrote the book in opposition to the excesses of Matthew
Hopkins, a self-appointed 'witchfinder general', who terrorised the
east of England between 1644 and 1646. Gaule himself believed
in witches, but he thought standards of evidence for their accu-
sation and prosecution should be higher. In that oddly familiar
description of a witch, he was making the point that elderly women
marginalised by widowhood and or poverty, or with odd appearance or behaviour, were all-too-easy targets.

A very common theme in the court records is that the accused
had been refused something, and that the cursing was in revenge
for this refusal. If you imagine a rather odd-looking, elderly woman,
prone to muttering, who is always round at the door asking for a
cup of this or a piece of that, it's easy to imagine how annoyance
could build up into bitterness. When your prize cow stopped giving
milk, or the milk in your cheese vats refused to turn into curd, and
you were looking round for someone to blame, the source of your
guilt and anger would be a perfect candidate.

The problem for people accused of cursing dairies is that
there is a lot that can go wrong in the production of milk and its
transformation into cheese, and even today it can be hard to work
out what has happened. Sally Hickey, author of the marvellously
entitled paper, 'Fatal Feeds – Plants, Livestock Losses and
Witchcraft Accusations', explores the idea that many if not all of the
livestock losses attributed to witchcraft could be down to animals
eating toxic plants. Remember the story of the dead cow with the
pinpricks on its heart? Unluckily for Elizabeth Castle, the accused,
these marks could have been pinpoint haemorrhaging caused by
nitrite poisoning from eating blackberry, turnip tops or unripened
oat crops. Poor fodder or the wrong sort of fodder could affect your
dairying practices as much as the animals themselves – sorrel, for
example, if eaten by an animal can make it difficult to churn their

Frontispiece from Matthew Hopkins' The Discovery of Witches (1647), showing witches identifying their familiar spirits.

milk into butter. One of the accusers in that case of Elizabeth Kewin of Kirk Arbory admitted that it could have been poor fodder that was causing her dairying difficulties rather than witchcraft.

Even if your animals are healthy, and their feed top quality, plenty can still go wrong in cheesemaking. Another culprit is phage – a sort of virus, some strains of which thrive on lactic bacteria. Now, if all the lactic bacteria which have been acting as a starter culture in your milk are eaten by opportunistic viruses, your milk won't acidify properly and turn into curd. With little or no lactic bacteria to compete with, or make the curd acidic enough to be inhospitable, your vat could then be colonised by all sorts of nasty creatures, creating weird flavours and textures or even making the milk dangerous to consume.

I have seen cheesemaking fail in a dairy, and it was as heartbreaking and as mystifying for the modern cheesemaker as it would have been for his seventeenth-century predecessors. What was especially painful about this incident was that all morning everything had seemed to be going perfectly well. We had soured and set the milk, taken the whey off and were about to start cutting and stacking the perfectly fine looking curd when, after testing the acidity of the whey, the cheesemaker sighed and said bitterly, 'It's dead,' meaning that it hadn't acidified enough, and not only wouldn't knit together into cheese but wouldn't reach the level of acidity that would make it safe for people to eat. After all that work, all we could do was feed the curd to the pigs.

Just to give you an idea of the scale of the loss, the amount of curd we had would have translated into something like £5,000 worth of cheese at wholesale price. What made it worse, in a way, is that this cheesemaker, with all the skill and knowledge born of more than thirty years of experience, couldn't say for certain what the problem was, other than that the starter culture had failed to do its work. I was fearful that I might have jinxed the process, since earlier on I had asked him what they did to protect themselves from phage in the dairy. The cheesemaker looked at me much like stagehands do when you say 'Macbeth' in a theatre. 'We don't use the P word in here,' he said. However, phage was an unlikely culprit in this case, as that microscopic monster tends to manifest itself slowly over a few days.

Intriguingly, if phage was a problem, the instructions for lifting a curse from your dairy in the seventeenth century might well have solved the problem. The first thing the owner of a cursed dairy needed to do was to stop making cheese and spend some time at church getting right with God. The next was to ritually and thoroughly cleanse their dairy, and then, when they began cheesemaking again, they should bring in a rowan branch. By ceasing to make cheese they would have denied the phage its food source, and by giving the cheese room and cellar a thorough scrub they would be removing all or most of it. Strains of phage evolve swiftly to consume the particular strain of lactic bacteria in a dairy, so by bringing the rowan branch into the dairy you could be introducing new strains of bacteria that were hitching a lift on the branch. These would not be to the phage's taste, making sure that as you resumed cheesemaking you weren't feeding the virus once more.

If you get phage in a modern dairy, the remedy hasn't changed much. You stop making and clean your dairy as thoroughly as you know how. The crucial step, though, is to hold off on cheesemaking for a few days, since if you have any holdout phage in a hard-to-reach place they will die off without any lactic bacteria to feast on. Also, just as in the old days they would introduce a new strain of bacteria on a rowan branch, in modern dairying you use a different strain of starter culture that the phage has not evolved to prey upon. In fact, most hard cheesemakers have a collection of cultures that they rotate, so a strain of phage doesn't get a chance to take hold.

There is a final explanation for failure in cheesemaking, both then and now – it's simply that someone has blundered. It's all too easy to be late in crucial steps of cheesemaking like adding rennet, cutting curd or pitching – that is, getting the curd out of the acidic whey. These sorts of mishaps can result in a lower yield, over-acidified rock-hard cheese or just plain nasty-tasting cheese. I'm afraid that when I read about the two servants who accused Margaret Harknett of cursing their dairy, my first thought was that they had messed up and, rather than confess to the boss, found a likely candidate to accuse. It's sort of understandable, since in those days failures in the dairy could result in beatings of the staff. This is uncommon in modern dairies.

Reginald Scott, the sixteenth-century witchcraft sceptic, not only entertained the possibility of slovenly work on the part of a dairymaid but had some good cheesemaking knowledge. He pointed out that there could be problems with cheesemaking if whey is kept too long 'or in an evill place or be sluttishly used so as to be stale and sour'. In an unappetisingly vivid description he noted that, if you use stale whey, your curd when heated 'congealeth, so it will rope like birdlime that you maie wind it about a stick...Which alteration being strange, is woondered at and imputed to witches.'

Then, as now, people were well aware that a conscientious and skilled dairymaid, or dairyperson, was vital to the success of your cheese. Even before the advent of microbiology, people understood the importance of hygiene in food preparation. Dairymaids need to be clean, since 'scabbed and scurvie hands...such filthiness of hands hinders curdling and makes cheese full of eyes,' according to Charles Etienne, a French writer of the early sixteenth century. Neatness about her person was a clue that she was capable of the kind of painstaking systematic and above all consistent work required to make good cheese. And there was a final requirement – that she be strong. To test this, farmers on the look-out for a new dairymaid at one of the local agricultural fairs would bring along the stone that formed their cheese press. When they spotted a clean neat woman, preferably with a good reputation for hard work, they would get her to try and pick up the stone. If she could do it, she was in.

Someone well aware of the value of a good dairymaid was the Suffolk farmer Thomas Tusser, author of *Five Hundred Points of Husbandry*, a comprehensive set of instructions in rhyming couplets, covering everything you need to know about running a midsized farm, first printed in 1557. He does, however, at times seem to be a bit hard on Cisely, his imaginary dairymaid, the list of whose potential failings make up his cheesemaking instructions.

Poetically, Tusser illustrates Cisely's list of possible faults with ten 'guests' drawn from folkloric and biblical imagery, and once you have unpicked the allusions all the faults are quite familiar to a modern cheesemaker or affineur. One of the problems Tusser lists is blown cheese, where unwanted bacteria have produced gas and making the cheese swell, 'Tom Piper hath hoven and puffed up cheekes, if cheese be so haven, make Cisse to seek creekes.' This can still happen even in the days of modern hygiene and I've seen more than one cheese in a cellar whose top has begun to bulge ominously. While the bacteria aren't harmful, they don't taste very nice, and, once again, the usual remedy is to feed it to the pigs.

As the problems that beset today's cheesemakers haven't changed much in five hundred years, neither has one of the most common tasks of the affineur – rubbing or brushing cheese. Tusser instructs: 'So Ciss that serves must make this note, what fault deserves a brushed cote.' I think the fault here might be an overabundance of cheese mite, the tiny arachnoid creatures that live off cheese and, if left unchecked, can eat a significant amount. Even in the days of modern technology, rubbing and brushing is the most effective way to keep mite down – it is never eliminated, just controlled. I quite liked doing this when I worked at Neal's Yard Dairy. Brushing and rubbing feels like a caring and nurturing thing to to with a young cheese while you shepherd it along its path to maturity.

Thankfully, unlike Cisely, my then boss Bill Oglethorpe didn't beat me if my work failed to reach the required standard. In fact, Bill's criticism never got more brutal than looking at me quizzically and saying, 'Gee, why did you do that?' Cisely, on the other hand, needed to keep up a high standard or she would face corporal punishment:

If though so oft beaten
amends by this
I will no more threaten
I promise thee Cis.

What distinguishes Tusser from Walter of Henley, his thirteenth-century predecessor, is the kind of farming he is talking about, and who he is talking to. These aren't the massive farms of the secular and monastic manors, but smaller farms run by a husband-and-wife team. His readers are the yeomen farmers and cheesemakers, whose ancestors in the previous century had taken advantage of the high wages and low land prices after the Black Death. The seventeenth century was the heyday of these yeomen farmers, so much so that this period has even been referred to as the 'yeoman revolution'.

As to what they were making, it seems that the most common form of cheese in the seventeenth century was new milk cheese, and it is at the beginning of this century that we start to find written recipes for that cheese. New milk cheese was so called because it used whole rather than skimmed milk from the morning milking, with a little cream from the evening milking to further enrich it. It was a labour-intensive, many-staged process, involving heating and cutting curd, repeated pressings and rewrapping of cheese on the first day, salting on the next, and turning on a draining table before the cheeses were put in a cellar or 'cheese-heck' to mature. This isn't the sort of cheese that a busy peasant housewife can make as part of her daily round of tasks. It needs a designated employee with some skill who can spend most of her working day making and looking after the cheese – a dairymaid, in fact. It also needs a farming enterprise big enough to hire a dairymaid.

Throughout the first half of the seventeenth century, the business of cheesemaking in Britain was dominated by the yeomen cheesemakers of East Anglia, and their most significant market, alongside the army and navy, was London. As we saw in the previous chapter, this mutually beneficial relationship had been established in the previous century and by now London cheesemongers were becoming titans of business. But they did not end up taking the East Anglian cheesemakers with them on their rise to power. By the middle of the seventeenth century, the East Anglian cheesemongers had fallen from grace and their position was being assumed by the yeomen of Cheshire. It was partly the hand of God – in the 1640s, an unfortunate combination of cattle plague and flooding had considerably reduced the cheese yield in the eastern counties. But the hand of the London cheesemonger can be seen, too. Keen to drive their producers to specialise, they began to insist that the East Anglian cheesemakers provide them with more and more butter rather than cheese. While East Anglian cheese was already skimmed (it was known as flotten cheese or 'flett'), in order to provide the butter the London cheesemongers demanded, the cheesemakers had to skim even more cream off the milk. The resultant cheese became less tasty because of the lower fat content – fat holds flavour – and rock- hard. It needed to be warmed for some time before it became edible and came to be know derisively as 'Suffolk Bang.'

The cheesemakers of East Anglia eventually realised what was being done to their business, and in 1690 petitioned Parliament:

> The Cheesemongers in London have of late Years encouraged the Farmers to make Flett Cheese, whereby the Quantity of Butter sold with such Cheese is increased to Four Firkins in a Load; but the Cheese thereby becomes only fit for Slaves; from whence the Commodity is grown into Disrepute, and, if not prevented, will become a general Prejudice.

But by then it was far too late. The reputation of East Anglian cheese had been dealt a mortal blow by the London Cheesemongers, as this contemporary verse about Suffolk cheese shows:

> Those that made me were uncivil
> They made me harder than the devil.
> Knives won't cut me, fire won't sweat me,
> Dogs bark at me, but can't eat me.

*   *   *

We have already exploded the notion that Cheshire cheese can be found in the Domesday Book. However, the county of Cheshire had been famous for its dairy farming since at least the thirteenth century, and by the sixteenth the reputation of its cheese was also getting about. In 1580, Queen Elizabeth's privy council dined on a number of excellent Cheshires and, in 1610, William Camden, the author of *Britannia*, the first topographical and historical survey of England and Wales, was able to report that 'Cheshire cheeses are more agreeable and better relished than those of any other parts of the kingdom.' But since transport was prohibitively expensive, at least by land, Cheshire's reputation must have been largely based on hearsay and on the odd delivery that made it to London, like the one in 1569 when the Corporation of Chester, the west coast port that was soon to become a powerhouse of cheese exporting, sent a gift of cheese to some gentlemen in London who had done them a favour.

This haphazard market suggests that in the first half of the seventeenth century cheesemaking in Cheshire was a subsistence business, with farmers making just enough to feed their family and estate workers, with any surplus going to local markets. Then, on 21 October 1650 – a date that should be celebrated more universally than in my own house – the cargo ship *James*, captained by one Robert Mills, arrived at the port of London with a shipment of twenty tons of Cheshire.

Everything changed. The *James* shipment had been financed by William Seaman, who was the London merchant of a Cheshire family. And after enduring all that Suffolk Bang, it must have been a revelation to the city's cheese fanciers – a full cream cheese made with whole milk, and thus an obviously premium product. It immediately commanded a penny a pound more than East Anglian cheese, but nobody seems to have been deterred, and from 1652 regular shipments of Cheshire cheese began arriving at the London Docks.

'Cheshire' seems to have been a loosely defined brand, and by no means limited to its supposed county of origin. Cheeses were gathered up from the neighbouring county of Shropshire and the

Welsh counties of Flint, Denbigh and Montgomery as the more astute dairy farmers of these counties jumped on the bandwagon. The cheeses were gathered at the port of Chester for shipping to London, and all were given the good name of Cheshire for this new and seemingly limitless market. The port books of Chester record that in 1664 some three hundred and sixty-four tons of cheese were shipped to London; by the 1670s this amount had grown to a thousand tons a year, and by the 1680s that number had doubled again. To provide this much cheese the dairy farmers in the areas that produced it had to change how they farmed.

If you were an ambitious Cheshire dairy farmer in this post-Jamesian moment, the first thing you were going to need was a bigger herd. In the seventeenth century an average dairy cow produced around two hundred and forty pounds (about a hundred kilos) of cheese a year, so to produce a thousand tons of cheese you would need ten thousand cows. Given the increase in the amount of cheese arriving at the London Docks between 1650 and 1688, the increase in the number of cows in the northwest over this period must have been in the region of twenty thousand. That's a lot of cows, and a lot of cows need a lot of land, so the next thing you'd be thinking, as an ambitious dairy farmer, is 'We're going to need a bigger farm.' Which is obviously what the Dewsbury family of Aston in north Cheshire thought. In the sixteenth century, the Dewsburys had held a farm of twelve acres, a respectable holding for a free peasant. By 1749, their descendants had enlarged the family holdings to fifty-six acres, putting them happily in the yeoman class.

Fortune favours the bold, and the Dewsburys must have made some bold moves in the property market over those two hundred years. Another bold mover was John Nixon, the first serious cheese producer in the same part of north Cheshire – at least, the first for whom records survive. On his death in September 1661, his probate inventory shows that he owned seventeen cows and had one ton of cheese, an indication that he had moved over to large-scale cheese production. His success suggests that, even as a tenant farmer, he had embraced farming methods required to produce large amounts of consistent-quality cheese: attention to animal health and welfare and a high level of skill and care in his – or rather his dairywoman's – cheesemaking. Mr Nixon had clearly paid close attention to Tusser.

Larger farms were created either by merging smaller ones or by enclosing land that had been previously held and grazed in common. In the mid-1680s, the Warburtons, lords of the nearby manor of Appleton since the early thirteenth century, created six new farms to which they let or sold leases and at the same time enlarged their four principal farms. Note that 'new' farms didn't mean more farms. In Crowley, another township in the same area, thirty 'old farms' became seventeen new ones by 1740s.

Enclosure of common land and enlargement of farms, which had become a significant force in the sixteenth century, was the cause of much of the movement of newly landless rural workers to the towns. It also made life much more precarious for the remaining rural poor, who previously had been able to keep an animal or two on common grazing land. The people of seventeenth-century Britain were resentful of what was being done to them, as this contemporary rhyme shows:

The law locks up the man or woman
Who steals the goose from off the common
But leaves the greater villain loose
Who steals the common from off the goose.

In 1607, the people of Northamptonshire, Warwickshire and Leicestershire, in the face of particularly rapacious enclosure, rose in what became known as the Midland Revolt. This was one of the last times that the peasantry and gentry engaged in open conflict and it ended with around fifty dead, and the execution of the ringleaders. The revolt was led by a tinker called Captain Pouch, who told his followers that the contents of his pouch – documents from the king and lord of Heaven – would protect them. He was

Ye Olde Cheshire Cheese pub on Fleet Street, rebuilt in 1666 after the Great Fire of London when its name was on trend.

captured, and met the customary grisly end granted to those convicted of treason – he was hanged, drawn and quartered. All that they found in his pouch was a piece of green cheese.

As well as flight to the towns, rural misery and the living disembowelment of Captain Pouch, enclosure led to the all but disappearance of peasant cheesemaking. In France the enclosure movement never got up to the kind of intensity or thoroughness of Britain and the lucky people of that nation retained much of their peasant cheesemaking tradition, embodied in the thousands of small soft cheeses characteristic of different regions like Camembert from Normandy, Epoisses from the Champagne-Ardennes and all the lovely lactic goat's cheeses of the Loire like Crottin and Sainte-Maure.

172

What was good for the cheesemakers of Cheshire and nearby counties was good for the port of Chester, too. Before the cheese boom, Chester's international trade amounted to little more than a couple of ships a year from Bordeaux or Portugal laden with wine and fruits, and the occasional ship from Norway carrying timber. In 1664, there were fourteen cheese ships trading between Chester and London, but by the 1680s this number had climbed to over fifty. And then there was the return trade, as ships empty of cheese sailed back up the coast with goods that had come to London from all over the world. Not only was it exciting for the people of the northwest to have all sorts of fancy foreign goods, this new coastal trade gave a great boost to local economies as apothecaries, grocers, ironmongers and haberdashers set up shop.

The London cheesemongers weren't doing too badly out of the trade, either. In the later part of the seventeenth century, nine cheesemongers dominated the London market, and the most powerful of all of these was John Ewer, who between 1685 and 1689 shipped forty-one per cent of all the cheese to arrive at the London Docks, an impressive two thousand, seven hundred and forty-one tons of it, all told.

Cheese shipping on this scale required an infrastructure of considerable size and complexity. Cheesemongers employed cheese factors to go directly to the farms and buy up cheese in advance, storing them in warehouses owned by the cheesemongers in Chester. This system ensured a quick turnaround for the ships arriving in the port to pick up their cargoes. The root of Ewer's domination was a comprehensive network of cheese factors scouring the farms for the best Cheshire for him to sell back in London. He also had good connections in the world of shipping; the records show he shipped almost all his cheese with the same five families of ship's captains, who appear to have barely ever shipped cheese for anyone else.

In 1689, Britain and France went to war – which was not a very notable event, since they'd been at war the previous year. What was remarkable about this war, though, from a cheese point of view, is that French privateers engaged in cheese piracy so vigorous that it put a stop to the coastal cheese trade. It would not resume until the war ended in 1713.

Whether the French were getting their Cheshire cheese via piracy or by legitimate trade, an odd little reminder of the days when Chester was a powerhouse of the British cheese trade still exists. In France you can still find in supermarkets a rather unenticing block cheese called 'Chester' which claims to be 'fromage anglais', though I've never seen it for sale on this side of the Channel.

In the early eighteenth century, war and piracy notwithstanding, Cheshire was top dog among the cheeses of Britain and Ireland. Cheddar was snapping at its heels and Stilton would be along soon. But for now Cheshire ruled. The twenty thousand pounds of cheese arriving at the London Docks each year might have taken up to four thousand small herds to produce and, even if we allow the possibility that some of the dairies made cheese from the milk of more than one herd, that's still thousands of different Cheshire producers, and thousands of different Cheshires, each with their own individual characteristics of flavour and texture. It would have been a lifetime's work to try them all, and what a life time.

But every cheese has its day and, although Cheshire survived happily enough up until the 1930s, it then – like most other traditional British cheeses – virtually went extinct. As we'll see in a later chapter (Chapter Seven, if you want to skip ahead), it fell victim to an unholy combination of factory production, American imports and the Milk Marketing Board. When I started at Neal's Yard, in 2002, there was reckoned to be just one dairy that was making traditional Cheshire – Appleby's in Shropshire.

So, of course, writing this book, I had to go and see them.

I arrived at Hawkstone Abbey Farm, as instructed, at dawn, peering into the dark as the taxi made its way along tree-hung Shropshire lanes. But the Appleby's dairy was a cheerful place, even at this hour, an airy, brightly lit building dominated by a particularly impressive vat. With its sides made of riveted sheets of metal, painted white and slightly dented, it looked like an old freighter, though with a comforting aroma of milk.

Under the friendly direction of Garry Gray, Appleby's head cheesemaker, I was set straight to work, putting the cloths into the cheese moulds. This is another of those typical cheesemaking tasks that appears simple but is actually quite tricky. The moulds are steel cylinders, about a foot high and eight inches across, with handles sticking out like ears. The cloths are nylon bags that line the inside, crucially without any creases – which would spoil the smooth surface of the cheese. Garry did his with an assured sweep of his hands, while I fumbled along, but, as he kindly pointed out, he'd been doing it for a long time. He began his career in 1986 at a local dairy factory, having just come out of a ten-year stint in the army – not an obvious apprenticeship for cheesemaking, though the exacting way of doing things and the robust attitude to adversity are common to both careers.

The next task was to fill the vat with milk. Just like its seventeenth-century ancestor, new milk cheese, Cheshire is made from a mix of higher-fat evening milk and lower-fat morning milk. This is one of the factors that contributes to Cheshire's goldilocks texture – crumbly, yet moist and giving. The dairy's evening milk had been in cold storage while the morning milk arrived fresh from the cows, in a little tanker towed by a tractor. Garry connected pump and hose to the tanker and the milk began to flood into the vat. As ever, I was struck by the beauty of fresh milk – its rich ivory colour and strange heft as it swirls around in the vat.

The milk for Cheshire needs to be heated to a temperature which the starter will find conducive to its work, just over 20° C, Garry told me. This meant opening a pipe to flood the jacket of the vat with steam, rapidly heating it up. So that the milk would heat evenly and the cream not separate, Garry switched on the stirrer. Imagine a pair of giant spinning egg whisks, moving up and down and around in a circle, and you will have an idea of what was going on. This mechanical stirring is a world apart from the simple kit and gentle treatment of milk that characterises soft-cheesemaking like Mary Holbrook's. In fact the milk in this vat was being stirred so vigorously that the surface became a mass of choppy waves.

While the milk was heating, Garry and I went to get the starter that had been incubating overnight in a ten-gallon milk churn. To ensure a clean slate, the milk had been pasteurised by the simple method of running hot water around the outside of the churn. To my surprise, Garry told me that Applebys buy their starter cultures from Barbers, Cheddar makers since 1833, and the guardians of traditional Cheddar-making cultures. How can two such different cheeses emerge from the same culture? One reason, I was about to observe, was that you use a lot more starter culture for Cheshire than for Cheddar. This means faster acidification, which in turn means more calcium loss; and cheese with a lower calcium content, like Cheshire, has a naturally crumbly texture.

Having added the starter to the milk, Garry added annatto, a flavourless food colouring derived from a South American thistle, which gives Appleby's its signature sunset-orange hue. The colouring of cheese is a surprisingly ancient practice. Before the 'discovery' of America, cheesemakers in Britain used the juice of marigolds, or a herb called ladies bedstraw. There are a few different explanations for why they might have done this. One is that in the days before winter feed solutions, like turnips and silage, winter milk was pretty thin stuff and the cheese a bit pallid. So the canny medieval cheesemakers dyed their winter cheese to make it look fuller and more summery. But I have also heard that Welsh cheesemakers, jealous of the lush pasture and richly hued cheese of neighbouring Cheshire and Shropshire, took to dyeing their cheese. Another theory, which I found in cheesemaker and micro-biologist Paul Thomas's book, *Home-made Cheese*, is that the higher acidity in Cheshire bleaches its colour (which derives from the carotene in the grass), and back in the 1660s, when Cheshire was breaking into the London market, cheese fanciers wanted an alternative to the pallid-looking Suffolk Bang. So Cheshire makers, perhaps encouraged by London cheesemongers, might have added a little of the newly available annatto to distinguish it.

When I asked Garry why Appleby's is coloured, he told me that, 'They won't buy uncoloured Cheshire down south, it's got to be coloured. But up here they won't buy coloured Cheshire, so we also have to make some white.' And, funnily enough, the week after my trip, I served a hefty chunk of Appleby's to some friends after dinner, giving as usual a rousing encomium to this prince among cheeses and referring to it as the last proper traditional Cheshire. At which my friend Helen, who is from Nantwich and grew up in Chester said, 'This isn't Cheshire, it's a funny colour.' Living proof of the north–south divide.

Having added the starter and annatto, we had to leave the milk to ripen for two hours, to reach the right level of acidity for the rennet to work. The timing was perfect, because, as I could see from the door that connected the dairy with the farmhouse kitchen, Aunt Sarah, who had promised to fill me in on Appleby's history, had arrived. I was particularly interested in what she might tell me, as Appleby's has, for a British cheese, an unusually long pedigree.

🧀 🧀 🧀

Many of the cheeses featured in this book were revived or created in the Great Cheese Renaissance of the 1980s (of which more anon). Appleby's, however, dates back to 1952, when Aunt Sarah's sister, Lucy, began making cheese at Hawkstone Abbey Farm, which she and her husband Lance had bought during the war.

Garry Gray adding the annatto to a vat of soon-to-be Cheshire.

I knew that Sarah and Lucy were from a farming family, and that Lucy had studied at agricultural college in Nantwich to learn the art and science of cheesemaking, and I wondered if they had any history of cheesemaking in the family. 'Oh yes,' Aunt Sarah said. 'At Lighteach farm, where we grew up, everything revolved around the cheese.' She pointed to the glass-panelled door that connects the kitchen with the dairy. 'We had the same arrangement at Lighteach, so mother could keep an eye on the vat.' Apparently the Ministry of Agriculture had asked Lucy to brick that doorway in, saying there should be separation between the kitchen with its open coal range and the dairy, but Lucy resisted.

Aunt Sarah, by the way, hadn't followed in the family tradition of cheesemaking like her sister, but the apple didn't fall far from the tree. She worked for the Milk Marketing Board visiting dairy farms to make sure that hygiene standards in milking parlours and cheese rooms were being maintained. Although she began working in the 1960s, many farmers still remembered the stringent standards required by the agricultural department during the Second World War and Sarah was known to them as 'The War Ag Lady'.

I asked if there was any truth in the story that Lance had chosen his bride because he could see that she was strong enough to turn Cheshire cheeses. Aunt Sarah laughed and said, 'It's the sort of thing he would say. Mind you, they were much bigger cheeses in those days.' The cheeses the Applebys make on the farm today weigh about eighteen pounds (nine kilos) each and turning a few hundred of them is a decent workout for a monger. Aunt Sarah showed me an old black-and-white photo on the kitchen wall of some cheese in their moulds, perhaps from the 1950s. They were gigantic. 'Sixty pounds, those ones would have been.'

I was stunned. Turning hundreds of sixty-pound cheeses would be a herculean task – and, when they were still in their moulds at a day old, they would have been full of moisture and even heavier. Getting them out of those moulds, or knocking out, would have required enormous strength or amazing technique.

Aunt Sarah didn't seem all that fazed by the memory when I mentioned that. 'Oh yes, the knocking out, that was hard.'

Classic cheesemaker understatement.

Sixty-pound Cheshire cheeses had come into being in the mid-eighteenth century. When Cheshires first came to the London markets, they tended to weigh in at around the nine- or ten-pound mark. But the logistics of the supply chain – stretching from the farms of the northwest to London – meant that they could be kept in warehouses in Chester for months. The cheese factors and mongers were paying the farmers on delivery to the warehouse, and as the cheeses sat there they lost moisture and thus weight, which meant a loss for the buyers and a loss of quality. As a result the London cheesemongers demanded larger cheeses that would dry more slowly, and offered to pay a premium for them. That was the pull. The push was that the London cheesemongers began to refuse to buy the smaller ones, and some started using nefarious means to delay delivery, putting the loss in weight onto the farmers. They did this by saying they had no warehouse space and no ships, telling the makers to keep the cheese in their store until transport became available. When you think of John Ewer and his eight fellow cheesemongers, with their fleets of ships and acres of warehouse space, this claim seems unlikely.

The cheesemakers responded by making thicker and heavier cheeses. Consequently Cheshire wheels doubled in weight between the mid-sixteenth century and the beginning of the eighteenth. This, however, bought its own problems. Larger cheeses had to have more moisture forced out in the press, otherwise it would cause them to rot. Also surface salting – the rubbing of salt onto the outside of the cheeses – no longer worked; the greater mass meant that the salt took too long to diffuse. Two technological breakthroughs, applied in the first half of the eighteenth century, addressed these problems. One was that cheesemakers built bigger presses, with stones weighing up to three and a half thousand kilos. The other was to add salt to the broken-up curd *before* it went into the moulds. Of course, this meant you could no longer select your dairymaids by getting them to pick up your press stone, so in Cheshire the farmers would take the candidate to the local church and get them to try and lift the lid of the massive parish chest.

But cheesemaking is a bit like wallpapering, in that you think you've smoothed a bit out and then you notice a bump appear elsewhere. The Cheshire makers now discovered that their problem wasn't getting rid of moisture, it was keeping the right amount of moisture in. Their solution was to rub the surface of the cheese with butter a few times, creating a protective coating. At the end of this period of development, the average size of a Cheshire had increased to a whopping sixty pounds (thirty kilos) and the larger presses and internal salting would have created a texture and flavour much more familiar to us today.

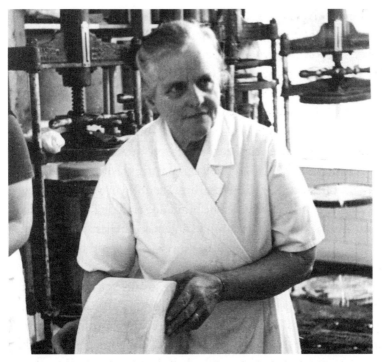

Lucy Appleby, founder of the dynasty, with a wheel of Cheshire. In the background are Edwardian cheese presses that are still in use today.

By the middle of the eighteenth century, cheesemakers from other counties had seen what a good thing the Cheshire were on to and began to make similar styles of cheese, copying these technological developments. These counties included Lancashire, Gloucestershire and Leicestershire, and if these names sound familiar to us cheese fanciers it is because their namesake cheeses still exist and form a class of cheese unique to Britain known as the territorials. These are all hard, cloth-bound cow's milk cheeses, often crumbly textured, mild yet complex in their flavour. So, nefarious though they may have been, the London cheesemongers assisted at the birth of a characteristic British style of cheese.

Back in the kitchen at Hawkstone, I asked how far the family tradition of cheesemaking went back, and in answer to that Aunt

Sarah, with quiet pride, brought something out of her bag to show me. It was a pair of silver medals in a small wood and glass case. On one side were engravings of a cow being milked, butter churns and a cheese press, and on the other these words: 'Agricultural Hall London 1877 Dairy Show, Award of Merit, Mr R. P. Walley, 1st Prize, Cheshire Cheese'. That was Mr Richard Pedley Walley – Aunt Sarah and Lucy Appleby's grandfather.

Lucy herself made cheese on Hawkstone Abbey Farm for some fifty years, keeping the flame of traditional Cheshire alight and fighting for the cause of traditional British cheese in general – she was one of the founders of the Specialist Cheesemakers Association, set up in 1989. In 2001, Lucy and her husband Lance were awarded MBEs for their services to British cheese. And the business is still very much a family one, with their son Edward and his wife Christine, and their son Paul and his wife Sarah, running the farm, and the dairy along with Garry Gray.

At that point I saw the merit of the door connecting kitchen to dairy, as Garry tapped on it to beckon me back to the vat.

The milk had now ripened and set with the addition of rennet. Garry had replaced the giant eggbeaters with many-bladed curd knives that were slowly whirling around and up and down the vat, cutting the curd into pieces not much larger than rice grains. While these two heavy steel lattice blades were moving through the curd, Garry was calmly squeegeeing the sides and the bottom of the vat to stop the curd sticking. Hard cheesemaking moves a lot faster than soft, and this curd had taken just forty-five minutes to set rather than the twenty-four hours a soft curd can take.

As the curd is cut and heated, it shrinks, expelling whey and becoming firmer. A couple of times Garry got me to dip a very, very clean hand in and feel it. It's quite magical feeling the curd change from moment to moment, and as it firms up it begins to disappear under the whey and sink to the bottom of the vat. Then it was time for the big reveal, as Garry opened the tap on the bottom of the vat to let the whey run off. As the greenish white liquid drains, there, like buried treasure, lay the curd, golden coloured from the annatto.

The next stage in Cheshire making is to cut the curd – which has by now set into one solid rubbery mass – into blocks about two feet long and eight inches wide. Garry had told me before how Cheshire is a physically demanding cheese to make, and now I saw why. He and his assistants Anna and Neil had to bend over the vat and flip these blocks over, not once but several times. It looked to me like Cheddaring, a crucial part of the making of Cheddar, when blocks of curd are stacked in the vat. But here is another crucial

Back-breaking work – the Appleby's team working in the vat.

difference that makes Cheshire what it is. Garry pointed out that they don't stack the blocks, but just turn them, which helps to drain more whey out. By not adding the pressure of stacking, they end up with the crumbly texture of Cheshire rather than the more dense texture of Cheddar.

In the next stage, the curd is torn up, salted and put through a curd mill, which looks like a mangle with spikes. Then the resulting curd is poured into the steel moulds that Garry and I had lined. The moulds are then taken into the press room, where I was to behold one of the most wonderful sights I have even seen in my cheesemongering career – a platoon of cheese presses. About four feet tall, made of cast iron and painted a lovely, glowing forest green, these beauties were made at the turn of the twentieth century and still work perfectly. They were all made locally, as you could see from the names stamped on their crossbars – Elsmere, Whitchurch and Nantwich. The cheese would remain in the presses for the rest of the day and night, periodically being taken out, turned and put back in, just like Tusser's dairymaid Cisely would have done with her new milk cheeses. After pressing, the cheeses are knocked out of their moulds, painted with an edible paste called Blanose, in place of the traditional butter, and wrapped in calico bandages.

Sadly I couldn't stick around to see the knocking out and bandaging, as there is only so much you can impose on a cheesemaker and farmer's hospitality. But, just before I left, Neil took me to see the store where the cheeses are matured. With something like two thousand cheeses sitting in neat ranks on their shelves (stillages, they are called), this huge room felt like a cathedral of cheese, albeit a cathedral with a tangy and herbaceous scent of mould. I was profoundly moved.

It was time to go and Anna gave me a lift to the station at Whitchurch, site of the great Cheese Fair. As we drove down the lane between the pastures, where the Applebys' herd were grazing contentedly, Anna pointed out the cattle troughs in each field. 'See what they are? she asked. They were the old cheese vats, in graceful retirement, still making a contribution to the working of this wonderful place.

☞ ☞ ☞

The cheesemakers of the seventeenth century lived in troubled times. Civil war broke out in in Britain in 1642 after a decade of conflict between the autocratic Charles I and an increasingly confident, rambunctious Parliament, and it was a savage conflict. While the names of set-piece battles at Edgehill, Marston Moor and Naseby may be familiar to us, it was mostly times of skirmish and ambush among the hedgerows, and sieges of country houses and towns. Proportionately more British and Irish people – military and civilian alike – died than in any conflict before or since. The Irish suffered most of all, with forty per cent of the Irish population wiped out, many of them in the massacres in Drogheda and Connaught led by the Parliamentary general, Oliver Cromwell.

According to some sources the cheese ration for both armies in the Civil War was impressive, up to a pound per day per man (compare this to the ounce a day for the legionaries of Rome). Without the cheesemaking capacity of the Roman army, the Royalist and Parliamentarian forces must have relied on 'requisitioning' for their needs. In response, all over England groups of 'clubmen' sprang up – armed local civilians gathering to protect their food stocks from the raiding troops. I wouldn't have liked to face the clubmen of Cheshire swinging their weapons with the strength born of knocking out and turning their heroic cheeses.

The war lasted for four years, with a brief reprise in 1648. The following year, Charles was beheaded at Whitehall in London on a cold winter's day – Charles wore two shirts so that he wouldn't shiver with cold and appear to be frightened. There followed ten years of godly government by Parliament and then by Cromwell as the dictatorial Lord Protector. This must have been a bit like living under the Taliban. The puritanical protestants banned the theatre, the celebration of Christmas and weddings, and closed the pubs. At the same time, however, Britain grew economically, as taxes on Royalists and the sale of church and royal lands filled the national coffers. The merchant and navy fleets grew (Cromwell has a good claim to the title father of the navy), and new colonies were developed in the Americas. With the death of Cromwell in 1658, things at last began to unravel and, in 1660, General Monck marched south from Scotland with the regiment he had formed, the Coldstream Guards. Fearing the chaos of a leaderless nation he somewhat brusquely called on MPs to resume their seats and in that same year Parliament declared Charles II king.

Charles II returned from his continental exile to begin what Daniel Defoe would perhaps affectionally describe as his 'lazy, long lascivious reign'. Another writer was actually aboard the ship as it made its triumphant landing at Dover, recording that 'the shouting and joy expressed by all is beyond imagination'. This was the MP, secretary of the Admiralty and diarist, Samuel Pepys. His diary is an unparalleled record of the bawdy years of the Restoration, and is famous not just for the sordid details of Pepys' love life but also for its reports of the Great Plague of London in 1665 and the Great Fire the year after. The Great Fire burnt for four days, consuming more than thirteen thousand houses, eight churches and the old St Paul's Cathedral. And it is the occasion for the most famous story about Pepys and cheese. In his entry for 4 September, when the fire had been burning for two days and was getting terrifyingly near to his house in Seething Lane, Pepys wrote this: 'And in the evening Sir W. Pen and I did dig another [hole], and put our wine in it; and I my Parmazan cheese, as well as my wine and some other things.'

If a wheel of Parmesan was the same sort of size as it is now, about ten inches high and sixteen across, then Pepys and Penn (father of the founder of Pennsylvania) must have been pretty accomplished diggers of holes. The fire was so close that, after dinner that night – presumably a sadly Parmesan-less dinner –

Pepys walked down to the Tower of London to watch men blowing up houses along that street to create a fire break.

On the next day, the fire got to the very bottom of Seething Lane itself and Pepys sent his wife with all their gold away to Woolwich. Happily for posterity the fire burnt itself out before it could consume Pepys' house and his diary, although I admit to feeling a little sadness at not knowing the fate of the 'Parmazan'.

A few years earlier, Friday 4 October, 1661 to be precise, Pepys recorded: 'And so home, where I found my wife vexed at her people for grumbling to eat Suffolk cheese, which I also am vexed at. So to bed.' By 'her people', Pepys means their servants, who it would appear, were ahead of the curve in showing their disdain for Suffolk cheese. Perhaps they'd rather have had some of that luscious new premium Cheshire. Pepys and his friends certainly liked it, as this entry from January 1659 shows: 'Then I went down into the Hall and to Will's, where Hawly brought a piece of his Cheshire cheese, and we were merry with it.'

I love that they were merry with it, as really great Cheshire often makes me merry, too. And the fact that, as well as recording the fires, plagues and kings, Pepys encapsulates the fall of Suffolk cheese and the rise of Cheshire.

🧀 🧀 🧀

CHAPTER SIX

Stichelton

The birth of a brand

1688–1837

STILTON IS A QUINTESSENTIALLY BRITISH CHEESE – and perhaps just as quintessentially a product of the eighteenth century. If you think of that period as a time of ruddy-faced country squires quaffing foaming tankards of ale and bumpers of brandy, then a rich, piquant and indulgent cheese like this fits right in. Of course, there's more to Stilton, and indeed the eighteenth century, than that. While the country squires no doubt did plenty of quaffing, and Stilton-eating while they were at it, this was a time of great and rapid change in Britain. It was a period of unification, agricultural revolution, improvement in transport, growth in commerce, leaps forward in science and technology, and a vastly increased presence for the country on the international stage. In 1755, the author of the annual directory *The Present State of Great Britain* felt able to boast that 'Our trade is the most considerable in the whole world.' And in 1787 *The Gentleman's Magazine* reported: 'Of all the cheese this kingdom produces, none is more highly esteemed than the Stilton.'

So what is it that makes a Stilton so great – and, indeed, what makes a great Stilton? First, there are the things all mongers can agree on. Stilton is made from cow's milk and comes in a cylinder about a foot tall and ten inches across. A good Stilton has a knobbly rind in a light tan shading to orange. Sometimes there are shades of blushing pink on this rind, a phenomenon that some cheesemongers like to call 'baboon's bum'. (If you see baboon's bum on a Stilton, buy some straight away – I guarantee that cheese will be a stunner.) To the touch, the rind of a Stilton should be lightly moist and, when finally you cut the cheese open, its paste should be the colour of old ivory piano keys, with blue veins radiating out in a marbled pattern. The shade of blue is important. Indigo is perfect. If the blue is too light, it will lack intensity. If it is very dark, it will taste sharp, overly spicy and perhaps even a tad metallic. And when you at last put some Stilton in your mouth, it should have a meltingly creamy texture, a bit like a soft fondant icing.

My favourite Stilton, which ticks all the boxes I have drawn above – and has a flavour that has hints of malty digestive biscuit, Marmite and bubblegum – is made by Colston Bassett Dairy in Nottinghamshire, by a brilliant cheesemaker called Billy Kevan and his team. They collect their milk from nearby farms in the area, giving it the terroir of the Vale of Belvoir, a place long famous for cheese. The dairy was established in 1912 and Kevan is only the fourth cheesemaker in a century. There's continuity for you.

There's an origin myth for blue cheese. I've been told variations of it by cheesemakers, mongers and affineurs from France, Spain, Italy, England and Wales and, as with all origin myths, each teller has patriotically located the story in their own country. However, they agree in the broad strokes, which are as follows.

One day, long ago, there was a shepherd out in the hills with his sheep and his lunch of bread and fresh cheese. He was about to tuck in when he saw a gang of bandits cresting a nearby ridge on their shaggy mountain ponies. (Here, by the way, the Italian story diverges from the rest. According to my Italian source, the shepherd decided to go off and see his girlfriend.) Anyway, whether for reasons of self-preservation or romantic intent, the shepherd left his animals to their own devices and his lunch under a rock. After a prudent interval he returned, only to find that his bread had gone mouldy, and the mould had got onto the cheese and flourished. The shepherd, like all peasants, was hungry, so he took a bite of the mouldy cheese – and, of course, it tasted great.

There might be some truth in this story – using mouldy bread to get your cheese to 'blue up' is an ancient method in blue-cheesemaking. As long ago as the eleventh century, the makers of Roquefort put mouldy rye bread in the caves where their cheeses were maturing. In more recent times, in the south-west of England, cheesemakers are said to have encouraged their cheeses to blue by dragging a bit of leather from a horse's harness through the vat of curd. A cheesemaker from Dorset, it is said, used to leave his old boots in the maturing room and was famed for his blue cheese.

As much as I would love to try blue cheeses made this way, modern environmental health officers are unlikely to sign off on it, and these days all the cheesemakers I know buy their mould in sachets, which also produces more consistent results. The mould responsible for making all blue cheese, by the way, is known as *Penicillium roqueforti*, so it was probably classified, if not discovered, by a Frenchman.

But enough of the continental peasantry and bits of mouldy old leather. Let's get back to Stilton and the eighteenth century. Which, as centuries do, sort of began a bit prematurely – in 1688, to be exact, with the Glorious Revolution (in which William and Mary came over from Holland to re-establish Protestantism, and the too-Catholic James II fled to France) – and ended, according to some historians, in 1837 with the death of William IV, the last of the Georgian kings. And this is not as barking as it sounds. Many of the developments, improvements and revolutions we think of as characterising the eighteenth century had already gained considerable momentum before its onset.

As we saw with the dairy farmers of Cheshire, enclosure and the commercialisation of agriculture was going strong in England in the latter part of the seventeenth century. In 1682, John Houghton in his *Collection of Letters for the Improvement of Husbandry and Trade* noted that 'since His Majesty's most happy restoration the whole land hath been stirred up by the profitable hints it hath received from the Royal Society'. Among the things that Houghton celebrated was the improvement of cattle feed through the cultivation of soil-enriching crops such as clover, and the use of winter feed like turnips that would allow milk production year-round. Notice the mention of the Royal Society, too, a learned society of natural philosophers that was founded in 1660, long before the eighteenth-century Enlightenment.

The long naval war between the English and Dutch had come to an end in 1674, so by the time of the arrival of William and Mary foreign trade was booming. New markets and scores of goods had been opened with the colonisation of the North American coastline and the West Indies, which was begun in earnest under the first Stuart kings and pursued by Cromwell's administration. The middle class were able to afford foreign luxuries like tea and fine china to drink it out of, and even the working poor could afford more material products, such as stockings, earthenware dishes and brass pots.

The seventeenth century had also seen the first stirrings of what became the Industrial Revolution. There was a lot of shipbuilding; the mines of England and Wales were producing more coal, iron and tin and the brewing of beer was becoming an industry; as, of course, was the making and wholesaling of cheese.

Politically, there were two key events that affected all this industry and trade. First, when William and Mary were crowned joint monarchs in 1688, a Bill of Rights established the sovereignty of Parliament and the idea of constitutional monarchy. This led to a degree of political stability. Second, in the year 1707 the Act of Union was passed, joining the parliaments of England and

Scotland. Wales had already been in the union since 1535. Ireland remained outside until 1801, when Great Britain became 'Great Britain and Ireland'.

One of the positive effects of the 1707 union was that it did away with internal customs charges between the two nations and beefed up the economy. For national trade to really work, though, you need to be able to get around, and in that same year the first Turnpike Act was passed, appointing dedicated trustees to run Britain's roads, which had been in a shocking state since the Romans left. The Act appointed dedicated trustees, usually clergymen, gentry or merchants – who, naturally, had a vested interest in better roads. They were duly improved, trade increased and goods could be sold further and further from their place of origin. The process of local cheeses going national, which had begun with Cheshire in the

The Great North Road leaving London at Highgate, prior to being turnpiked.

seventeenth century, got a turbo-charged boost. Soon it would be meaningful to talk about Stilton as a great British cheese.

Oh, and another thing that happened in 1707 was that Fortnum & Mason opened. You can imagine that they – Mr Fortnum and Mr Mason, that is – were as keen as anyone to get the roads sorted out and goods moving around, standing in their nearly empty shop tapping their fingers on the lovely slate counters as they awaited the arrival of nice things to put into little pots.

Now that the stage has been set, it is time for the story of the birth of Stilton. A version of events, taken as gospel by many mongers and cheesemakers, relates that in the early eighteenth century a man called Cooper Thornhill owned the Bell Inn in the village of Stilton. One day his sister-in-law, Mrs Pawlett, who made smashing cheeses on her husband's farm in Wymondham (over the county border in Leicestershire), sent him one for a present. Seeing a business opportunity, Thornhill made a deal with Mrs P. to sell her cheese exclusively at The Bell, to the increasing number of travellers using the improved Great North Road, which joins London to Edinburgh, via Stilton. People from London got a taste for the cheese and the lucky landlord's fortunes were made. At last, Mr Fortnum and Mr Mason had something nice to put in their fancy little pots.

A proponent, if not the author of this account, was the marvellously-monocled Patrick Rance, author of *The Great British Cheese Book* and champion (as we shall see) of British cheese in its darkest hour (the 1970s). Rance's account of Stilton's beginnings is redolent with the gruff certainty that characterises much of this army-officer-turned-cheesemonger's writing; the facts, he claims 'are historically beyond dispute'. He further asserts that Mrs Pawlett's cheese was originally made at Quenby Hall from a recipe called 'Lady Beaumont's Cheese', and 'never made in, or even near, Stilton'.

But not everyone is convinced. Step forward the equally authoritative and only slightly less gruff Trevor Hickman. Stilton, he declared, wasn't born at Quenby Hall but in the town of Stilton itself, then in Huntingdonshire.

There is a tantalising nugget which supports Hickman's argument that Stilton was made in Stilton. It is reported in Mr John Pitt's *Report to the Board of Agriculture* published in 1793, that a regular at the Bell Inn, a Mr Croxton Bray, who died in 1777 aged about eighty, remembered the people of Stilton collecting cream from nearby villages to make the cheese. So, according to Mr Bray, Stilton was made in Stilton in the early eighteenth century. The trouble with this story is that it sounds a bit like something some old fella down the pub told you. Wait a minute – it is.

Whatever the truth, Stilton was soon getting a mention in Daniel Defoe's snappily entitled *A Tour Through the Whole Island of Great Britain*, the first travel guide to Britain, published in 1724. However, I'm not convinced that the cheese known as Stilton back then is one we would recognise. Defoe described Stilton as 'our English Parmesan'. Parmesan is hard. Stilton, as we know it now, is not. But it is possible that Defoe meant it was the English signature cheese. On the other hand, a recipe appears in Mr Richard Bradley's *General Treatise of Husbandry and Gardening* of 1723 for 'the famous Stilton cheese' that instructs you to boil the cheese in whey, press it and mature it for a year – which would certainly make for a hard cheese. Confusingly, in a book published in 1732, the same Mr Bradley says of Stilton that 'one may spread it on bread like butter'. Now that sounds more like the soft creamy Stilton we know and love. Perhaps they had stopped pressing it by then or were maturing it for less time. Or perhaps a wily cheesemaker was keeping her trade secrets when she told Bradley her recipe the first time. It is all a bit of a mystery.

Let us turn to something we can be a bit more sure about, the Bell Inn in Stilton. The great thing about the Inn, as opposed to Lady Beaumont's recipe or an actual Stilton from the early eighteenth century, is that it is still there. Handily, the date 1642 is inscribed on a gable end. And the landlord of The Bell during Stilton's rise to prominence was indeed Cooper Thornhill. That much is documented. But what part did he really play in bringing Stilton to the nation? Remember, according to Rance, Thornhill married the sister of Mrs Pawlett, cheesemaker extraordinaire. This dynastic cheese marriage secured Thornhill a reliable supply of the best cheeses.

Hickman doesn't mention marriage but suggests Thornhill might have advised Mrs P. on how to improve her recipe. Unwise as it may sound to blunder into a woman's dairy and start being free with your opinions, this wasn't unheard-of behaviour for cheese factors at the time. They often tried to persuade the (mostly female) cheesemakers to adopt more 'scientific' practices in order to produce more consistent cheeses. At the time this was often couched in terms of male rationality attempting to overcome rustic female habits. But it was mainly about money. As transport and trade improved across Britain, cheese became a more and more profitable commodity. In 1725 *six and a half million kilos* of Cheshire cheese alone passed through the London Docks. In order to shift volumes of cheese like this, you need it to be of excellent and consistent quality, and you need a regular supply. It's all very well selling Messrs Fortnum & Mason a hundredweight of prime Stilton once, but if you want to stay on the cheese cash turnpike you need to make sure every batch is just as good. As a result, cheese factors were off scouring the countryside for excellent cheese, but also trying to figure out what made it excellent and how to repeat that success.

This was very much a manifestation of Enlightenment thinking: the idea that every natural process and human endeavour could be understood and improved by the gathering of empirical evidence and the application of rational thought. The study and improvement of cheesemaking was a part of a larger project to improve farming driven by theoreticians – usually urban, and invariably men –

who became known, perhaps insultingly, as 'book farmers'. In the world of cheese, the best known of these was Josiah Twamley, who published *Dairying Exemplified* in 1784. To his credit, in his preface he acknowledged and celebrated the skill and experience of the women cheesemakers whose dairies he had visited.

With all that in mind, let's return briefly to Cooper Thornhill and what involvement he may have had with Stilton's rise to prominence. What we know about him is that he was a renowned horseman and, as such, pulled off some major feats. On 29 April 1745, he rode from Stilton to Shoreditch and back, and then back again, in 'eleven hours, thirty-three minutes and fifty two seconds', winning a five-hundred guinea wager. That's about a hundred times the annual wages of a stable hand of the time. Why am I telling you about Thornhill's riding prowess? For one thing it's incredibly cool (and do note that Cooper would never have been able to pull it off without the improved turnpike road). But the other thing is that it was reported in his obituary in the *Oxford Journal* for Saturday, 10 March 1759. That is the only thing they mention about him. If Stilton cheese was such a big deal back then and Thornhill was largely responsible for making it famous, you would think they would have mentioned it in his obituary.

Equally, remember that Defoe was writing about Stilton as 'our English Parmesan' in 1724, but it was not until 1733 that Thornhill put an advert in the *Stamford Mercury* announcing his takeover of the Bell Inn. It's one of those wordy and slightly diffident adverts so beloved of eighteenth-century businessmen: 'there is now good Entertainment for People of Quality...there being laid in a Stock of the best Wines, &c. and all other Things necessary for entertaining'. No mention of Stilton. If I was married to the sister of the best Stilton maker in Britain and had an exclusive contract to supply her cheese, I'd be making a fuss about that. The first mention we find of a connection between Thornhill and Stilton is in the *Derby Mercury*, in December 1790, thirty years after his death. The article says that Mrs Pawlett provided cheese for Thornhill, but 'of what

This print from 1840 shows staff of the Bell Inn loading the boot of a coach. Notice a nicely wrapped Stilton cheese in the foreground.

country was not publicly known hence it obtained, of course the name of Stilton cheese'.

Perhaps Cooper Thornhill's link with the Stilton story was an early marketing tool. Stilton gets to share some of Cooper's fame as a horseman and hospitable host of a well-known inn. Plus, if you are making a cheese called Stilton and you aren't in Stilton, it would be handy to have some sort of historical backup. Advertising was becoming more and more effective in eighteenth-century Britain, leading Samuel Johnson to say 'the trade of advertising is now so near perfection that it is not easy to propose any improvement' (but then he'd never seen Cadbury's drumming gorilla ad). Anyway, the linking of Thornhill and Stilton may be more wishful thinking than historical fact.

Happily there are some certainties in life, one of which being that you can now go and get a nice big lump of Stilton from a proper cheese shop, cut yourself off a decent chunk, put it in your mouth, let the creaminess melt across your tongue and the flavours of malty biscuit and *Hubba Bubba* intoxicate your taste buds.

🍏 🍏 🍏

Another thing to remember about the eighteenth century is that the British were at war for most of it. Usually with the French, sometimes with other peoples around the world like the Cherokee and the Maratha Empire of India, sometimes with the Irish and sometimes with each other.

One of the lesser-known wars of this period was the Cheese War of 1766, which happened in and around Nottingham and adjacent counties in the October of that year. Like so many other conflicts, this *fromage* fracas had its origins partly in the Seven Years' War. This conflict, beginning in 1756 and ending in 1763, was a strong contender for the title 'Actual First World War', as it was fought in Europe, North America, Central America, West Africa, India and the Philippines. The main combatants were, as usual, Britain and France, but assisting on the British side were Prussia, Portugal and the Iroquois nation and, on the French side, the Holy Roman and Mughal empires. The war ended in such an embarrassingly comprehensive victory for the British and their allies that they actually felt obliged to give some territory back to the losing side. Even so, Britain ended the Seven Years' War with great swathes of North America under its control, which meant new markets for British produce. But the war also left the country heavily in debt. As a result, taxes and prices rose in Britain, and as ever these burdens fell heaviest on the poor.

Now, in Britain at the time, the poor were not to be messed with. If this was an epoch of wars, it was even more of an epoch of rioting. Rising prices were often a spark for these outbreaks – for example, Norwich was racked by riots over the price of mackerel for six days in 1740. The Cheese War, too, was about money. It broke out at the annual Goose Fair in Nottingham, on Thursday 2 October 1766 and hostilities opened in the town square, where a group of Lincolnshire cheese factors were attempting to pack up a load of cheeses they had just bought. Some local 'rude lads' surrounded them and told them that 'they should not stir a cheese till the town was first served'. A word of explanation here: these food-related disturbances were not just about high prices, but also a reaction to the increase in national trade. Locals in a town with a market attached saw that food was being taken away from them to be sold to other towns and cities, and feared this would cause shortages as well as higher prices.

This was not an unusual event. It was quite common for groups of locals to overcome a cheesemonger, sell their cheese to the crowds at the old price, and then give the cheesemongers the money. In Nottingham that day, however, things got swiftly out of hand, as locals set up armed guards at the borders of the city to search wagons for cheese. The cheeses involved were large round wheels, probably something like Red Leicester, and local youths started trundling them off down the streets, knocking down the mayor in the mayhem after he came out to remonstrate. Unrest continued all night with the mob 'becoming more outrageous.' When some of them were arrested and held in a coffee house, the mob broke them out. The next day the local militia – infantry and cavalry – were called out and shots were fired into the crowd. The only recorded injury was to a farmer called William Egglestone, who later died of his wounds. William was actually guarding his own cheese, and so is probably the only recorded incidence of death by cheese-related friendly fire.

The crowds in the city began to disperse, but all was not over. Some of the rioters went down to to the river, where they found a boat laden with cheese trying to make its escape. The owner attempted to placate them by offering them money and promising to sell this cheese at a lower price, to which the ringleader replied, 'Damn his charity, we'll have the cheese for nought.' A revolutionary slogan without the mass appeal of 'liberty or death', but pretty punchy nonetheless. The mob made off with the cheese, thus carrying out the first recorded act of cheese river piracy (though not the last – this actually happened a few times across Britain during the cheese rioting season).

However, the most extreme action of the Cheese War of 1766 was yet to come. The mob had got wind of a warehouse full of cheese and decided to lay siege to it. It was defended by armed men who fired 'small shot and grape shot' at the rioters, and finally drove them off. Having done so, the owners of the warehouse got a posse together on horseback and pursued the mob into the nearby town of Donnington. It seems that, during a period of rioting, local Justices of the Peace were not always keen to come down too heavily, and the Donnington JP refused to grant the posse search warrants. Incensed, they seized some of the rioters they had identified as ringleaders, took them to the gates of the JP's house and started breaking open the gates and 'using many unbecoming expressions', according to a local paper.

The townspeople didn't much like this attack on their local JP and joined with the rioters in assaulting the cheese factors and their posse, 'volleys of stones falling from the hills around them where women and children were arranged in ranks five or six deep'. The posse were driven out of town and fled back to the warehouse where they were once again besieged. This time the defenders were so panicked that they were driven off and the mob at last gained possession of the cheese. After this victory the town church bells were rung and a hogshead of beer broached for the people – which suggests the collusion of the local vicar and innkeeper.

The violence and cheese raiding went on for days, with many more warehouses and boats in the area being raided and pirated.

There are also accounts of the hijacking of armed cheese convoys moving between towns. Eventually, the dragoons – heavy cavalry – managed to restore order and the arrests and trials began. The mob managed to rescue some of the accused from the buildings they were being held in, but many others had to go on the run. One source claims that four hundred men fled into hiding.

As to what happened to those who were caught and successfully tried, at least two were whipped and some may have been hanged. Records are not very forthcoming. I do know that plenty of people have been transported for stealing cheese over the years, though. Indeed, my friend Dave, an Australian cheesemaker, names his cheeses after men who were transported to his home country for this very reason. He makes quite a few different styles of cheese and hasn't run out of names yet.

You might be wondering why this chapter is called 'Stichelton' and not 'Stilton'. What is this Stichelton? Is it a funny way of spelling Stilton, or a cheese in its own right? In order to explain that, we're going to have to touch on the somewhat arcane world of PDOs and pasteurisation, and pay a visit to a nice American man called Joe.

A PDO, or Protected Domain of Origin, is a classification given to a product that has an association with a particular area or place, like West Country Cheddar or Melton Mowbray pork pies, and is made in a traditional way. The system was set up by the EU in 1991 as a way of protecting the livelihood of people who make these products and is a sort of descendant of the French AOC (Appellation d'origine contrôlée) system. PDOs are registered with the EU, which enforces international compliance. This means that if someone tries to make goat's milk Stilton in a factory in Azerbaijan, they're going to have to go up against Brussels and its battalions of lawyers. This is a Good Thing and what might happen to this system in a post-Brexit world is an open question. Perhaps we will be trying the Azerbaijani version after all.

Anyway, back in 1996 the Stilton Cheese Makers Association (SCMA) registered a PDO for Stilton. Fair enough. But its detail specified that the cheese must be made with pasteurised milk. This may have been a reaction to a series of food safety scares that beset Britain that decade (remember mad cow disease?), many of which involved listeria monocytogenes, which can be present in milk. I touched upon pasteurisation with Steele's (in Chapter Three), and will come to it again when we're looking at the twentieth century. So for now we will leave Louis Pasteur and just recall that pasteurising milk involves heating it to a temperature where all the bacteria in the milk are killed – a process that will also wipe out the diverse population of safe bacteria that are partly responsible for complex flavours in cheese. In order to get us on the train up to Collingthwaite Farm and its resident cheesemaker, Joe Schneider, it's enough to know this: Stichelton is made with raw milk and so at present cannot legally be called Stilton.

Stichelton Dairy and Joe's house are on the Welbeck Estate, which covers 15,000 acres and straddles two counties, Nottinghamshire and Derbyshire. The family, consisting of Joe, his wife, their two daughters and a black Labrador called Poppy, live in the principal's house on the estate. It's a beautiful eighteenth-century house built in warm butterscotch sandstone, with a high-ceilinged vestibule, wrought-iron banisters on the stairs, a labyrinth of corridors and rooms and – most welcome for me, after a somewhat chilly trip from the station – a huge fireplace in the living room, which had a fire burning welcomingly in the grate.

I soon found myself on the sofa in front of this fire, a bottle of the Kernel Brewery's heartening (7.8 per cent) India Export Porter in hand and Poppy the Labrador obligingly warming my feet. Cheesemakers know how to give you a hospitable welcome and Joe Schneider is up there with the best. As his name might suggest, Joe is an American. He was born in upstate New York and, after studying construction engineering in the States and making feta cheese in Eindhoven, he found himself on the Daylesford Estate in Gloucestershire making a Cheddar-style cheese. It was then that he got a call from Randolph Hodgson, owner of Neal's Yard Dairy, hero of the cheese renaissance, and my old boss. For years Randolph had been trying to get the Stilton Cheese Makers Association to relax the ban on unpasteurised milk and let people make raw milk Stilton, but to no avail. Tiring of the struggle, he decided to get someone to make a raw milk Stilton-style cheese instead. So Randolph and Joe set up a dairy at the Welbeck Estate farm and Joe started making cheese there in 2006.

Developing a new cheesemaking business is never a matter of just finding a recipe and following it. Joe said that figuring out how to make his cheese was a matter of 'making slow, attritional improvements, as well as enjoying a few lightbulb moments'. By the third year he was nailing it, and now, after a decade of experience, Stichelton is consistently delicious, with all the complex balanced flavours and creamy texture you expect from a Stilton-style cheese. Joe says about making Stichelton, 'It's like the Holy Grail of cheesemaking, to bring back the quintessential English cheese and make it with raw milk on a small working farm.'

As they developed the recipe, Randolph and Joe were also casting about for a name for the cheese, originally thinking of Notlits, which is Stilton backwards. Then they discovered from a knowledgeable regular at Neal's Yard Dairy that the original name of the town of Stilton was Stichelton, a form recorded in the twelfth-century Lincoln Rolls, and so a cheese was born...or renamed.

Over dinner, our conversation touched on the politics of PDOs, moral philosophy and business practice, and reasons for being a cheesemaker. I remember one particular gem of Joe's, when I asked him what he thought of a proposal to create a cheesemaking apprenticeship scheme. Some cheesemakers were worried that an apprentice might steal all their secrets and set up as a competitor.

Joe Schneider in the maturing room at Stichelton Dairy.

'When I was starting out, I would have given my right arm for a chance to learn like that, as would everyone else,' said Joe. 'You can come to my dairy, take pictures, take notes, copy everything you like. You won't know how to make my cheese. I don't know how I make my cheese.'

Another thing that unites cheesemakers, along with warm welcomes and nice houses, is early starts. As a French cheesemonger said to me appallingly early one morning as we roared up the queasily switchback mountain road in his SUV, 'The milk doesn't wait.' After plenty of peaty single malt whisky and a heavy but short night's sleep, I found myself at 5 a.m. in Joe's Land Rover heading out to the dairy, feeling a little fuzzy-headed. Stichelton Dairy is in an ancient stone barn next to the cattle sheds, barns and milking parlour of the Welbeck Estate farm. To give you an idea of its scale, Joe has a twenty-minute commute each morning from his house to the dairy, without leaving the estate.

As we've seen, the first thing you do when you arrive at a dairy for a day's work is switch on the pump that shifts the milk from milking parlour to the vat in the dairy. The second thing is to put the kettle on. This is not because cheesemakers are lazy; it is because when milk has to travel, it likes to do so in a slow and dignified manner. Joe therefore installed a pump that is very, very slow and gentle so as to not upset the milk and to give him the best chance of making the creamiest cheese. It is so slow that no one else in the dairy industry uses pumps like this and Joe had to have this one specially designed. This is an example of the attention to detail which is a trait that all great cheesemakers share. If they weren't cheesemakers, they would probably be nuclear safety inspectors.

After the tea had been consumed and the vat was full of milk, we went into the cheese room itself. White-walled, with red tiled floor, huge windows and lots of light, it is, like all the artisan cheese rooms I've been into, a lovely place to work. It was now time for the Washing of the Hands. This is such a detailed and time-consuming process that I often wonder if it wouldn't be quicker and simpler to just plunge oneself into a vat of bleach. It involves washing the arms up to and beyond the elbows, which, the first time I was told to do this, made me worry that I would be called upon to perform some sort of gynaecological procedure on a cow. If you're ever at all worried about the safety of cheese, raw milk or not, you can comfort yourself with the knowledge that cheesemakers are extremely hygienic people.

Then it was time for the actual cheesemaking to begin. We added starter culture, rennet and blue mould to the tranquil vat of milk. I'm always amazed by the awesome magical power of starter and rennet, the bacterial culture that acidifies the milk and the enzyme that coagulates it. We used tiny amounts – about 50 ml of each in liquid form – which we then added to 2,700 litres of milk in a shining rectangular steel vat the size of a couple of billiard tables laid end to end. But these magical liquids contain the power to convert this huge amount of milk to cheese.

Having added the starter and rennet, we had to wait for them to do their work. There is a lot of waiting in the making of Stichelton – it's a style of cheesemaking called a punctuated make, just like Mary Holbrook's soft cheeses from Chapter One. Periods of doing things are punctuated by periods of waiting for stuff to happen. Happily there are plenty of other things to do in the waiting periods. Firstly, there is the rubbing up. Yesterday's cheeses are slid out of their 'hoops' – three-foot-long blue plastic cylinders with holes all over them – to let the whey drain out. At this stage the cheeses are buttery yellow-white with little cracks up and down their outsides. These are smoothed over with butter knives to create a nice even surface and stop any air getting in or creaminess getting out – that's the rubbing up. This is done standing around a table in a companionable group, chatting away as cheesemakers must have done for hundreds of years. As with so many tasks in cheesemaking, though, it is much harder than it looks. Joe's fellow cheesemakers smoothed the sides of the cheese with an easy flick of the wrist, averaging one every five minutes. I think I managed one every twenty and soon my wrist was aching and my back was nagging at me from bending over to peer at my work .

By the time we'd done with the rubbing up, the curd had set into a form like a very wobbly crème caramel. Joe and his head cheesemaker Ross then began to cut it with multi-bladed curd-cutters. The curd-cutting allows the whey to drain off. This was far too skilful and crucial an operation to let a novice loose on, so I just watched, mesmerised, as the team dropped the curd knife into one end of the vat and then, walking alongside the length of the vat at a measured pace, drew it through the curd in one smooth motion.

After cutting comes another period of waiting as the curd drains. So our next fill-in job was the turning of the older cheeses. As cheese matures it loses moisture and, if you didn't turn your cheeses regularly all the moisture would puddle on the shelf, giving you sticky-bottomed cheeses. They would also slump and lose their elegant shape, as well as developing an uneven texture and flavour. Young cheeses contain more moisture and have to be turned more often than their older siblings, maybe twice a day at first. A fully mature three- to four-month-old Stichelton weighs about eight kilos; a younger one with more moisture, considerably more. There are hundreds of them in the Stichelton store and turning

Joe Schneider (right) turning curd with Randolph Hodgson, the founder of Neal's Yard Dairy.

them is a constant and physically demanding job. The cheeses are fragile, and if you bash them about you'll crack them and let air and unwanted moulds in, and moisture out.

I greeted the next period of cheesemaking, the ladling, with some relief. Not that ladling is exactly a stroll. Having done a fair bit of ladling with other cheesemakers, I knew how painstaking and how painful ladling can be. Here, however, the degree of painstaking and painful was something else. The curd for Stichelton is cut into cubes about an inch across and if ladled carelessly they would break into crumbs and lose their creaminess. Using a scoop that looks like a dustpan, the correct method is a shallow and gentle skim across the top of the curd, then an upwards flick, before turning around to gently deposit the scoop of curd on the draining table. Oh – and each scoopful should contain the same amount so that they drain at the same rate, and it all has to be done at pace, since you can't let it hang around in the vat too long or it becomes too acidic, resulting in sharp, hard cheese. They let me have a go, but it was a challenge – and within minutes my wrist and arm were on fire. I could only marvel that Joe and his team do a whole vat of Stichelton every day.

You might at this point wonder why cheesemakers put themselves through such an incredibly demanding process. Surely there must be some sort of technological fix? There is indeed, and in fact Joe, and the makers of Colston Bassett, are the only Stilton (or Stilton-style) makers who still ladle by hand. The others use a sort of dump-truck arrangement: the vat drops at one end and the curd slides off in one mass onto the draining table. Joe had a graphic way of showing me why he doesn't do this: he took a handful of curd and threw it on the cheeseroom floor, where it broke into liquified crumbs. 'You can't do that with my curd,' he says. 'It's too delicate. The other cheesemakers have changed their cheese to fit their technology. I don't want to do that.' Which means that Joe can only make a comparatively small amount of cheese – about five thousand kilos of Stichelton a year. The larger

Stilton makers, who supply the supermarkets, make around sixty thousand kilos.

With the ladling all done, the curd sits on the draining table losing whey and setting into a rubbery mass. This takes a while and is a great opportunity to have some lunch. After lunch the set curd is broken into fist-sized lumps and fed through a curd mill, a sort of mangle with teeth that tears it up into half-inch bits, into which liberal handfuls of salt are mixed. The salt sucks out more moisture and slows down the action of the starter culture. Without salt you would get soggy cheese that tastes bonkers.

The salted, milled curd is packed into steel buckets and from them tipped into the blue plastic hoops that shape it into the finished cylinders of cheese. You wouldn't think it, but even this bit takes some skill. The curd has to be tipped into the moulds in an even, slow movement. Too fast and it gets compacted and makes hard cheese that doesn't blue up as thoroughly as Joe would like. The hoops of nascent Stichelton are then stacked up on boards to drain and later that day they are put on the hastener, a set of shelves in a relatively warm room.

To get the veins of blue to develop evenly all through the cheeses, they have to be pierced. This allows the air into the cheeses that the mould needs in order to grow. Originally Joe did the piercing by hand, using an ice pick, but this didn't create a very even blueing, so he changed to a system where the cheeses sit on a powered turntable. As it turns, banks of steel rods shoot out and pierce the cheeses, creating a consistent pattern of holes. This results in better, more even blueing and less psychotic cheese-stabbing.

To make really great blue cheese, you need to control the rate that the blue grows in the cheese and the overall amount of blue. Remember that what you are looking for in the flavour is the interaction between the blue and the cheese it has grown in, not just the flavour of the blue, which can be bitter. Joe does this by leaving his cheese to mature for several weeks before he pierces it, so the cheese itself develops a complex rich flavour. He also only pierces two times in the three to four months that the cheese matures, so that the blue doesn't run wild. The result is an exquisitely balanced flavour with none of the metallic bitterness that heavy blueing can give.

When you put all of the aspects of Joe's method together – the slow pump from the milking parlour, the raw milk, the gentle hand ladling of the curd, the patient wait until the cheese is ready to pierce, and the constant monitoring and turning over the months that the cheese matures – you get a great cheese. The flavour is intense but balanced between all its elements, not too salty, not too acidic and not too blue.

I have an old cheesemaking book open on my desk as I write this called *Practical Cheesemaking*, written in 1917 by C.W. Walker-Tisdale and Walter E. Woodnutt (they had proper names in the old days). I can recognise all the steps for Stilton making in this book just as I saw them at Joe's dairy, and I like to think that the cheesemakers of 1917 would have been impressed with Joe's cheese. There is a photo of some Stilton in the book showing just the same texture on the rind and marbled spread of blue veins throughout the cheese that I would expect to see in a great Stilton or Stichelton now.

After the cheesemaking, Joe had another little job for me, which was to help him shift a pallet load of fifty-kilo sacks of salt from one end of the barn to the other. A task he had thoughtfully been saving for my arrival. One thing you get asked all the time when you are a cheesemonger is 'How come you're not really fat? I'd be so fat if I had your job.' This is why.

After that, Joe and I had a bit of a stroll around the farm, and went to chat with the cowman. The herd are Holstein Friesians, beautiful creatures, like illustrations in a book of fairy tales. Checking in with the herd is part of Joe's cheesemaking philosophy. By keeping up with his cows, he can get an idea of what may be happening with the milk and keep ahead of any problems – an important part of making a safe, healthy raw milk cheese.

Among many other questions I asked Joe as we wandered about was this: 'Do you still want to be allowed to call your cheese Stilton?' After all, he is selling all the Stichelton he can make and it's become a successful brand in itself. Joe's answer, though, was yes: 'I want to be able to call it Stilton, because I *should* be able to call it Stilton.

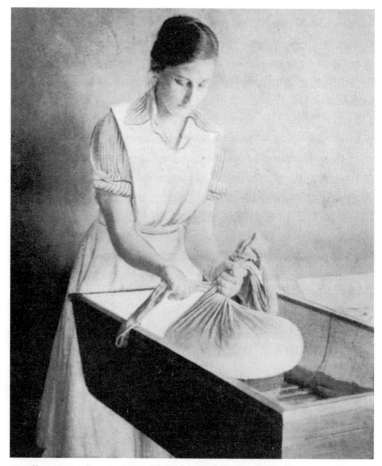

An illustration from Practical Cheesemaking *(1917) shows a Stilton maker tying curd in cloth to drain.*

Listen, I'm American, it doesn't matter to me, but for you British people, this cheese, made in its traditional way with raw milk, it's part of your culture, it's your birthright. It's just wrong that you can't make an unpasteurised cheese and call it Stilton. PDOs are there to protect traditional local foods and methods of producing them. How can pasteurisation be part of a traditional process? It only got started properly in the twentieth century.'

Joe campaigns continually to get the PDO changed, but in a kafkaesque twist you can't apply to alter a PDO unless you're a member of it. So Joe has had to go and see the Minister of State for Agriculture, Fisheries and Food to try and get government support, and to demonstrate outside Parliament for his cause, handing out bits of cheese, of course. So far, it hasn't worked.

I got on the train back down to London with pleasantly sore cheesemaking muscles, a new collection of cheesemaking anecdotes, but no less a sense of confusion about the intertwined issues of PDOs and pasteurisation. It seems to me that PDOs are a force for good when they protect traditional producers. At the same time it seems a shame that a cheesemaker who wanted to explore older ways of making cheese would not be allowed to retain that PDO.

The other thing I had with me on the train was a great big hunk of Stichelton, a present from Joe. So I texted some friends with the message, 'Huge lump of Stich from Joe! Come and meet me at the Queen's Head.' The Queen's Head is a real ale pub near King's Cross station. Now, you might think that if you had a big bit of Stilton-style cheese you would be best off heading for a wine bar and ordering a large glass of port, but this is not the correct thing to do. It is purely an accident of history. Let me explain.

In the early eighteenth century, when Britain was, as usual, at war with France, good French claret was hard to come by and we had to settle for Portuguese wine. The wines of Portugal weren't all that great at the time and an enterprising wine shipper had the bright idea of adding brandy to them. The brandy stopped the wines fermenting, and left them heavy and sweet, and so port was born. It wasn't all that popular at first, as this epigram by Scottish dramatist John Home suggests:

Firm and erect the highland chieftain stood
Old was his mutton and his claret good.
'Let him drink port' an English statesman cried.
He drank the poison and his spirit died.

By the 1720s, when the first ports had had some time to age and mellow, port became immensely popular and fashionable. This was precisely the time that Stilton was becoming famous. So if you were

'I can't believe it's not Stilton!' Joe Schneider, militant lactivist, outside Parliament.

keeping up with the latest developments in high society, you would have had port and Stilton on your dining table. It wasn't that people figured out they were a great match; it's just that they were both very much on trend, so the Stilton/port pairing became the thing to do. And if you wanted to be really cool, you wheeled your Stilton up and down the table in a special Stilton truck. They still pop up on eBay from time to time.

I love port, and I quite like it with Stilton, but for me a far better match is a glass of proper stout or porter. Neither will overwhelm the flavour of cheese in the way that the port can. The rich texture of both beer and cheese complement each other beautifully and the bitterness of the hops clears the palate, setting you up for another generous fondanty mouthful of cheese.

Even without the port, when I finished my journey from Welbeck I felt like I was back in the eighteenth century: seated at the table of a warm and hospitable hostelry, surrounded by friends, still red-cheeked from the cold of the Midlands, well provided with foam-topped pints of porter and a big hunk of Stichelton – though thankfully not, for now, at war with the French.

CHAPTER SEVEN

Westcombe Cheddar
Ploughman's lunch
1837–1901

THE PLOUGHMAN'S LUNCH IS A BIT OF A FAKE. It was an advertising concept, dreamt up in 1960s Britain to persuade us to eat in pubs – a hitherto unknown concept, in a world when pub grub was a choice between crisps or pork scratchings. The UK Milk Marketing Board put money into marketing the concept and the great British public was hooked. A pint and a ploughman's became a regular lunch order: a slice of cheese, a hunk of bread, a dollop of Branston pickle, perhaps even a pickled onion. And the cheese, more often than not, was Cheddar – Britain's favourite then and now. In 2018, Cheddar, astonishingly, accounted for around half of the UK's £2.6 billion cheese market – and, with variants from Canada to New Zealand, it is beaten in worldwide sales only by pizza-base Mozzarella.

Alas, much of that billion pounds' worth of Cheddar is factory block – pre-wrapped in plastic and, lacking depth and complexity, very much in need of the Branston. There is a note of doom sounded in the report that those sales figures come from, which is that, perhaps due to Cheddar's 'popularity as a versatile ingredient' (i.e. a 'cooking cheese'), only thirteen per cent of consumers see it as a fitting cheese for special occasions. Like the Victorian Mrs Beeton, more than a third considered continental cheeses like Brie or Camembert as cheeses ripe for that role. Fancy cheese still rules, and there is much work to be done. For there is another Cheddar, which we shall consider in these pages. And it has ardent and loyal supporters. It is this cheese that Patrick Rance, the monocled champion of British cheese, had in mind when he described Cheddar as 'our most generous gift to humanity'.

When I began my mongering career on a bright winter's day in 2002, I was standing behind a wide slate counter in the Covent Garden branch of Neal's Yard Dairy, framed by a tower of Cheshire on my left and Stilton to my right. But the very first question that was fired at me by a customer was this: 'Which is best today? Keen's or Monty's?' I had no idea what he was talking about. And then I turned to follow his gaze, towards a rampart of Cheddars on the shelf behind me and saw one called Keen's, and another called Montgomery's. I turned back to my new customer and said: 'I have no idea. Shall we try them?' I was about to enter a brave new world, of proper artisanal Cheddar.

Traditional Cheddar comes in imposing foot-high cylinders weighing in at twenty-four kilos and bound in cloth that has been rubbed in lard. They tend to have the grey colour of an old battleship from the mould that has grown on them as they mature. Their traditional place of origin is Somerset – if not actually in the village of Cheddar, then certainly at the feet of the Mendip Hills.

Opening one of these cheeses is a bit of an undertaking and requires some practice to do right. You take a good, sharp bread knife and score a line through the cloth along the vertical axis of the cheese, then take a long cheese wire with a handle at each end, trap one end under the Cheddar, lay it along the line you have scored through the cloth and in one smooth movement pull the wire through the cheese. If you have done your job right, the cheese will be divided into two equal halves, and here is your reward: when you pull the halves apart, the cheese reveals itself to you in

Now that's what I call Cheddar. A very decent slice of Monty's.

its full glory, a rich, warm yellow like a Van Gogh sunset. If no one is looking, you can pick that half up and immerse yourself in its sharp and earthy aroma.

Cheddar should be firm, hard enough to make your fingertips whiten if you press it, but not too dry. There should be a trace of moisture left on your fingers afterwards. While there is much talk of super-strong Cheddar that makes your mouth hurt, I prefer balance in a cheese. So, as much as I want an enlivening tingle of acidity in a Cheddar, I like that to be tempered by its rich buttery texture and complemented by a range of flavours – beefiness, grass, earthiness, a little sweetness and lots of length. I want that flavour to go on – as with any cheese, length is a sign of quality.

And, even if two Cheddars come from the same region and benefit from the same terroir, they'll taste different.

The two cheeses my new customer had asked about – Keen's and Montgomery's – are a case in point. Keen's has a moister texture, with a hint of sulphur and a sharp acidic bite (perhaps a result of the higher moisture, because more moisture means more bacterial activity and thus acidity). Monty's is harder and drier, with a more balanced acidity and rounder flavour. I think of Keen's as the brass section and Monty's as the woodwind in the great Cheddar orchestra and, just as neither section is better than the other, I don't prize one Cheddar above the other. Sometimes I am in the mood for a bit of the restrained, elegant Monty's, made on Manor Farm near North Cadbury, perhaps washed down with a glass of Riesling, its gentle off-dry sweetness perfectly complementing the savoury flavours in the cheese. Other times, a hunk of Keen's, made on Moorhayes Farm near Wincanton, with a glass of cider from nearby, is what I'm after.

With artisan hard cheese, it is often the case that ageing (done properly) makes for quality. But that is not always true for Cheddar. I have heard people speak of five-year-old Canadian Cheddars in hushed excitable tones. And, in America, a cheesemaker called Ed Zahn from Milwaukee discovered some Cheddar in the back of his storeroom, inadvertently buried since the early 1970s, and even though it was a factory block, extreme age had conferred complexity and depth of flavour. Wanting to ensure a fair distribution of this happy historical accident, Ed sold it to personal callers only, in small pieces. Sadly, I missed out.

But in general twelve to eighteen months is a good age for a cloth-bound Cheddar, like Monty's and Keen's. Or, indeed, Westcombe (of which more later), the third member of what I think of the Somerset Cheddar triumvirate. I smile a little sadly when a customer tells me, 'I'm sorry, I only like boring cheese like Cheddar.' There is nothing wrong with good Cheddar. And it comes, like so many of the British Isles' finest cheeses, from one of the most beautiful stretches of countryside – those misty, lush-pastured valleys around Glastonbury, where King Arthur is said to have held court.

🧀 🧀 🧀

As much as the ploughman's lunch might have been dreamt up by a marketing department, Cheddar was a staple food for the sturdy ploughmen of old England, and indeed all agricultural workers. And even in its early days, it was a fine food for the gentry. This is a cheese with a pedigree.

The 'excellent and prodigious great cheeses' of Cheddar are given an honourable mention in William Camden's *Britannia* (first published in 1586). 'Great', in Camden's description, probably meant 'big'. He says that it took two men to lift a Cheddar to the table. But he also describes their flavour approvingly, as 'a delicate taste, equalling if not exceeding that of the Parmesan'.

At the time, though, transport being what it was, little cheese made its way out of the county of Somerset, and if it did it was to be found on the the tables of the rich. In the eighteenth century, everything changed and, with better roads, communications and a buoyant economy, Cheddar's fame grew nationally, alongside Cheshire and Stilton. That eighteenth-century cheese fancier, Daniel Defoe, in his *Tour Through the Whole Island of Great Britain*, writes of 'large Cheddar cheese, the greatest and the best of the kind in England'. He describes a communal system of cheesemaking in which all the dairy farmers around the village of Cheddar pool their milk to make these large cheeses, of a quality such that 'without all dispute, it is the best cheese that England affords, if not, that the whole world affords'. By the last quarter of the eighteenth century, Cheddar had caught up with Cheshire to share its place as the most widely sold cheese in the British Isles.

Our timeline for this chapter begins in 1837, with the accession of Queen Victoria to the throne of Great Britain and Ireland, and ends with her death in 1901. Victoria's sixty-four year reign was a period of change on a scale never before seen in the British Isles, or indeed anywhere else. The population grew from around twenty-five million in 1837 to forty million in 1901, and it was urbanising rapidly. By the end of the Victorian era, three-quarters of the population lived in towns and cities.

The year 1837 was eventful beyond Victoria's accession. In Bristol, the *Great Western*, the first ship purpose-built to cross the Atlantic, was launched; meanwhile, in London, Euston Station was opened as the capital's first mainline railway terminus. (In the same year, incidentally, Lea & Perrins started production of their Worcestershire sauce, that indispensable ingredient for the really good cheese toastie.) Revolutions in science, industry and agriculture were in full spate, the culmination of changes that can be traced back beyond 1712, when Thomas Newcomen invented the steam engine, at least as far as 1662, when the Royal Society was founded. Robert Hooke, one of the Society's founder members, is held in some esteem by cheese historians. Hooke's great work was the *Micrographia* of 1665, a cornerstone of scientific knowledge which includes, among much else, detailed drawings and descriptions of a cheese mite, the implacable little enemy of all cheesemongers. Whilst writing the book, Hooke invented new compound microscopes and coined the term 'cell', and he later invented a thermometer and a hygrometer for measuring humidity – instruments that would be vital in making cheese in the nineteenth century.

The Agricultural Revolution, as we have seen, had been rumbling away since the beginnings of enclosure, but in the nineteenth century things really got going. In 1838, the Royal Agricultural Society was founded to encourage the scientific and technological improvement of farming, and by 1851 James Caird, a Scottish agricultural writer, could record that 'all over England, wherever farms were making profits, new machines were bought, old hedgerows were removed and new farm buildings were put up'. Caird identified the greatest advances in farming as taking place in the Midlands and the West Country, where the domination of wheat was being seriously challenged by potato farming, pig farming and dairying. His influential book, *High Farming*, gave its name to these radical changes.

Dairy farming – and in turn cheesemaking – benefited from the discoveries, or one might say the ideology, of High Farming. Systematic breeding produced the Shorthorn, a mixed-use cow that produced plenty of top-quality beef, in addition to giving copious quantities of milk. Winter cropping of roots such as turnips, a move

The Shorthorn cow – the bovine face of the nineteenth century.

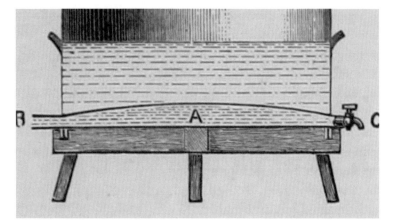

Cockey's cheesemaking apparatus – an early bit of technology in the move from farmhouse to factory.

championed by the aristocratic farmer 'Turnip' Townshend, meant more and higher-quality milk in the winter, not only increasing year round production but making cheese more consistent across the seasons.

The equipment and technology of cheesemaking also improved, seeing innovations like the multi-bladed 'American' curd knife and Cockey's Cheese-making Apparatus, whose double bottom foreshadowed the jacketed hot-water or steam-heated cheese vats still in use today. Buildings were improved too, as dark, earth-floored dairies were replaced by new 'sweet, airy and wholesome' buildings – this being the advice of Joseph Harding, a towering presence in Cheddar-making. All these improvements had one goal – to improve the commercial prospects of dairying by making more consistent, higher-quality cheese.

Nineteenth-century cheese books also mention purpose-built Cheddar stores, cut into the side of hills, where temperature and humidity could be kept more constant than in a free-standing barn. At Westcombe Farm, Tom Calver, overriding the understandable scepticism of his father, has built one of these inside the low hill that looks over the farmyard, and seeing it was one of the highlights of my visit. From the outside, with its neo-brutalist concrete wall and high arched doorways, it looks like a James Bond villain's lair. Inside, it is a cathedral of Cheddar. As Tom opened the enormous motorised door, thousands of Cheddars were revealed, maturing on wooden racks stretching fifty feet or more into the dim heights of the roughened concrete ceiling.

Like his Victorian forefathers, Tom has used all the benefits of modern science to maintain the temperature and humidity that the cheeses need. Instead of fans – which dry out the air – the store is cooled with water, which runs through pipes hanging just under the ceiling. Cool air falls and warm air heated by the fermenting cheeses rises, creating excellent air circulation. The electric heat exchanger is fed from cold water from a natural spring in the hillside and this elegant system runs on half the power needed to run an electric kettle. Just as the Victorians were influenced by new ideas coming from over the Atlantic, Tom got the idea for this incredible place from a similar store built by Mateo Kehler at Jasper Hill Farm in Vermont, but its design owes much to modern alterations to the Napoleonic Fort Saint Antoine in the French Alps, where thousands of wheels of Comté are quietly maturing as you read this paragraph. Tom even had special cheese-maturing concrete shipped in from France. Cheesemakers do this sort of thing.

And there is something else that is truly amazing – though I suspect the Victorian scientists would not have been so surprised. Tom has a cheese-turning robot. A steel and glass rectangle about seven feet tall, this robot can turn hundreds of cheeses a week. A mobile conveyor belt slides onto the shelf under the cheese and rolls it out, so the cheese isn't dragged over the shelf, then any mite is brushed off and the cheese is flipped, before being dropped gently back down without any rocking on the edges. Tom and I

The Westcombe robot setting about its business. The future is now.

agreed that, with the best will in the world, at the end of a long stint of cheese turning, we wouldn't do such a good job. The cheeses look healthy and happy, and when I run my finger along a shelf it is almost totally free of mite. I'm impressed.

But, to return to the Victorians. The gospel of High Farming was spread by the journals of agricultural societies such as the Bath and West Society, which had been established back in 1777, and the Highlands Agricultural Society, which was just seven years younger. These prominent societies were to become the model for the Royal Agricultural Society of England, granted a royal charter by Queen Victoria in 1840.

226

It was the Bath and Western Society that published the report of a pivotal moment in the fortunes of British cheesemaking, which was the visit of the 1857 Deputation of the Ayrshire Agricultural Association to English cheesemakers. The deputation consisted of two men, David Cunninghame and James Drennan, who visited farms in Gloucester and Wiltshire. There they saw regional variations in cheesemaking practice and learnt from the knowledgable, confident women who ran the farmhouse dairies. Even in this era of high farming however, some of the old ways persisted. At one farm, in the Vale of Berkeley in Gloucestershire, they witnessed the dairymaid 'cutting out the witch', which meant taking a small cone of curd from one of the new-made cheeses. This, along with the horseshoe above the dairy, they were told, 'forms a perfectly sufficient safeguard against witch-craft'.

The highlight of the Ayrshire Deputation's journey was the visit to Marksbury Farm in Somerset, owned by Joseph Harding, who was already famed for his Cheddar. At Marksbury they observed the practice of Mrs Harding, 'who has had long experience in cheesemaking', and were clearly impressed by how she and her grand-niece could tell the temperature of the curd to within a couple of degrees just by running a hand through it. These women were making cheeses which weighed a barely believable seventy to a hundred pounds; these days full-size Cheddars are around fifty pounds and are hard enough to shift. Even the hardy Scots cheesemakers thought that the cheeses could be made a bit smaller for ease of handling.

Cunninghame and Drennan were also excited by the modern cheesemaking technology employed at Marksbury, in particular the rotating curd-breaker, noting that 'in England as well as Scotland the farmer's wife is generally the dairy manager; and mechanical improvements which lessen her labour are generally very desirable'. Quite so. The most valuable finding of the Ayrshire Deputation, though, was the 'Harding System', with its careful monitoring and control of the speed and the temperature at which the curd sets.

This was what they and so many other cheesemakers were looking for – a standardised system that could be easily replicated and which would produce consistent, quality cheese. And the Scots wasted no time. In 1858, Harding-style cheese took the prizes at the Highland Agricultural Show.

Rather generously, given that cheesemakers can be protective of their trade secrets, Joseph Harding wrote a book, *Practical Aspects of Cheesemaking*, which was published in 1859 by the *Ayrshire Advertiser*. He also came out of semi-retirement, with his wife Rachel, to demonstrate cheesemaking all over Britain. In Pembrokeshire they showed that skilful cheesemakers can make good cheese on what was thought to be poor land. In Cheshire they tactfully refrained from championing the Cheddar method and restricted themselves to general teaching points. In Ayrshire, *The Scotsman* reported that 'if our Scottish cheese could be manufactured of equal quality with Mrs. Harding's, the balance at many a farmer's bank account would speedily assume more importance'. They were quite right. Top-quality Cheddar was selling at ten shillings a hundredweight more than its closest competitor, Cheshire.

Harding was an enthusiastic advocate of setting up dairy schools to train people 'in the art of good cheesemaking, combining science and practice'. The first permanent dairy school – and the first to take women students – was established at Munster in County Cork in 1880. An early example of that Irish county's disproportionate influence on the fortunes of British and Irish cheese, it was well regarded enough to send cheesemaking teachers to the Cheshire Dairy Institute in Worleston in 1886 – predecessor of the Reaseheath Agricultural College, where Lucy Appleby would eventually go to hone her cheesemaking craft.

Alongside these permanent schools were travelling dairy schools that based themselves for the summer on a different farm each year. The students were the wives, sons and daughters of tenant farmers, who paid a hefty eight guineas for the term. One of the relationships that formed during these seasonal schools was between a precociously

Visionary cheesemakers Rachel and Joseph Harding. That dog must have had a nice life.

young cheesemaking teacher, twenty-two-year-old Edith J. Cannon, and a Welsh-born chemist to the Royal Association of British Dairy Farmers, Dr Frederick J. Lloyd. Since the Harding method's rise to fame in the 1850s, a few other systems of Cheddar-making had become available to the inquisitive cheesemaker, and the Cannon System was reckoned one of the best. It had been developed by Somerset cheesemaker Mrs Cannon, whose husband owned Milton

Farm near Castle Cary, and whose daughter Edith, who had begun cheesemaking on the farm at the age of fourteen, won first prize at the Frome Agricultural Show in 1887. The Bath and West Society were impressed with her systematic method, and adopted it for their roving cheese schools, along with the cheesemaking prodigy, Edith.

Dr Lloyd was a classic Victorian scientist, keen to develop, at the request of the Board of Agriculture and the behest of Joseph Harding, nothing less than a complete understanding of the chemistry of the cheesemaking process so that 'cheese could be made (as it ought to be) on principles scientific, and consequently unerring'. This mighty undertaking took him seven years – a task, he lamented, 'infinitely more laborious than I had anticipated'. The study culminated in *A Report on the Results of Investigations Into Cheddar Cheese-Making*, published in 1899. It was, according to J.G. Davis, a cheese scientist of the 1940s, 'the greatest single contribution ever made to the science of cheesemaking'.

It's not an unmighty undertaking to read the thing, either. With scientific rigour, Lloyd collected thousands of data points, recording which fields the cows had been grazing in for each day's make, as well as acidity levels, temperatures and timings. In the process he made a number of suggestions for technical innovations that are still in operation. These include the make sheet for recording the critical variables of each day's work (which almost all the cheesemakers I know still use) and a graded cylinder for measuring rennet accurate to one-hundredth of an ounce (Lloyd grumbled that 'some cheesemakers use merely an old tea cup and wonder why they do not get the same results with their cheese day after day'). But his most significant contribution to cheesemaking technology was the introduction of the acidometer, and I'm afraid that when I saw the picture of it in his report I let out another of my yawps, now notorious in the Rare Books Reading Room of the British Library. It was the exact same design I have seen in so many of the dairies I have visited – it hasn't changed in a hundred years.

As for understanding the processes underlying cheesemaking, Lloyd had two crucial insights. One was about the importance of the development and control of acidity. The other was about the role of bacteria. As Lloyd put it, in his introduction:

> Investigation soon proved that during the making of a cheese there were other than chemical agents at work whose influence for good or bad might be quite as powerful as if not more powerful than, the skill of the maker...Bacteria, those infinitely minute vegetable growths which are now found to play so important a part in both the welfare and ills of mankind, were not absent from the dairy, and were fighting either for or against the skill and intelligence of the cheesemaker.

Our understanding of bacteria can be traced back to the 1670s, when a Dutchman called Antonie Van Leeuwenhoek, inspired by Hooke's *Micrographia*, and using his own home-made microscopes, identified what he called *animalcules* in samples of water. Further study of bacteria languished for a couple of hundred years and it wasn't until 1857 when a French doctor, Louis Pasteur, was studying problems in beetroot winemaking that the microbe again reared its tiny little head. It was this study that led Pasteur to the development of a process that has led to more arguments in the world of cheesemaking than any other – pasteurisation (more on which later). Another vital figure in nineteenth-century bacteriology was the German scientist Robert Koch, who in the 1880s developed a method for isolating and culturing pure strains of bacteria. This discovery would not only help cheese scientists like Dr Lloyd to identify strains of bacteria active in cheesemaking but would also pave the way for the development of starter cultures, which would lead to far more consistent cheesemaking.

Aware of the importance of bacteria in cheesemaking, Lloyd decided to put his findings to the test by making a Cheddar using only measurements of acidity, temperature and time, entirely disregarding the smell, taste and feel of the curd. It was the cheesemaking equivalent of flying a plane on instruments alone. His conclusions appeared to be vindicated when, at the end of that Cheese School year, his scientific Cheddar was judged to be excellent, however, being a research scientist rather than a cheesemaker, he did have some help, having been advised on the technical aspects by Edith J. Cannon.

It sounds as if Lloyd was a rather difficult man. His obituary describes his 'peculiarities of temperament and a certain aggressiveness,' which may have hampered his career. But he obviously had a considerable regard for the craft and talent of young Edith, which shines through his stately Victorian prose. Lloyd professes his admiration for Edith's ability to tell when the curd is ready to mill by taste alone – 'how very few makers possess sufficient delicacy of taste to form an accurate opinion on such basis' – and celebrates the consistency of her cheesemaking. And, even better, when he refers to the Cheddar system in use at the Dairy Institute, he calls it 'Miss Cannon's method'.

When I decided to visit Tom Calver at Westcombe and make his cheese, this chapter's signature Cheddar, it was partly because his cheese is delicious and also because I knew and liked him. But what I hadn't known was that my choice was totally serendipitous. For when I called him to fix up a visit, I asked him if he knew much about Edith Cannon. 'Well, she used to make cheese here on the farm,' he said.

My reaction was stunned silence at this magical serendipity. After I had put the phone down, I shifted into a more vigorous and louder celebratory mode, the cheesemonger's equivalent of yipping and chasing my tail. Attracted by the commotion, my wife came in to the study (our bedroom) to see what was going on.

'Are you in pain?'

'Nope!'

'Have we become suddenly very rich or very poor?'

'Nope!'

'Then what, Ned?'

'EDITH CANNON MADE CHEESE ON TOM'S FARM!'

I'm sure you will appreciate the moment. And, for me, it felt a bit like a pilgrimage as I took the train to Castle Cary, deep in Cheddar country. It's a wonderful journey, by the way, as the train heads out of Bristol along the route of a canal, passing Victorian mills before following the valley of a meandering river, with sheep grazing on the pastures and trees covering the slopes on either side.

After a tour of Westcombe Farm, Tom asked if I would like to help milk the cows in the afternoon. I have to admit that I was a little intimidated (cows are big beasts), but it was an impossible offer to turn down. Not only I would be assisting celebrity milker Nick the Herdsman, but Nick's cows live over at Milton Farm, where Edith Cannon was born and began her cheesemaking career. So Tom and I drove the few miles from Westcombe and Tom pointed out a large stone farmhouse. 'That's where she was born. And see that window there? That's the cheese room where she started making Cheddar.'

Tom gave me a moment to recover before taking me off to meet Nick Millard, aka Nick the Herdsman. He had told me about Nick on the way, leaving me with the feeling that herding careers were a bit like those of cheesemakers and mongers – which is to say that they don't follow an obvious linear path. Nick had begun his adult life as a drummer in a pop band, but after tiring of world tours had quit life on the road for agricultural college. He had recently moved to Milton Farm from Bwlchwernen Fawr Farm in west Wales, where he was looking after the herd that provide the milk for Hafod, a supple earthy Welsh Cheddar.

In the warmth of the milk parlour, amid the clattering of the milking machine and the lowing of the cows, we talked of animal husbandry. Nick was trying to reduce the use of antibiotics to a

Edith Cannon about to cut the curd with her cheese harp or curd breaker. At just the right time, of course.

minimum, focusing more on the health and comfort of the cows. They certainly seemed pretty happy, if perhaps a little taken aback to find a novice milker nervously trying to put the cylinders of the milking machine on their udders. Nick knew each cow's quirks and occasionally would stop me and say, 'I'll do this one, she's a bit frisky.' Which was nice of him, as my inexperience earned me a few kicks to the hand even from the staid ones. Milking is like a very high-stakes game of Operation.

As we were finishing up the last row of cows, Nick pointed to a pretty brown-and-white Ayrshire. 'That's Edith,' he said. 'She's carrying a baby Shorthorn.' This is the breed whose milk Edith

Cannon made Cheddar from more than a hundred years ago. Nick and Tom plan to move the herd over to Shorthorns from Friesian Holsteins, the black-and-white cows familiar from picture books, and had named this cow in her honour.

❦ ❦ ❦

There is no question that Lloyd's influence on Cheddar-making was huge, but it is not an untroubled legacy. The cheese science writers Bronwen and Francis Percival say in their recent book, *Reinventing the Wheel: Milk, Microbes and the Fight for Real Cheese*, that what we have come to think of as proper Somerset Cheddar is perhaps a rather homogenised and often over-acidic cheese, and is more F.J. Lloyd's creation than Edith Cannon's. They point out that the Lloyd method reduced the focus of Cheddar-making to the monitoring and speedy development of acidity, and that, while this is a good way of keeping unwanted spoilage bacteria down, and getting consistent results, it doesn't necessarily make for great cheese. Some consumers have come to imagine that 'strong' and 'acidic' equals 'good' and ask for Cheddar that will 'take the roof of my mouth off'. To me, that's all wrong.

Still, Lloyd's motives were sound. As well as understanding the processes that underlie Cheddar-making, he was trying to come up with a method that was consistent and teachable. And, to do him justice, Lloyd celebrated difference, writing that 'the methods of manufacturing Cheddar are as numerous as localities where it is made'. He couldn't have known that his work would contribute to the homogenising of Cheddar.

If the farmhouse Cheddar we know today owes more to Lloyd than to Cannon, Edith still left a rich legacy for the cheesemakers who followed her, and there's a little of her craft in all modern artisan Cheddar. There is more than a little of it at Westcombe, where Tom Calver has begun experimenting with the Cannon method. I asked him what the difference was, and he proudly showed me some wooden racks leaning up agains a wall of the dairy. 'We drain the curd on these,' he said. 'What difference does that make?' I asked. 'I'm not sure yet, but for one thing you don't have to bend down into the vat to work it.' Saving cheesemakers' backs would be a worthy enough development, but Tom wants to go a little further in trusting experience and instinct rather than relying on measurement. This isn't mere romanticism. As other Cheddar makers have told me, by the time the curd is nearing the point where it needs to be milled, there is little whey left to get an accurate reading from the acidometer, and, flying blind again, a good cheesemaker will trust their instincts.

I was pleased to discover that there were women in management roles in Victorian England, and that they were getting the respect they deserved for their experience, at least from Dr Lloyd and the Ayrshire Deputation. As we saw when we looked at witchy and folkloric beliefs around cheese, dairying had traditionally been the province of women across the British Isles. In Scotland, it was common for a dairyman to be hired on the condition that his wife and daughters would do the milking, and a less able man might be hired on the strength of his family's milking skills. By the end of the nineteenth century, however, the women of Scotland, Wales and Ireland were losing their status and even their jobs in the dairying industries.

In Ireland, the disappearance of women from dairying seems to have been particularly extreme. In 1881, women made up more than forty per cent of the dairy workforce, but by 1911 less than less than one in six dairy workers were women. The reasons given by the National Education Commission were shamefully explicit: 'taking into account the vast importance of the industry, and that intelligent direction in the dairy would be useful, the training of men in dairy management...is deserving of serious consideration'. Men were uncomfortable with the idea of a woman managing men, as a letter to the *Irish Homestead* newspaper noted: 'young intelligent men...through lack of sufficient training...are subject to the anomaly of being subordinated to the dairymaid.' And, flying in the face of centuries of work experience, women were suddenly considered too weak to do the heavy lifting required. Given that back in Somerset in the 1880s they were making Cheddars weighing up to forty-five kilos, that seems a bit rich. Nonetheless, by the 1900s it was all but impossible to find trained dairymaids in Ireland, Wales or Scotland.

Industrialisation played a major role in the removal of women from dairy. Where traditional practices were maintained, so too were traditional roles, but when cheese or butter-making shifted into the factory, women lost out. In Ireland, where butter making was far more important economically than cheesemaking, the threat of competition (mainly from Denmark) drove the rise of the creamery, where local milk was bought in from a number of farms. By the turn of the century, farmhouse buttermaking was largely a thing of the past. Over in Britain, the adoption of industrial cheesemaking had a less drastic beginning, but the process was no less inexorable.

For this we have to blame the Americans and the generosity of spirit of a Somerset cheesemaker.

In 1851, the world's first cheese factory was set up by a farmer called Jesse Williams in Oneida County in New York State. It was actually a bit of an accident. The year before, Jesse's son George, perhaps intimidated by his father's skills (Jesse's cheese was famous throughout the county), pulled out of a contract with a buyer and instead pooled his milk with his father's. Jesse, a quintessential American go-getter, reasoned that if he could combine the milk of two farms, why not go even bigger? He persuaded his friends and neighbours to give him their milk in return for a percentage of

The Williams Cheese Factory in Oneida, New York – the world's first industrial dairy, set up to mass-produce cheese.

profit from the cheese, and set up a factory and a store that was well supplied with cool spring water. On 10 May 1851, the Williams Cheese Factory commenced production and the world of cheese was changed forever.

Back in Britain, the cheesemakers, blissfully ignorant of the disaster looming on the horizon, were probably feeling pretty good. The country was coming out of an economic downturn that had followed the end of the Napoleonic Wars, agricultural prices were up and so was production. Their confidence would have been misplaced. In 1859, two thousand three hundred tons of American cheese was exported to Britain. And this was merely a foot in the door. In the decades leading up to the 1850s, Britain had shifted from protectionism to free trade. This move began in the 1820s, when merchants from several of Britain's major towns petitioned the House of Commons to end protectionism – whose most famous manifestation was the Corn Laws, which restricted the import of corn and other foods. They were repealed in 1846, having been given final impetus by the Irish Famine of 1845, which made British Prime Minister Robert Peel decide that the way to alleviate the suffering of the Irish was to increase the supply of food – a misguided policy, as corn remained too expensive for the poor. The Corn Law issue split the Tory Party and this resulted in a Whig government under George Russell. As ardent free traders, the Whigs refused to countenance subsidising foodstuffs or halting the export of food from Ireland, thus increasing the severity of the famine. By 1849, when the famine ended, more than a million people had died and a further million had emigrated.

The last nail in the coffin of protectionism was the repeal of the Navigation Acts, which had forbidden foreign ships from offloading in British ports. Free of tariffs and other trade restrictions, and with new steamships providing a boost to transportation, American factory cheese began to flood into the British Isles. Then, in 1861, came the American Civil War. American dairies were now short of workers, as huge numbers went off to fight, and this led to the development of less labour-intensive factories – and cheaper cheese. By 1864, there were two hundred and five cheese factories in New York State, making thirty per cent of America's cheese, and their exports to the British Isles had grown by one thousand per cent since the beginning of the decade.

British cheesemakers, it seems, were confident that their cheese would win out on quality. But, while the new factory-made American cheese may not have been as delicious as a really good West Country Cheddar, it was a whole lot cheaper, wholesaling at between ten shillings and one pound less per hundredweight than British cheese. The difference was decisive. A Chesterfield cheesemonger reckoned that, for every ton of Derbyshire cheese he sold, he shifted eighty tons of American.

A little ironically, given his exalted position in British cheesemaking, Joseph Harding helped this process. In 1866, he hosted a visit at his dairy from a representative of the American Dairyman's Association to learn about his method. Harding's visitor, the splendidly monikered Xerxes A. Willard, hadn't been blown away by other dairies he had visited, reporting that 'their appliances are inferior, their work more laborious and they have but really one style of cheese that competes with the best grades which our factories make. This is the Cheddar.' However, Harding's dairy was a different proposition and he realised he was in the presence of greatness, singling out in his report 'the famous cheesemaker Joseph Harding'. Indeed, on his return to the States he attempted to forge a dynastic link, writing to Joseph: 'I hope your daughter Miss Harding is well and has not forgotten us. I believed she almost promised to give her hand to an American, if I should send one over possessed of requisite qualifications. Tell her I have not abandoned this idea of finding such a gentleman, for if we can only secure the Best Cheddar Dairy Girl in England on this side, our country surely can take the palm at cheesemaking.'

The marriage didn't happen, but Xerxes did 'borrow' elements of Harding's system and promoted them at dairy conventions. Even ten years later, though, he was to lament that American factories, for all their technical innovations, like steam-powered gang presses that could take many cheeses at at time, had 'not yet been able to surpass in excellence the fine specimens of English Cheddar. It is a very high standard of cheese.'

Harding may have been blithely giving way the secrets of British Cheddar, but not everyone was quite so sanguine about the growth of factory cheesemaking across the pond. One of the most concerned was Augustus Henry, the sixth Baron Vernon. Known as a keen improver of agriculture, Augustus suggested in 1868 to the Royal Agricultural Society of England (RASE) that it might be a good idea to pop over the Atlantic and have a look at what the

Americans were up to. Clearly what his informants saw gave them the willies, and in 1870, at a meeting of the Derbyshire Agricultural Society, an experimental cheese factory was proposed.

Things moved fast, and Britain's first cheese factory, built on the Derbyshire estate of Lord Longford, opened for business on 4 May 1870. Seeing as no one in the British Isles knew how to run a cheese factory, the Society hired two American brothers, revelling in the names Cornelius and Levi Schermerhorn, to come over, one to run the Longford factory and the other to run its urban counterpart in Derby. The RASE had contracted to buy milk from farms in a three-mile radius of the factory at a guaranteed price, and as a further sweetener the farmers would get the whey back to feed their pigs. Milk was delivered to the factory in purpose-built cans provided to the suppliers. On arrival, the milk was poured into vats cooled by running water which, in a rather elegant system, on its way out turned a small wheel that operated rakes which agitated the milk and kept the cream from separating. All the benefits of modern technology were used, the vats were steam-heated, and the new gang presses were brought in. Things seemed to go pretty well at first, and in 1872 the Longford factory sold eighty-two tons of cheese – that's a pound of cheese a week for over three thousand people.

Inspired by this success, other factories appeared in Derbyshire, Staffordshire, Gloucestershire and even in those strongholds of traditional cheesemaking, Somerset and Cheshire. By 1878, there were twenty factories in five different counties making cheese from the milk of six thousand cows. But the ride was bumpy. The first batches of cheese weren't very good, as this contemporary description shows:

> The cheese made under the supervision of the Shermerhorn brothers was too much like American cheese, and had its defects as well as its merits. Its texture was not compact; it had a peculiar taste and smell; and lacked fine flavour.

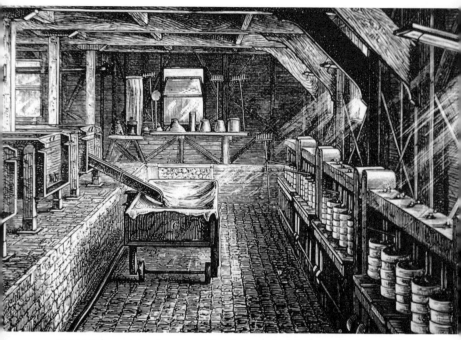

Britain's brave new cheese world – the Longford factory, which made cheese for just two years before moving across to 'railway milk'.

This problem was fixed by draining off the whey more quickly. However, not everyone was enthusiastic about all this new-fangled factory malarkey. One factory opened in Holm in Derbyshire was known locally as 'fools corner'. The counties of Somerset and Cheshire seemed particularly reluctant to take up the new ways, which may not just have been about hidebound tradition, as their fine cheeses were still commanding a decent price on the national market. Even in Derbyshire, where the factory movement started, it never developed a large enough network to make the system viable.

One reason for this might have been that it was hard to get individual dairy farmers to cooperate, since their business had long been about making better cheese and selling it for a better price than their neighbours. The cheese factors weren't necessarily keen on the factory system either, as they had such a lock on the British cheese industry. One way that this manifested itself was that cash-strapped farmers (surely a tautology) would borrow money from factors as an advance on cheese. The condition of the loan would be an agreement to sell the whole season's make to that factor but with no agreement on the price.

But, whether or not the cheese factors had a hand in the premature demise of Victorian factory cheesemaking in Britain, the whole system was doomed before it began by a product that would also contribute to the near demise of farmhouse cheesemaking – railway milk.

The railways bloomed fast in Britain. Locomotion No. 1's first trip with a load of coal and passengers took place in 1825. By the 1840s, there was a network of more than two thousand miles, and by the beginning of the 1850s, almost six thousand. And, while the original motivation for the railway was to carry coal, it was swiftly discovered that passengers would be as lucrative and important a freight. And that there was another commodity just waiting for the age of the train – milk.

There was already an urban market for milk and, of course, London was the big one. Before the railways, urban milk was provided by urban cows which at first grazed on open land; in 1810, a herd of five hundred grazed on the green pastures of Islington. But, as London grazing land was snapped up by developers for building, herds moved into permanent accommodation in vast cattle sheds and their diet went from nice fresh grass to urban waste scraps and spent brewers' grain, which cows love, but it only makes up part of a healthy balanced bovine diet. The quality of urban milk dropped sharply, a fall that can't have been helped by the common practice of adulteration. Water was the least harmful of the adulterants and its use was so common that the water pump became known as 'the cow with the iron tail'.

The first trainload of milk arrived in London in 1845 from the bucolic farming districts of Romford and Brentford in Essex. In 1865, the trade really kicked off when cattle disease tore through the overcrowded London cowsheds. From 1865 to 1866, the amount of milk brought into London doubled from three and a half million gallons to seven. Railway milk was here to stay.

New technology for transporting milk arrived. The old milk cans, which allowed the milk to get churned up on the journey, were sarcastically named 'churns' and the name stuck when they were replaced with better ones. Special train wagons with heat-reflecting white-painted roofs and louvred walls kept the milk cool on its journey into the fast-growing cities. Light, well-sprung vehicles replaced the juddering old carts taking the milk from farm gate to railhead; these were called 'floats.' And, meanwhile, the railway network was spreading its tendrils ever closer to remote dairy farms.

The cheese factories were quick to switch over to liquid milk sales. The flagship Longford factory was selling all its milk to London by 1874, its experiment with centralised cheesemaking having lasted just two years. Dairy farmers were also shifting from cheesemaking to liquid milk sales, starting with those closest to railways. In Derbyshire, where railways had arrived as early as 1846, there was 'an almost total abandonment of farmhouse cheesemaking by dairy farmers living within five miles of a railway line', according to agricultural historian David Taylor.

Not everyone bought into the liquid milk craze. J. Sadler, writing in the Bath and West Society Journal in 1908, said of the Cheshire dairy farmers: 'any man who had the temerity to relinquish cheesemaking and send his milk away was regarded with something approaching suspicion: it was surmised that either he was getting near the rocks financially or that his people could not make good cheese'.

However, these holdouts were bucking the trend. A series of bad harvest years culminated in 1879, a 'year without a summer', and agricultural depression followed, its effects worsened by increasing American imports, which kept prices low. And now America wasn't the only country shipping cheese, as the colonies were getting in on the act. Joseph Harding's own son Henry had gone out to Australia to run the cheesemaking at a dairy in New South Wales and from there had introduced to the rest of Australia many of the modern Cheddar-making practices developed by his father and honed by Dr Lloyd. In 1895, prices collapsed, and by the turn of the century many of the local cheeses of Derbyshire, Shropshire, Warwickshire and Leicestershire had disappeared. In 1905, writing in the journal of the Royal Agricultural Society, the agricultural historian J. Skertchly recorded, sadly, 'The old Derbyshire plain cheese has become a thing of the past.'

Stilton alone seemed untouched by the catastrophic currents of industrialisation and modern international trade. It was a premium product, and its affluent consumers were prepared to pay a premium price for it. And up in the Yorkshire Dales – a bit like Asterix and his one small village of Gauls still holding out – Wensleydale had carved itself a niche. Its makers were cash-poor and bartered their cheeses with local grain and agricultural supplies merchants, who in turn sold the cheese on twice a year to dealers from the rapidly growing Teesside towns. We will explore how this plucky little cheese survived the further decline of farmhouse cheesemaking in twentieth-century Britain in the next chapter.

Cheddar and Cheshire, the product of their eponymous counties, strongholds of farmhouse cheesemaking, seemed indestructible, though production of the latter largely shifted into Shropshire. Over the last quarter of the nineteenth century they dominated the British farmhouse cheese market, with Cheddar, by the end of the century, taking almost half the market for itself.

Even so, by 1900, cheesemaking in Britain and Ireland seemed to be on the way out. Since 1870, cheese and butter making had dropped by around forty per cent, while the production of liquid milk had tripled. Only a quarter of all the milk produced in the British Isles was being made into cheese.

But, before we turn to the twentieth century, let's pause to take a look at what kind of cheese the Victorians had been eating – or at least *ought* to have been eating if they wanted to create the right impression. For this our guide shall be the forthright, didactic and only occasionally misguided Mrs Isabella Beeton, editor of that eminently Victorian instructional tome, the *Book of Household Management*, published in 1861.

Conveniently, Mrs B gives us a list of 'the principal varieties of cheese used in England', and, interestingly in this age of Cheddar, it's Cheshire that tops her list, 'famed all over Europe for its rich quality and fine piquant flavour'. Cheddar only makes number five and her description of it is intriguing. She says that it 'much resembles Parmesan', suggesting that it wasn't well enough known to be described in its own terms, though she concedes it 'has a very agreeable taste and flavour' and 'has a spongy appearance'.

If this signifies a surface full of little holes, then Victorian Cheddar looked nothing like its modern descendant. It sounds like the work of gas-producing bacteria, which have a place in the making of cheeses like Emmental, where they not only create the holes but also impart a sweet flavour. In Cheddar-making, though, they would nowadays be considered unwanted guests.

The rest of Mrs Beeton's British cheeses – Gloucester, Sage Derby and Stilton – we know well enough, but there's one exception, 'New Cheese', which she says was made in Lincolnshire either from pure cream or a mixture of cream and whole milk, and served at a week old with 'radishes, salad, &c.' If this were a little older, old enough to develop a rind, it would sound like Saint Félicien, a luxuriantly

CHEESE.

1—Gorgonzola. 2—Double Gloucester. 3—Koboko. 4—Parmesan. 5—Dutch. 6—Roquefort.
7—Schabzieger. 8—Dunragit. 9—York Cream. 10—Port du Salut. 11—Cheddar.
12—Pommel. 13—Camembert. 14—Mainzer. 15—Cheshire. 16—Stilton. 17—Cream
Bondon. 18—Gruyère. 19—Wiltshire Loaf. 20—Cheddar Loaf.

Mrs Beeton's cheeseboard – or, at least, the classic cheese page from the 1901 edition. This features seven British cheeses: (2) Double Gloucester, (9) York Cream, (11) Cheddar, (15) Cheshire, (16) Stilton, (19) Wiltshire Loaf and (20) Cheddar Loaf. Mrs Beeton included recipes for Welsh rarebit and macaroni cheese.

creamy cow's milk cheese from the Lyonnais region of France. I can't suggest a traditional British equivalent, because the small soft cheeses of Britain, under threat since the beginning of enclosure, pretty much disappeared in the mid-twentieth century. It is telling that Lincolnshire New Cheese is no longer around.

Mrs Beeton isn't averse to having a few fancy foreign cheeses on the cheeseboard. Parmesan is still top dog, 'the most celebrated of all cheese', in her somewhat unpatriotic words. She does display some good cheese knowledge, though, ascribing the excellent flavour of Parmesan to the 'rich herbage' in the Po River valley. Dutch cheeses have their place, too, although here Mrs Beeton says something rather odd: that they get their flavour from the 'muriatic acid' used instead of rennet to coagulate the milk. This is hydrochloric acid, and I have never, ever heard of anyone being so lunatic as to use it to set milk when there is rennet around. I'm not even sure how well it would work, but even if it did, I can't imagine the Dutch doing such a thing.

Having got off to such an impressive start in the Middle Ages, by the nineteenth century the cheesemaking industry of the Netherlands was a mighty behemoth, and the government was heavily involved in its regulation. Cheese control stations were established in all the dairying areas, and the 'outdoor staff' at each station had the job of regularly visiting every dairy in their area and giving each cheese a government certification stamp if it passed muster. This was largely to stop people selling skimmed-milk cheese as whole milk, but, if they were that bothered about fat content, I doubt the outdoor staff from a cheese control station would certify cheese with hydrochloric acid in it.

Actually, using hydrochloric acid in cheesemaking wasn't entirely unheard of, although not in place of rennet. It gave bland cheeses bite and was used by unscrupulous cheesemakers to make young cheeses taste mature so that they could sell them more quickly. If overused it made people very ill indeed. Hydrochloric acid and red lead, used to dye Double Gloucester, were among many toxic substances, including strychnine, arsenic, copper sulphate and mercury, that were added to food in the nineteenth century until the Sale of Food and Drugs Act 1875 largely put a stop to all that. Hooray for regulation.

Also entirely acceptable on the aspiring young Victorian's cheeseboard, according to Mrs Beeton, was Swiss cheese, Gruyère in particular, and I absolutely agree with her.

According to Mrs Beeton, cheese should be served cut into small squares and handed around the table in a glass cheese dish, unless it is too crumbly, in which case it is brought to the table whole and cut by the host. Accompaniments include rusks, cheese biscuits, butter, salad, cucumber or watercress, and indeed these 'should always form part of a cheese course'.

Now, the issue of who should eat cheese, and how much they should eat, was 'a vexed question', according to historian Judith Flanders, who points out in her book *The Victorian House* that 'young ladies were expected to refuse savouries and cheese', adding yet another item to the long, long list of reasons why I would not like to have been a young lady in Victorian times. Mrs Beeton is cautious, framing her commentary in terms of a health warning: 'cheese in its commonest shape, is only fit for sedentary people as an after dinner stimulant, and in very small quantity.' But I think her real fear shows in who she thinks can consume cheese in bulk as a meal: 'Bread and cheese, as a meal, is only fit for soldiers on the march or labourers in the open air, who like it because it holds the stomach a long time'. Of course, the aspirational Victorian, searching Mrs Beeton's book for clues as to how to comport themselves around the cheeseboard, would hardly want to be taken for a soldier or a labourer.

Or, indeed, a ploughman.

CHAPTER EIGHT

Hawes Wensleydale

Farmhouse to factory

1901–74

WE LEFT THE CHEESES OF BRITAIN AND IRELAND in a parlous state. And as the Victorian era closed – with the death of the queen in 1901 – another event took place that would be momentous for cheesemaking. This was a conference on tuberculosis, addressed by Dr Robert Koch, a pioneer of bacteriology. It was Koch who in 1882 had identified the cause of TB as the *Mycobacterium tuberculosis* bacterium, which the scientific community had accepted. But in his 1901 address to the British Congress on Tuberculosis he made a highly controversial claim: that *Mycobacterium bovis* (*M. bovis*), the strain that causes TB in cattle, couldn't make the jump between species, and that bovine TB was thus harmless to humans. Many were not convinced.

In the nineteenth century, TB accounted for as many as one in four deaths in Britain, so this was a major controversy. In the proceedings of the congress, one Dr Robertson demanded that 'something should be done to undo the mischief caused by Professor Koch's statements'. Something was done: a Royal Commission was established to explore the link between bovine and human TB, and its reports of 1907 and 1911 firmly identified bovine TB as the main cause of non-pulmonary TB in humans, and milk as its primary vector. The obvious way to protect against this terrible disease was the pasteurisation of milk, heating it for a short time to kill off the dangerous bacteria. But pasteurising also kills off harmless bacteria, including those that help turn milk into cheese. It also required a lot of expensive kit that was beyond the means of many small dairy farmers. Britain thus divided into two camps: one for compulsory pasteurisation of all milk, and one for a less draconian solution, based on the improvement of herd health and hygiene practice. The great pasteurisation debate would have profound effects on the dairy and cheesemaking industries.

Louis Pasteur was an extraordinary scientist who made breakthrough discoveries in the role of germs in disease and their prevention through vaccination, fermentation and – the patented discovery that bears his name – pasteurisation. He came up with pasteurisation initially as a means of deactivating unwanted microorganisms in, as we noted, wine. But its application to milk was soon realised, and in 1882 the first commercial pasteuriser was developed in Germany – Albert Fesca, its inventor, called it a 'continuously working apparatus for the preservation of milk by heat'. At first, it appears that pasteurisation was more of a commercial issue than a health and safety one. Danish milk sellers were quick to adopt it, treating their product to give it a longer shelf life, while industrial buttermakers, who bought milk from numerous farms, pasteurised their milk to make a more uniform product.

The Royal Commission reports gave impetus to pasteurisation in the British Isles, to protect the health of the population. However, there was a commercial interest at play, too. One of the effects of the First World War on the dairying industry was the amalgamation in 1917 of Wiltshire United Dairies, Metropolitan and Great Western Dairies. This was meant to be a temporary measure to keep their businesses going in the face of labour and horsepower shortages, but proved to be so successful that the merger was made permanent under the name United Dairies. (The name persisted until 1959, when United amalgamated with its long-term rival Cow & Gate to form Unigate, whose dairying operations continued until 2000, when they were sold to Dairy Crest.) In 1920, this new-born dairying behemoth began introducing pasteurised milk to British cities, chiefly because it had a longer life.

Pasteurisation suited large dairies very nicely. But smaller producers couldn't afford the bulky and expensive pasteurisation machinery and so had to take their milk to a central depot, add it to a bulk tank, and get back an equivalent amount of pasteurised generic milk, losing the unique character of their milk and its direct connection with the land – milk 'direct from the cow'.

Raw milk partisans had a few health and safety arguments in their armoury, some of which were based in fact and some of which were utterly bonkers. Among the former category was that early methods of pasteurisation were not very reliable, and improperly pasteurised milk could be particularly dangerous, as reservoirs of pathogens like *M. bovis* could, with little or no competition from other strains of bacteria, reproduce in dangerously high numbers. There was another more global concern, which was the danger of making pasteurisation the one and only control over unwanted bacteria; if pasteurisation failed, the results could be troublesome. (In 1976, this worry was shown to be a very real one when Canada's worst ever outbreak of salmonella was caused by an ostensibly pasteurised cheese. An employee had unwittingly shut off the pasteuriser, but milk still flowed into the vat, from herds that were later found to be carrying salmonella. Twenty-seven thousand people were infected.)

Back in 1916, realising the danger of relying solely on pasteurisation for safe milk, the anti-pasteurisation movement set up the National Clean Milk Society, whose wholly worthy project was to encourage research into better production methods.

As laudable as the clean milk project was, there was also a mystical dimension to the movement, evoking the ancient magical aura that surrounded milk and its associations of whiteness and purity. This was as bad as it sounds. The idea had its roots in the Boer War, at the turn of the century, when army doctors found that around fifty per cent of recruits were too malnourished to fight. But, by the 1930s, as the raw milk vs. pasteurisation debate rumbled on, it had full-on fascist associations, borrowing the Nazi rhetoric of 'blood and soil' to account for the supposed failing health of the British race. In 1938, in an article for the *British Medical Journal*, the secretary of the Cheshire Medical Committees wrote: 'Much of modern food is processed, preserved, refined, sterilised, dead... Contrast the insipid pasteurised fluid of today to the milk of our forefathers.'

One of the more disturbing members of the raw milk movement was Viscount Lymington, aka Gerald Wallop, a member of the British People's Party, who visited Hitler and Mussolini before the war. He was a founder of Kinship in Husbandry, a group of rural revivalists who counted among their number Jorian Jenks, a close associate of the British fascist leader Oswald Mosley. Jenks was also a founder of the Soil Association, which was tainted by far right elements in its early stages. Thankfully such tendencies disappeared with Jenks' death in 1963, as the Soil Association took on a measured environmentalism under its next president, Barry Commoner. A later director was Patrick Holden, on whose farm in Wales the lovely Hafod Cheddar is made.

The pro-pasteurisation movement in Britain was coordinated by Graham Selby Wilson, Professor of Bacteriology at the London School of Hygiene, and Viscount Dawson of Penn, the King's physician. It had general establishment support and in 1938 the British Medical Association ran a poster campaign warning of the danger of raw milk. However, in an indication of the power of the

Employees looking into pasteurisation tanks at the world's then-biggest milk depot at Wood Lane, Shepherd's Bush, London, 1935.

raw milk lobby, some papers refused to publicise the campaign for fear of being sued.

The war years can be seen as a watershed in the history of pasteurisation. The war effort required unprecedented levels of government control over food production, and opposition to this control was reduced in the immediate aftermath, as the nation embarked on the struggle to rebuild. Just after the war a spokesman for the milk trade, Ben Davies, declared that 'the old debates about the pasteurisation of milk are over'. Helped by an increasing move towards centralisation and standardisation in the dairying industry, pasteurised milk spread from the larger cities to the smaller ones and out into the villages. However, although raw milk became increasingly rare over the next decades, Mr Davies was a little overconfident in his pronouncement. Raw milk for drinking and for cheesemaking has never been banned in England, Wales or Ireland, and the debate has continued into our current century, although happily with zero involvement of fascists.

One thing that slowed the introduction of pasteurised milk to cheesemaking is that the early nineteenth-century 'flash pasteurisation' method was carried out at such a high temperature that it damaged the milk, making cheesemaking difficult. Lower-temperature, less damaging methods came in around 1910 and evolved into the process which is still used now – high-temperature short-time or HTST-pasteurising, where the milk is held at 72° C for just fifteen seconds.

The equipment, to begin with, was heavy, bulky and cripplingly expensive, and very few farmhouse cheesemakers used it. The early adopters of pasteurising for cheesemaking, therefore, were the factories, and it seems that their main reason for adopting the technology was consistency rather than health and safety, since they were getting milk from various sources and at varying degrees of freshness. As to the implications for quality, there are tantalising hints that this was a worry. As early as 1919, some Stilton-makers experimented with making raw and pasteurised batches in tandem. On tasting the results they firmly went with the raw milk/clean milk plan. Arguments over the health implications of raw versus pasteurised cheese really took off during the food scares of the 1980s and '90s, and it's a sign of how serious these were that the Stilton makers then decided to adopt pasteurisation.

But, before we get there, it is time to go back to the 1900s and follow the course of British cheesemaking as it weathered the storms of war and depression through the twentieth century.

In the 1900s, whatever promise a new king (Edward VII) and a new century held for everyone else, things were looking no better for cheesemakers than they had been in the previous century. Imports now accounted for two-thirds of the cheese sold in Britain. By now the cheesemakers weren't just competing with American factories, but the dominions had joined in too – first Canada, then Australia and New Zealand.

Ever since the Americans had improved their factory cheese with the help of Joseph Harding, the imports were cheap, consistent and good enough. They were also changing tastes, and the more flavourful, perhaps more challenging, and certainly more expensive, farmhouse cheese was becoming a boutique product. Cheese factors, seeing British tastes changing, encouraged native producers to modify their own cheeses; many of them, having been in relationships with these factors for generations, complied. In the north a new, fast-ripening product appeared, known as 'Bastard Cheshire'. It was 'white, characterless and flavourless', according to Val Cheke, who must have known the cheese, in her 1958 *Story of Cheese-Making in Britain*.

It wasn't just imported cheese that was killing the local industry. Diet was changing, too. Refrigerated ships, a technological development of the late nineteenth century, were bringing cargoes of frozen mutton and beef from Argentina and the dominions, and the meat was sold at prices that the less well-off could afford. The whole structure of rural life and employment was in flux, as well. Family farms broke up as the next generation looked towards forms of urban employment that were less uncertain, less back-breaking and frankly more remunerative than farming. In many areas of Britain it was now becoming hard to find milkers and dairymaids.

In the north of England, atavistic holdouts still made a relatively successful living out of cheesemaking, mostly in small cooperative factories. And, as we saw in the previous chapter, Stilton, a premium-priced cheese for the connoisseur, also remained largely immune from the battering being dealt out by imported cheese, and the districts that produced it around Melton Mowbray and the Vale of Belvoir continued to prosper. Perhaps deliberately, aware of the advantage of making a quality product, the makers of Stilton seemed to have stuck to their old 'empirical' methods so looked down on by Harding and Lloyd. The amount of rennet was 'guided by experience', as was the right time to break the curd, and sometimes curd from different days was held over and mixed together to get the right balance of acidity and mellowness. In the hands of a skilled cheesemaker, this is a recipe for success, but not a recipe for the kind of economy-of-scale-type production that was required to produce cheese at a price and volume that could compete with imports.

With all the insouciance implied by the term 'laissez faire', the pre-war Liberal government seemed unaware of the plight of British cheesemaking, indeed of agriculture as a whole. In 1905, the Royal Commission on the Supply of Food and Raw Materials in Time of War published a report which recommended that 'it may be prudent to take some minor practical steps to secure food supplies for Britain'. This was to turn out to be the most colossal understatement of all time. Not only was the government still exhibiting that reluctance to get involved that characterised Liberal policy, they had complete confidence in the Royal Navy's ability to keep the sea routes open, and made no plans to ease Britain's reliance on foreign imports.

And then, in Sarajevo on 28 June 1914, Gavrilo Princip shot the Archduke Franz Ferdinand and his wife Sophie, and for the next four years, as the First World War raged, the government started paying a bit more attention to British farmers and the food they produced. As well they should have, since sixty per cent of Britain's food came in by sea in 1914. Still ridiculously casual, the government at first suggested that it might be a good idea to plough up more pasture for arable land. Farmers weren't particularly keen to implement this directive. Farming is a long-term game full of unforseeable risks, and farmers as a result are somewhat conservative in their decision-making. Ploughing up all that land would require investment, and what was the point if, as everyone was saying, 'it would all be over by Christmas'?

The three-quarters of a million men who joined up in the first two months of the war didn't have to wait until Christmas to feel the effects of food shortages. The government had called for a hundred thousand volunteers and the army's supply systems were feeling the strain of the extra six hundred and fifty thousand who had enlisted. Unrest among the troops was common and, although this often took the form of peaceful demonstrations, with soldiers carrying banners bearing simple messages like 'Pay' and 'Food', things sometimes took a more rowdy turn. In November 1914, at Upwey camp in Dorset, a sergeant removed the cheese from the men's rations. A fight broke out, during which one soldier was shot and another injured when he was struck from behind with a fifteen-pound block of cheese.

As imports dwindled to a trickle, the Board of Trade commandeered all the cheese imports from the Dominions to feed the army, with the civilian population of Britain having to make do with what was left. The army's daily ration of cheese in 1917 was one ounce a day if you were at the rear or in the communication trenches, and two ounces at the front line. I'm sure that extra ounce made all the difference when you were dodging the whizz-bangs in the trenches.

In May 1915, Germany began attacking all ships bringing cargo to Britain. Now, at last, the government began to exert more control over agriculture and food production. Each county was required to set up a War Agricultural Committee to organise efficient production. The 'ploughing up' campaign converted more than two million acres of pasture to arable land, and yet, in 1917, in the wake of poor harvests, Britain found itself with only three weeks of food reserves left. Drastic measures were needed. The Board of Agriculture set up the Women's Land Army, with the stirring call, 'Women of England! Wake up and hear your country's urgent call for help.' Between then and November 1919, when the Land Army was disbanded, twenty-three thousand women joined up, many as dairy workers.

It was hard graft, as Agnes Greatorex from Cardiff remembered: 'We had to get up at five in the morning for milking, and then we'd have to take it up to Glan Ely hospital. After that – especially during the winter – we'd have to muck-out the cow sheds. Then we might get half an hour for breakfast.' But Agnes, like many of her fellow women, discovered an independence and confidence in the work, saying, 'when I became a land girl I thought that's it, I'm independent. I had a pound a week, not as much as the men but a lot still – there was no one to boss me, no more running around at the beck and call of the cook.'

After the war, the government could no longer ignore the call for women's suffrage, and in 1918 the Representation of the People Act gave more than eight million women the vote. In 1919, in a further victory for women's rights, the Sex Disqualification Act made it illegal to exclude women from jobs because of their gender.

As much as things might have seemed to be looking up for farmers during the war, by 1920 things were looking bleak again as post-war prices collapsed. At first it looked as if government had changed its ways, and the Agricultural Act of 1920 continued wartime subsidies for farming, but in 1921 these were withdrawn – an action remembered by farmers as 'The Great Betrayal'. Over the next decade, the agricultural price index fell by more than half. And then, in 1929, the American stock market crashed, signalling the beginning of the Great Depression. Although to be honest I'm not sure British farmers really noticed – things could hardly get any worse for them.

The National Government of 1931, under the Labour prime minister Ramsay MacDonald, saw the need for intervention.

However, there was a dilemma. The government had to keep food prices low, particularly for the industrial workers who were bearing the brunt of the Depression. Forcing prices up with controls on imports, therefore, did not seem like a good option. In a reversal of earlier policy, much of the arable land was returned to pasture. Even the beef farmers of the Midlands and Norfolk and the arable farmers of Wales went over to milk production. This was thought of as a return to 'dog and stick farming', as a dog and a stick are all you needed to manage your animals.

Farming wasn't inherently unprofitable, even in the inter-war years, but the farms that did well were larger ones which embraced modernity in the guise of new technology and the new chemical fertilisers. This wasn't a good outlook for small family-run farms producing traditional cheese. Some did stop making cheese and go over to liquid milk sales, like the Court family, in Wiltshire, cheesemakers for generations. Arthur Court, in his memoir, *Seedtime to Harvest*, recalled, 'I am not sure whether mother was glad about that or not...at least she could go to the Women's Institute meetings and not have to rush to get her cheese finished first.'

On the positive side, there was an injection of new blood into the British dairying industry between the wars. Val Cheke writes stirringly about the steep increase of students at agricultural colleges just after the First World War. Men traumatised by the war 'turned to agriculture as an antidote, and who saw in its fields a hope of peace'. Many, perhaps even a majority, of the new students, Cheke notes, were women who'd had a taste of farming in the Women's Land Army. Rural tradition and contemporary attitudes to women meant there was some resistance to the influx of young women. Many farmers saw the new recruits as 'town lassies' with new-fangled modern ways, but the students nevertheless had a considerable influence on the modernisation of dairying, as can be seen by the record volume of orders for the latest cheesemaking equipment, such as acidometers, hygrometers and thermometers,

*Women's Land Army recruits – this time in the Second World War –
being taught how to milk by a government boffin.*

which the dairy managers were 'bullied into ordering' by their
young and confident staff.

🧀 🧀 🧀

In 1930, a report was published by the UK Ministry of Agriculture
and Fisheries on the state of the dairying industry. Its findings
would shape policy in response to the Depression and beyond –

including the requirements of rationing in the Second World War and the shift from postwar austerity to consumer culture. And, while it is easy to say this with the clarity of hindsight, it was a policy that just about did for British cheese.

You can see trouble coming in the first paragraph of the 'Cheese' section of the report. The author begins with the observation that since the Industrial Revolution the main business of dairy farming has switched from making cheese and butter to selling liquid milk. With improved farming practices and the changeover of so many arable farms to dairy, the market is now flooded with surplus milk. Within the terms of this argument, cheesemaking is described as 'the process generally adopted for the conversion of milk surplus'. Not a vital rural industry, not an ancient and valuable cultural practice, not the production of a nutritious staple food, nor of a gourmet product. Just conversion of a surplus.

The report goes on to state that farms were still switching from cheese to milk production, because milk converted into butter or cheese 'has a lower value than when it is sold for liquid milk'. This seems incredible. How could you possibly get less money for delicious, nutritious, easily portable cheese than for mere milk? The explanation is that the cheese market of the British Isles was glutted with imported cheese. New Zealand, from a standing start in 1900, was now the main culprit, producing half of all the imported cheese arriving at the London Docks. Factory-made New Zealand Cheddar was fourpence a pound cheaper than its British farmhouse equivalent in 1929, and that was enough to make a difference to the mass consumer. This is not to say that less affluent cheese fanciers didn't care about flavour, or lacked loyalty to their local cheeses. Whenever the price difference between imported and local varieties shrunk to below a penny or two, the customers in the north and the Midlands would buy home-produced Cheshire; and, in the south-west, home-produced Cheddar.

Perhaps you are wondering what had happened to British factory cheese since its bold beginning and swift decline in the 1870s? Well, it didn't *entirely* die. The original purpose-built factories had nearly all turned into depots for the collection of milk, and more had been built for the same purpose. But, as the demand and price for liquid milk fluctuated wildly, a milk depot would at times find itself with a surplus and, rather than pouring it down the drain, they would make cheese. This must have been poor fare, as the milk had often been hanging around, and the cheesemakers weren't very skilled. There was, however, another kind of cheese factory that focused on making cheese. These were 'creameries', run by local farmers, who pooled their milk and picked their best cheesemakers to run them – dairy workers, often from farming families and with centuries of accumulated cheesemaking skill.

The Ministry report recommends the factory over the farmhouse as the best way to make cheese but at least advocates the creamery-type operation over the dual-purpose butter/cheese factory. Their other recommendation, intended to protect the producers from the wilder fluctuations of milk prices, is for 'the creation of some comprehensive organisation of milk producers generally'. So, in a nutshell: make more uniform cheese, make it a bit better, make it in factories, set up some sort of milk marketing board. And that is exactly what happened.

It might seem that I'm not very keen on whoever wrote the report. Actually, that's not really the case. Its authors have an admirably thorough knowledge of the state of British cheese and cheesemaking in 1929, detailing who was selling it and how, and what people were buying. The specialist retail cheesemonger was a rarity then, as now, and the report warns of the difficulty, outside large cities, of maintaining 'a turnover sufficient to cover the overheads of a shop devoted solely to cheese'.

Building a beautiful display of cheese is an important part of a cheesemonger's craft. It's also a lot of fun, so I was a bit sad to read that back then it was 'a difficult matter to make an attractive display of cheese'. The mongers faced a dilemma we still have today: that unopened wheels of cheese don't look all that inviting and need to be cut open so that people can see the appetising cheese within. The problem is that, once you open the cheese, the cut face starts to dry and crack, losing its enticing appearance and some of its flavour. Once this has happened the only solution is to 'face' the cheese – to cut the dry layer off and expose a fresh face within – which means expensive wastage. In a small shop with low turnover, this loss is critical; hence the difficulty of operating a specialist cheese shop outside the big cities. Nowadays we've got cling film, which helps a lot, although when sales are slow even big-city cheesemongers waste a lot of faces. Cling film, by the way, was discovered in America in the 1930s, and first use to spray fighter planes and jungle combat boots, so if anyone ever asks you what America has done for our cheese, you can tell them.

One of the many fascinating things revealed by the report is that Gorgonzola was inordinately popular in inter-war Britain, almost as much in working-class areas as in posher districts, maybe in part because it was several pence a pound cheaper than domestic Cheddar. Gouda was particularly popular with Jewish customers, who were also partial to a bit of Caerphilly. Processed cheese had already reared its tasteless rubbery head, and sold well to all classes. It came in pre-packed units, and as a block that retailers could cut, which meant little to no wastage. Older mongers 'professed to regard the development of the packeted trade generally as a symptom of declining tradesmanship', showing that we grumpy mongers haven't changed a bit.

'Fancy Cheese' is what they called the continental imports. Roquefort was also popular in the working-class districts as a change from Gorgonzola; Camembert was on sale in half-pound boxes just like today; Brie and Port Salut were also available. But Italian cheese was much more popular. In fact, Britain was Italy's biggest market for their soft cheeses – Bel Paese, Stracchino and Bella Milano were all good sellers, as well as the harder Pecorino and the ever triumphant Parmesan. Boss of the continental importers, though, was the Netherlands. Gouda and Edam had been market leaders in Britain for hundreds of years. The Dutch had been canny cheese marketers since the Middle Ages, but in the late nineteenth century they took their export cheesemaking a step further. With considerable government support, the Dutch cheesemaking industry shifted from farmhouse to factory production, with a

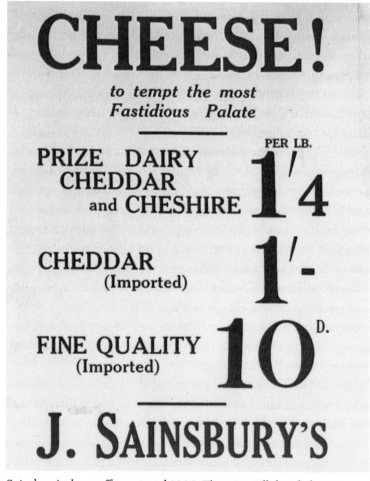

Sainsbury's cheese offers, around 1930. The prices tell the whole story, with premium prices for 'prize' local cheese and cheap imports.

strong focus on the export market. In Friesland, where most of the Netherlands' factory cheesemaking was based, recipes for Cheddar and Cheshire were developed specifically for the British market.

☞ ☞ ☞

With a market swamped with exotic imports and cheap factory cheese, quality British farmhouse cheese was becoming harder and harder to find. It is not surprising that, to quote a contemporary writer, 'English cheese is without honour in its own country and amongst its own kin.'

The writer was poet, critic and bon-viveur John Squire, in his introduction to *Cheddar Gorge*, a collection of essays on English cheese published in 1937 and reprinted in 2018 with all its homely E.H. (*Winnie-the-Pooh*) Shepard illustrations. Sad, funny and stirring in equal parts, the book is a paean for those cheeses that still survive, a warning of what there was to lose and a eulogy to what had already gone. In Squire's own words, 'There are few parts of England which do not remember cheeses extinct or nearly extinct...if we don't celebrate it both at home and abroad, it will cease to be. The world will be the poorer.'

The contributors to *Cheddar Gorge* might be amateur enthusiasts, but they have made a thorough study of their topic. The usual suspects – Stilton, Cheddar and Cheshire – make up the first three chapters, still in the podium positions they took in the latter half of the nineteenth century. John Squire himself pens the Stilton chapter, befitting a man who was to call for a statue to be erected to its inventor. Stilton, he maintains, is 'the perfect rounding off of a meal, the sunset of it'. Sadly, he notes that it is now mostly made in 'company-owned factories', though some is still made on the farm, by 'old village wives who can make magnificent cheeses by rule of thumb, or no apparent rule'. He describes, tantalisingly, a room dedicated solely to the maturation of Stilton in the blue-painted cellars of Fortnum & Mason, the cheeses looked after with special turning implements 'with as much pride as a groundsman takes in his wicket at Lords'.

Cheddar, by contrast, is described as an 'everyday cut-and-come-again cheese', though the author clearly thinks this is a good thing, with the cheese 'a never failing companion to a glass (or two) of vintage port'. Cheshire is apparently 'no food for weaklings', which appears to allude to its indigestibility. Double Gloucester gets a ringing endorsement as 'perhaps the single hard English cheese that can be compared for richness and delicacy of flavour with the great blue cheeses'. But the writer observes that there are now two sorts of Double Gloucester: one white or yellow, loaf-shaped and 'to speak frankly, of the poorest quality'; the other 'red, millstone in shape...and exquisitely flavoured, pungent without being sharp'. The difference is that the better cheese has been carefully chosen for the London gentlemen's clubs and matured until it has reached its peak. The lower-grade cheeses are sold young in the country for a much lower price. I'd like to go back and tell him that it will all be okay – that there are five well-established producers of farmhouse Double Gloucester now, each exquisite.

You might, if you've only been exposed to factory Double Gloucester, be a bit surprised by the author's passion. And I imagine you'd be even more taken aback by the writer on Leicester, who regards this as one of 'the noble cheeses' worthy of 'the same care and reverence accorded to a bottle of crusted port'. He, too, bemoans the domination of factory-made Leicester, sold young, and says that there are only twelve farms still making the cheese. Not long after the war there would be none at all, but this cheese, too, is staging a comeback.

To have tasted the best Dorset Blue Vinny, 'made of whole milk by a well to-do farmer...is to be spoilt for ever more', we read in *Cheddar Gorge*. It was hard to find when the book was written, and still is –there's only one maker, as far as I know. This is the cheese that I mentioned in the Stilton chapter that used to get its blueing from a

'Variety is a good thing.'

An illustration by E.H. Shepard from Cheddar Gorge – *a 1937 eulogy to the cheeses of Britain in what seemed to be their twilight days.*

bit of old harness tack dragged through the vat or a pair of old boots left in the cheese room. Traditionally it was made from skimmed milk after the farmers of Dorset had made their famous cream. The milk had to sit for days, unrefrigerated in the old days, for the cream to rise to the top, and would have got pretty sour by the time it came to cheesemaking, and high-acid milk also makes for tough cheese. Caerphilly was almost lost in the 1930s, at least in Wales. The writer says his London cheesemonger gets his Caerphilly from a factory in Leicestershire, run by Welshmen, or from Ulster, although this is said to be 'too creamy'. This might sound odd, but when you read his description of Caerphilly you can see that its virtue then was as a young, fresh, light-textured cheese, and inexpensive. Thank god for the Trethowans, is all I can say.

Although the Scottish chapter is written by a Scot, or at least someone with a Scottish name, it's a bit down on Scottish cheese. It seems that 'Dunlop is the only Scotch cheese.' Crowdie doesn't count apparently, and the writer doesn't see fit to mention Caboc.

He blames the land, saying that, aside from the rich pastures of Ayrshire, the home of Dunlop, Scottish land lacks the richness of English fields. It appears the man had never heard of cheese made from the milk of hardy sheep or goats that can sustain themselves on scrubby forage.

The poet Oliver St John Gogarty, the author of the chapter on Ireland, is more upbeat. He says much Irish cheese was made during the First World War for export to Britain, although a lot of it was 'hastily produced and of poor quality'. But it appears that at the time of writing Irish cheesemakers had solved the quality problem and the industry was going great guns, producing more than two and a half million pounds of cheese in 1936, which makes Ireland a global player. Its cheeses, Gogarty says, were not indigenous to Ireland, but were more often known as 'Irish Cheddar, or 'Irish Stilton'. But, more cheerily, he adds that many cheeses are now known by their places of origin, as 'Ardagh, Galtee and Whitehorn', among others. This was pleasing to hear. I like to think that Ireland took the idea of these cheeses and then made them its own.

*

There is often an elegiac quality to the prose in *Cheddar Gorge*, whose writers are aware that their day might be the twilight of British cheese culture. That said, there were clearly some absolutely bangers around and a prime example is Wensleydale, as described in glowing tones by the hugely prolific cookbook writer Ambrose Heath. He quotes a scholar called Osbert Burdett, best known for his work on William Blake but also the author of *A Little Book of Cheese*, who calls Wensleydale 'the superlative Yorkshire cheese, a rival to Stilton in the friendly sense that Bordeaux and Burgundy are sometimes said to be rivals'. If you are familiar with Hawes Wensleydale in its premium 'Kit Calvert' variant (of whom more very soon), a firm yet supple pure white cheese with a delicate slightly herbaceous flavour, the comparison to Stilton will seem a bit odd.

Heath admits that there is a young, firm and white Wensleydale on the market, but says that it doesn't compare with the 'finished glory of the ripened Wensleydale.' This, is seems, was a creamy blue cheese, 'soft and flaky, [that] will spread like butter, and has the delicate blue veining well distributed throughout the curd. The flavour is rich, sweet and creamy – not acid or bitter.' Doesn't that sound marvellous?

Cheddar Gorge was published on the eve of the Second World War, and four years after the creation in 1933 of the Milk Marketing Board, which is often seen as the death knell of traditional British cheese, particularly once it became an instrument, during the war, of the Ministry of Food, which limited the country's cheese production to a single, insipid, brand – Government Cheddar Or that's what we're often told. Happily, though, the story is a bit more nuanced than that, and we can trace some of its nuances through the changing fortunes of this chapter's signature cheese, Wensleydale.

It is a story that begins with Kit Calvert, who was born in 1903 in Burtersett. He was the son of a quarryman, not a high-earning job, but in 1931 he inherited a little money and bought a farm in Hawes, a small market town at the head of Wensleydale. This was a bold move in the midst of the Great Depression, and it was a very small farm, with sheep for meat and cows for milk. He and a friend hawked his mutton and lamb from door to door around the town and his wife sold milk from their cows by the jug from their farmhouse. And, like other farmers in the area, he sold milk to the local creamery to be made into Wensleydale cheese.

This creamery had been set up in an old woollen mill, bought for the purpose by a local merchant, Edward Chapman, in the 1890s. Chapman had tired of the old way of buying cheese in the Dales. The problem was that some of the farmers' wives had good 'cheese hands', in the local terminology, but some did not. To avoid causing upset, and to keep everyone's business, Chapman had to buy all the cheese at the same price. He decided instead to set up a centralised cheesemaking operation where he would have control over the quality of the product. Not long after, another local businessman, a Mr Rowntree, set up several creameries at the other end of the valley, at Masham, Coverham and Thoralby. Calvert recalled that just after these creameries were set up, motorised transport allowed the liquid milk market to penetrate into dales such as Wensleydale. Had they got there before the creameries got going, cheesemaking would have died out completely, he believed.

In the winter of 1932, Dales cheesemaking came under increased threat when the owner of Hawes creamery declared bankruptcy and the local farmers were left with unpaid bills for their milk. Calvert stepped up, recruited five fellow farmers and agreed with the main creditor that they could borrow the creamery and make cheese there until the creditor's debt had been recovered. They took over in February 1933 and began making Wensleydale, but soon ran into a problem – the bizarre economics of 1930s cheese that we came across in the ministry report. The six-man Wensleydale consortium had agreed to pay the other farmers five pence a gallon for their milk; one gallon of milk makes one pound of cheese; and the price for Wensleydale in June 1933 was three pence a pound. It didn't add up. Then, at a meeting, one of the six mentioned a rumour that some sort of government board was being set up to address this problem. They agreed to hang on and see what would develop.

The Milk Marketing Board (MMB) was set up on 1 October 1933. Its mission was to stabilise the milk price and guarantee a sensible price for farmers and cheesemakers. For Hawes creamery this came in the nick of time; orders were on the rise in the run-up to Christmas and Wensleydale prices were up, with Wensleydale being the Christmas cheese of choice for the northern counties, and the milk price set by the MMB was low enough to ensure a decent profit. After Christmas the six had sold enough cheese to clear their debts. The first Hawes creamery consortium couldn't hold on for another year, though, and decided to wind up their business. They offered to pay their creditors, the local dairy farmers, twelve shillings in the pound and a whole Wensleydale cheese for every pound of debt on top of that. At the meeting where this was announced, one of the farmers cried 'give me forty pound and keep t'bloody cheese, its more than I expected to git.'

The creamery reverted to its original owner for a brief period, but he couldn't make it work, and once again the threat of closure loomed. Losing the market the creamery provided was a bleak prospect for local farmers, still suffering from the depression, and with no reserves. For Calvert it wasn't just about economics, either; it was about preserving the cultural life of his beloved Dales. He knew that if the creamery closed down, cheesemaking would likely go too.

One pivotal day in the market square of Hawes, Calvert found a representative of the MMB, Mr R.A. Pepperall, addressing worried farmers, telling them to come into a room in the hotel in small groups to sign contracts with a Mr Crosby, representative of a company called Express Dairies. Express had been set up in 1864 by George Barham, inventor of the new milk churn, and was named after the express trains that took milk into the big cities. Calvert told the farmers not to sign anything until he had agreed it. Mr Pepperall argued that the Board was the only possible outlet for their milk, to which Calvert retorted, 'No it isn't.' 'What's the other one, then?' 'The sewer,' said Calvert.

But that wasn't Calvert's plan. At a meeting with his fellow farmers the same day, he announced the establishment of Wensleydale Products Limited, pledging one hundred pounds himself and asking for others to invest. None came forward. Undeterred, he went into Hawes and got backing from the hotel owner, the grocer and the chemist. With this initial finance in place, there was a further challenge to overcome. The Milk Marketing Board would want its payment for the milk before any of the next batch of full-size Wensleydales would be ready for sale. Unfazed, Kit

The original Wensleydale Creamery, an old woollen mill bought by Mr Edward Chapman in 1898.

got the creamery to make a load of 'smalls' – one- and two-pound cheeses – and got the local farmers' wives and kids to sell them at their farm gates and at local beauty spots. This marketing ploy generated enough cash to make their first payment to the MMB, and Wensleydale Products Limited was in business. In fact, pre-Second World War Wensleydale smalls proved such a hit in the run-up to Christmas that unscrupulous factors took to buying up cheap mini-Caerphillies made in the cheese factories of South Wales.

The Second World War began for Britain on 3 September 1939, announced in famously leaden tones by Prime Minister Neville

Chamberlain. There followed the eight-month 'Phoney War', but there was nothing phoney about the first year of the war for the country's cheesemakers. With the outbreak of war, the MMB diverted all milk production to liquid milk and there was no Wensleydale for Christmas that year. This would be a foretaste of things to come. Rationing of bacon, ham, butter and sugar began in January 1940, with cheese following in the spring of 1941. The initial standard ration was a measly one ounce a week, which would barely cover a cracker, though over the course of the war it would fluctuate, at one point reaching a bountiful eight ounces, but usually hovering around two to three ounces. Actually some people got a larger ration of cheese, which at times reached the princely amount of a pound a week. Beneficiaries of the big cheese ration included vegetarians, as a meat substitute, and Jews and Muslims, who received cheese in place of pork products. And, happily, outdoor workers – canal boatmen, fishermen, forestry workers, quarrymen – also got more, because they couldn't eat in canteens and would have to survive on cheese sandwiches.

Not that the cheese was particularly tempting. The Ministry of Food's Cheese and Butter Division, under Professor E. Capstick, not only controlled how much cheese everyone got, but what kind of cheese it was. Luxury cheeses like Stilton and shorter-lived products like the soft Ely cheeses were banned, and only durable cheese was allowed. There is a prevalent idea that this was a single 'National Cheese' or Government Cheddar, but Val Cheke, writing only a decade after the war, recalls a rather more expansive list of 'scheduled cheeses' that included Cheddar, Cheshire, Dunlop, Lancashire, Leicester, Derby and Wensleydale. At first, the miners of Wales kicked up such a fuss about their beloved Caerphilly, 'an essential factor to their existence', that it too was allowed, but it soon fell victim to the exigencies of rationing, and the miners had to be content with an extra allowance of 'mousetrap cheese' – another wartime nickname that may have referred to the small size of the ration rather than the quality of the cheese.

By pruning cheese varieties and blurring the distinctions between them, the war not only wiped out some of our cheeses but changed the very nature of those that survived. One of the main requirements for rationed cheese was that the cheesemonger could cut it into the small units required for each person's ration. This is quite hard to do well. At the Dairy we used to serve a very parsimonious regular who would ask us for the smallest piece we could cut. This became something of a competition and the winning piece was twenty-six grams, just two shy of the 1941 ration of one ounce. To do this with minimal wastage (another key requirement for a rationed cheese), you need a firm cheese. Crumbly cheeses like Caerphilly or Cheshire or pre-war Wensleydale won't cut it. So, cheeses either went under, like Caerphilly, or changed.

After Wensleydale had been adjudged insufficiently firm for ration requirements, the members of the Wensleydale Cheese Joint Conference, a consortium of Wensleydale makers and factors from all over the Dales, arranged a meeting with Professor Capstick, head of the Butter and Cheese Division. The professor explained that the cheese would have to fit into the rationing system or be benched for the duration of the war. When he asked what the members thought of the system, one of them (I suspect it was Calvert) replied with signature Yorkshire pithiness, 'Nowt.'

Thankfully, the professor had gone to school not far from Wensleydale and understood the subtleties of that single syllable. Another meeting was arranged and a special scheme created that allowed Wensleydale to find its place in the portfolio of National Cheese. Part of this scheme was that the makers would have to change the recipe to make a harder, lower-moisture cheese, hopefully only for as long as the war continued. They called it Austerity Wensleydale.

Another requirement was that the makers of any National Cheese had to guarantee its supply. To do this, all the creameries and farmhouse cheesemakers of the Wensleydale Joint Conference Ltd opted to pool their resources. One of the benefits of the company was that, with warehouses distributed around the towns and villages of the Dales, they were protected from losing all their stock to a single bomb. The need for mutual support was swiftly demonstrated when a gigantic Luftwaffe bomb exploded next to the Masham Farmers' Cooperative Dairy, severely damaging the vats.

This wasn't the only time the Luftwaffe threatened Wensleydale cheese. Later on in the war, during the V-bomb attacks on the south-east, mothers and children were evacuated from the Home Counties to the north. All milk production was then diverted to liquid milk, and cheesemaking in the north was stopped until the spring of 1945.

Though Kit Calvert fought hard and often to save Hawes creamery, and to keep cheesemaking alive in the Dales, there was one thing even he couldn't save – farmhouse Wensleydale. This was also known as Pickled Wensleydale because it was cured in a brine bath before maturing. Creamier, richer and more complex than the creamery's regular Wensleydale, Calvert said it was 'accepted by connoisseurs of territorial cheese as the aristocrat of the table'. This was the cheese that got Ambrose Heath so excited. The problem was that the farmhouse cheese nearly always came in over the sixteen per cent moisture level that was the maximum allowable for ration cheese, so the graders were forced repeatedly to reject it

This not only meant a poor price for the cheese but a bitter blow to the cheesemaker's self-esteem. Calvert's imagined farmhouse cheesemaker's reaction to this slight sounds authentic: 'He doesn't know his job. I've made cheese for forty year. Won prizes for shows throughout the dale and here comes a nincompoop from nowhere who's never tasted a real Wensleydale and say my cheese is not fit to eat. If that's what we've come to, I'm finished, I'll make no

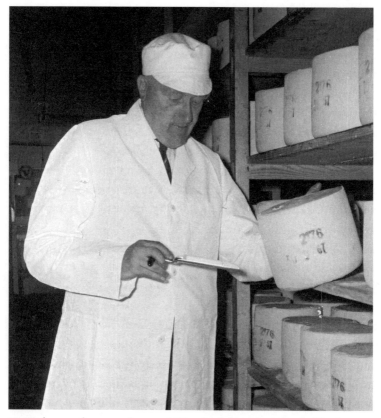

Kit Calvert – the man who saved Wensleydale – photographed in the 1970s, ironing one of his cheeses to taste it.

more.' This was clearly the reaction of many Pickled Wensleydale makers. Before the war there were more than a hundred farmhouse producers, but when peace broke out there were only nine left and these did not survive for long, mainly because food rationing – including cheese – survived until 1954. In 1939, there were more than a thousand farmhouse cheesemakers registered in Britain. Twenty years later, there were just one hundred and forty.

However, with rationing about to end, Calvert again displayed his unwavering confidence, moving the Hawes creamery out of the old mill to a state-of-the-art building on the outskirts of town. This was opened on 27 March by our old friend Mr R. A. Pepperall, now Chief Regional Marketing Officer of the Milk Marketing Board. The new creamery could handle eight thousand gallons a day and the old five-hundred-gallon tinned-steel vats were replaced with stainless steel vats twice their size, equipped with mechanical cutters and stirrers. The people of the north could once again get their Christmas treat as the production of Wensleydale smalls resumed; the new creamery sold seventy thousand of them in its first year.

With his usual forceful enthusiasm, Kit Calvert was embracing new technologies. One of these was a process developed by a company called Cryovac, which wrapped food products in plastic and, by extracting the air from the packaging, increased their shelf-life. Calvert saw the product on a shoulder of lamb in his local butcher and immediately saw the opportunity for cheese. Excited by the idea of enticingly wrapped cheeses on the shelves of the new self-service shops that heralded the age of the supermarket, he showed one to the board of directors of what was now called Wensleydale Products Ltd. The directors rejected the plan, saying that housewives wouldn't want to pay any extra for packaging, but Calvert just ignored them and went ahead. That year the company sold three hundred thousand smalls. Once again, Calvert had triumphed.

🧀 🧀 🧀

When I went to visit Hawes Wensleydale Creamery in summer 2018, it had moved again, to a brand-new, purpose-built creamery and visitors' centre – the 'Yorkshire Wensleydale Cheese Experience.' Now, I freely admit I am not a fan of 'experiences' and was ready to scoff. But it was fantastic: a museum stuffed with fascinating exhibits for the keen student of cheese history – including a gigantic stone cheese press with an air of the prehistoric megalith about it – and glass walls that allow you to watch the cheesemaking. Through the steamed-up glass you see white-coated, hair-netted workers bent over vats holding thousands of litres of curd that can produce up to ten tons of cheese a day. Cheesemaking at Hawes, however, maintains the tradition of the creamery – a sort of halfway house between farmhouse and factory production. The company cultures its own starter cultures, and the salt is still mixed by hand into milled curd, contributing to a creamier texture than mechanically mixed curd.

Twenty-three different varieties of cheese are made here, including their prime Kit Calvert Wensleydale, based on a recipe found on a crumpled bit of paper in his own handwriting. This cheese has a firm yet supple texture, is 'as pale and creamy as a milkmaid's shoulder' (to use a traditional simile) and has a simple clean flavour, with very little acidity and a slight hint of dill. As to what to drink with it, as a territorial cheese Hawes Wensleydale is amenable to matching by terroir, and so the products of a local brewery are a good bet. I like Black Sheep Ale, flagship beer of Black Sheep Brewery in Masham. Untouched by the craft beer revolution's predilection for intense New World flavours, and hopped with that quintessentially British hop, East Kent Goldings, this beer has gentle notes of spice, honey and a hint of earthiness, just right for a down-to-earth cheese like Wensleydale.

The Wensleydale Creamery also make a smoked cheese (which I'm beginning to allow myself to feel okay about, given that the Romans ate the stuff), and the more troubling Wensleydale-with-cranberries. However I might feel about the adulteration of cheese with fruit or other substances, the cranberry mix makes up a quarter of their sales. So, since it's keeping all the cheesemakers and local farmers going, I suppose I'm okay with that, too. The creamery and visitors' centre gets twenty-five thousand visitors a year – quite a draw for this part of the Dales.

Not that any of this has been plain sailing. In 1992, Hawes and its Wensleydale came under threat again, as, with profits low, its owner, Dairy Crest (then a division of the MMB), planned to shift Wensleydale production to Lancashire, a move that would have had the proud Yorkshireman Calvert out of his grave and on the warpath once again. The creamery manager, David Hartley, with the support of local business owners, led a management buyout, and Hawes Creamery stayed in business. The spirit of Kit Calvert rode again.

And the new owners, rather pleasingly, got an unexpected helping hand, from an animation studio in Bristol. In 1995, Wallace and Gromit joined Calvert in the pantheon of Wensleydale saviours when, in their film, *A Close Shave*, Wallace declares Wensleydale his favourite cheese. Kids across the land started asking for Wensleydale in their packed lunches and Hawes' sales skyrocketed. Hawes then got permission from Aardman Animations to license a Wallace and Gromit Wensleydale, which it began exporting to America, Canada and even France.

Kit Calvert ran the creamery at Hawes until his retirement in 1967, and in 1977 was awarded an MBE for his services to the nation. When he died in 1984, at the age of eighty, he was taken to his final resting place on a cart drawn by his pony, Dolly. Not one to take retirement easy, Calvert had run a secondhand bookshop in Hawes in his later years and otherwise occupied himself by translating biblical verses into the Dales dialect. The opening lines of *Psalm 23* go like this:

The Lord is my shipperd,
Ah'll want fer nowt.
He lets m'bassock i' t' best pastures
an' taks m' bi't watter side whar o's wyet an' peaceful.

CHAPTER NINE

Lanark Blue

The Great Cheese Renaissance

1974–99

Wᴇɴsʟᴇʏᴅᴀʟᴇ's sᴜʀᴠɪᴠᴀʟ ᴡᴀs ᴀɢᴀɪɴsᴛ ᴀʟʟ ᴛʜᴇ ᴏᴅᴅs. But, in a curious reversal of the pre-war situation, by the 1960s the creameries (rather than cheese factories) were dominating the market for domestically produced cheese. And to their credit the people at the Milk Marketing Board tried to help with publicity campaigns about farmhouse cheese, albeit with an emphasis on nutritional value rather than flavour and tradition. The liquid milk market, meanwhile, was even more saturated than ever, due to the increased take-up of milking machines, and because there was a new breed in town – the black-and-white Holstein Friesian. This super-milker first arrived in Britain just after the war in the form of a pair of bulls gifted by the farmers of Canada, and within a decade almost half the national dairy herd were Friesians. The new animals produced more milk than the old Dairy Shorthorns, although some would argue that their milk is less good for cheesemaking than that of other breeds. Stichelton is made from Friesian milk, mind, so let's not get too far into that debate.

The cause of farmhouse cheese wasn't helped either by the arrival of supermarkets, the first of which appeared in 1951 in Streatham, south London. For the supermarket, there is little to love about traditional cheeses. Their self-service model required the cheese

This Guinness advert from 1965 highlights seven British cheeses: Cheddar, Stilton, Cheshire, Wensleydale, Leicester, Blue Vinny and Lancashire. All of them enhanced by a half of Guinness.

to be pre-cut and wrapped, and had no call for a cheesemonger to tell you why this week's Wensleydale is a bit sharper, or how that attractive streak of blue in the corner of the Cheshire is a sign of authenticity. For all the discourse about how people's tastes changed, favouring milder flavours over characterful cheese, I do wonder how much our tastes were changed for us to suit the needs of supermarkets.

The cheesemonger and writer Patrick Rance was unsurprisingly no fan of the new style of shops, describing their rise in the 1960s as 'a tidal wave of concrete sweeping over the life, charm and traditional trades of many town centres.' Rance also thought that this mode of selling favoured hard styles of cheese that would 'submit, uncrumbling, to the violation of automated cutting and packing' and that the few more characterful farmhouse cheeses left were graded and sold before they matured. In 1974, Rance went on a tour of all the cheesemaking areas of Britain, equipped with a list of all the farms still making cheese. It wasn't a very long list: there were only sixty-two left.

But things were set to change from a combination of unlikely sources, the counterculture, an ex-army officer (Rance himself) and what was then called the EEC

🐄 🐄 🐄

The beginnings of the counterculture in the UK had been rumbling away since the 1950s and the British embrace of the American Beat movement, but really you could trace a particularly British strain of anti-establishment bolshiness back to the Civil War – the Levellers and the Diggers, nonconformists and proto-anarchists who weren't satisfied with demanding a different way of life but actually went and lived it. Although that lot were pretty thoroughly squashed by Cromwell's government, their memory lived on in an American group of the mid-1960s, called the San Francisco

Diggers, who combined protest against the status quo with local community projects providing free healthcare and housing in that cauldron of hippie activism, Haight-Ashbury. One British activist who went to San Francisco to see what was going on for himself was Nicholas Albery (later, in 1977, he created Frestonia, a road of squatters, artists, musicians and activists in north-west London). Albery brought word of what he had seen in San Francisco back to London and told his friends, one of whom was Nicholas Saunders.

Saunders, 'an alternative entrepreneur of genius', was born just before the war and co-wrote and self-published a guide called *Alternative London* in 1970. Billed by its authors as a 'book for young people coming to London who want to take part in the new culture', it contained advice on squatting, sexual health, drugs, immigration law, transport (you could cadge lifts through London in newspaper vans back then), cheap food and joining left-wing political groups. Saunders' distribution system for his book tells you something about the man; he would take carrier bags out to the park and enlist cash-strapped hippies to sell them by hand. Then, in 1975, he decided on a new venture – to open a wholefoods shop; in his own words, 'one that was cheap, efficient and would not make customers feel bad because they could not recognise a mung bean'. A noble endeavour.

The place Saunders picked was a warehouse in a squalid, dark, rat-infested derelict bit of Covent Garden called Neal's Yard, so neglected that it wasn't even in the A to Z of the time. In 1976, against the ruling of the local council but with the agreement of his new neighbours, he opened Neal's Yard Wholefoods Warehouse.

From the start Saunders' ambitions were a combination of good business sense and high ideals. He was influenced by the enigmatic mystic George Gurdjieff, who said 'fulfilment doesn't come from making work effortless, but by doing work which is demanding' – to which Saunders added, 'variety, learning and responsibility'. Famously this attitude to work was characterised by how the sacks of nuts and pulses were brought up to the first-floor

Nicholas Saunders looking down over Neal's Yard, late 1970s.

packing room. In an 'exhilarating exercise in trust and awareness', this was achieved by the 'human counterweight principle'. The humans stood on the first floor, holding onto a rope on a pulley, the other end of which was attached to a sack, and to haul it up the human counterweight jumped out of the window. There was other imaginative and practical stuff, too, like designing packing areas to make boring work more sociable, and working out a fair and transparent pricing system. There was, for example, a higher charge for wrapping some goods based on both their size and stickiness.

After nine months the shop was doing so well that Saunders divided up the profits between the workers and dropped the prices. Not your normal business practice, but it worked, and over the next three years Saunders added a bakery, a flour mill, a coffee shop and a dairy. The Apothecary which Saunders set up in 1981 has become Neal's Yard Remedies, the coffee shop is now Monmouth Coffee, and the dairy is now that temple of British and Irish cheese,

The exhilarating human counterweight system in action at Neal's Yard.

key player in the cheese renaissance, and site of my transformation into a cheesemonger – Neal's Yard Dairy.

Saunders himself described the dairy as 'a more ambitious and less viable project than the others'. It opened on 5 July 1979 with, in the words of its first manager and then long-time owner, Randolph Hodgson, 'very little to sell'. The original plan was to make and sell Greek yoghurt (little known in Britain at the time), soft cheese (because it used less milk than Cheddar) and ice cream. The first summer was a success, with all that lovely ice cream and fresh cheese, but winter was a bit of a disappointment. So, in the second year, Randolph and his new colleagues decided to get some cheese in.

They bought Cheddar, Stilton and Cheshire from a wholesaler, who just dropped the cheeses off at the shop. No tasting, no selection, no stories about the generations of craft that had created the characters of these cheeses. Those three cheeses were the standard range in a proper cheese shop back then. In a later radio interview, Randolph remembered going into into Paxton & Whitfield, the iconic London cheesemongers, when he was a student studying food science. He saw 'vast arrays of cheese from Italy or France and even Spain, but very little from Britain'.

One day, though, a new batch of cheese arrived at the Dairy – a West Country Caerphilly style called Devon Garland that was made by a lady called Hilary Charnley. Wanting to find out more about the cheese and its maker, Randolph went to see her. Ms Charnley told Randolph about other small artisan and farmhouse cheesemakers in the area and Randolph went to see them, too. (I am making a distinction here between 'artisan', by which I mean a cheesemaker who hasn't come from a local or family tradition and who is making a new cheese, and 'farmhouse', by which I mean a cheesemaker who is carrying on a local tradition.) Randolph began to widen his search out into the West Country, tasting and selecting cheeses on the farm and maturing room and bringing them back to the Dairy to sell.

And he found he was not alone in his cheese quest. Someone else had been seeking out the remaining British farmhouse cheeses or their newer artisanal cousins, and bringing them to the notice of the British cheese fancier. Step forward, Patrick Rance.

🧀 🧀 🧀

Major Patrick Lowry Cole Holwell Rance, to give him his full name, was born in 1918, the son of a priest 'who ministered to dairy workers at St Margaret's Leytonstone', and his earliest memory was of being given a lump of cheese in the vicarage kitchen. After fighting in the Second World War, Rance left the army, and in 1953 bought a shop called Wells Stores in the riverside village of Streatley in Berkshire. When he and his wife Janet took over the shop, it had three cheeses for sale: Edam, New Zealand Cheddar and Danish Blue. Rance made it his mission to seek out the remaining farmhouse cheeses of Britain, bring them to the people and support their makers.

In Rance's obituary, written by Egon Ronay for the *Guardian* in 1999, Ronay speaks of 'his life's towering achievement...the almost single-handed creation of the British farmhouse cheese industry.' With a little less hyperbole, Randolph said in an interview for Radio 4, 'What Patrick did was to show us that actually we were a nation of cheesemakers and this was something to be proud of.' He was also, it seems, a very nice man. Bill Hogan, an American-born Irish cheesemaker, said of Rance: 'There was no snobbiness to him, he was very accessible, almost childlike. The more you knew him the less military he became...he had the same ability that children have to just taste things objectively.'

Rance didn't just inspire existing cheesemakers, he gave immense support to new ones. For example, in 1972 Charles Martell took over a farm in Gloucestershire, with the intention of reviving the near-extinct breed of Old Gloucester cows and making proper Double Gloucester cheese from their milk. Rance sent him a blank cheque. Martell said that at the time he 'hadn't a clue how to make cheese', but the cheque started him off. Martell's (now Charles Martell & Son, by Royal Appointment) is still going strong, and even if you haven't heard of his Gloucester cheeses – he also revived the once defunct Single Gloucester – you probably know his pungent oozy washed-rind if for no other reason than its name, Stinking Bishop.

By the late 1970s, when Neal's Yard Dairy was still just a twinkle in Saunders' eye, Rance's shop offered two hundred British, French, Swiss, Italian and Dutch cheeses. And, whilst spearheading the British farmhouse cheese industry, Rance also found time to write, in 1982, *The Great British Cheese Book*. Campaigning and informative, this was still the most important work on British cheese when I started mongering in 2002.

It was natural that Randolph, on his own quest to seek out the more traditional and more interesting cheeses, found his way to

Patrick Rance, the man who rediscovered Britain's cheeses. People really did wear these shirts in the 1970s, though the monocle was exceptional.

Wells Stores, and as he and his colleagues started to develop Neal's Yard Dairy into a cheese shop, Rance provided much inspiration and help, with no concern for rivalry. On his odysseys around the counties of the south-west, Randolph would stop off at Wells Stores to see if Rance wanted to purchase any of the treasures he had discovered. But these visits were about much more than mere business transactions. Having had his pick of the findings, Rance would enquire, 'Would you like some soup, dear boy?' and they would take soup, a glass of wine and taste the cheeses in the shop. Randolph described it as 'the biggest cheeseboard in the world'.

That's proper mongers for you. Tasting became a key part of the Dairy culture. When I worked in Neal's' Yard, we would taste and discuss each cheese as we put them out first thing in the morning. It's that process that develops your palate, helping you to understand cheeses and so help customers find the cheeses they really want.

The other thing that Randolph and Rance talked about while they were tasting these cheeses was where to find more varieties of British and Irish cheese for the Dairy's offering. Randolph was keen to widen his search further afield than the south-west of England and Rance was characteristically generous with his knowledge. Not that the expeditions were always plain sailing. Randolph remembered being chased out of a farmhouse kitchen by one cheesemaker when he said that he wanted to buy her cheese, perhaps being mistaken as an agent of the Milk Marketing Board, which still exerted rigorous control over the sale of cheese in the 1980s. Randolph would buy Cheddars from a huge warehouse in Wells that were marked only with a serial number for each producer. One of his favourites was number 774, and after some prying he was able to discover that this stood for Manor Farm in North Cadbury, home of the Montgomery family and their eponymous Cheddar, which is now one of the most famous farmhouse cheeses in the world. Not only were Cheddars anonymous back then, but due to a philosophy of grading imposed by the MMB that prioritised quick sale and younger, blander cheeses, the British public were barely aware of the potential of this great cheese. On the farm Randolph met Mrs Montgomery, who showed him cheeses that had been refused by the grader but were to her (and his) palate delicious. He recalled that 'It was with Mrs M that I learnt so much of the difference between the modern view of how Cheddar should taste and the more old-fashioned flavour of the traditional cheese'.

Randolph was keen to widen his search further afield than the south-west of England, and Rance was characteristically generous with his knowledge. Soon Randolph's quest took him across the Irish Sea to seek out the artisanal cheeses that were beginning to appear in Ireland. There were moments of magical synchronicity, as when the husband of a Cork cheesemaker on a trip to London happened upon Neal's Yard Dairy and popped in for a chat. 'My wife's making cheese on our farm', he said to the man behind the counter, 'on the Beara Peninsula.' Randolph took the man's arm, said 'come with me', and took him into the back where a map of Ireland was laid out, with the very farm circled – 'I'm just packing up the car to go there.' The man was Norman Steele, his wife was Veronica, and that is how her cheese, Milleens, found its way to the slate at Covent Garden.

Randolph and the other cheesemongers at the Dairy weren't just finding cheeses and bringing them to the people – they were,

Randolph Hodgson at the original Neal's Yard Dairy.

like Rance, supporting fledgling and traditional cheesemakers in a number of ways. In a move similar to Rance's gift of a blank cheque to Charles Martell, when one cheesemaker had a sudden cash-flow problem, the Dairy bought the whole year's make of their cheese, in advance, before it had been made.

Another way that the Dairy helped new cheesemakers was in developing their methods and recipes. To some extent this came in the form of feedback from the Dairy's cunning sales strategy of giving every visitor a nice piece of cheese to taste. This in itself had grown out of the very beginnings of the Dairy, when they were making soft cheese in the shop. As they learnt their craft, the new cheesemakers noticed that their products changed from day to day, and rather than conceal this variation, they celebrated it, discussing the differences with their customers. This qualitative survey could be backed up by quantitive data in the form of sales figures that allowed Randolph, or the buyer or affineur, to talk to a cheesemaker and work together to develop their cheesemaking methods to optimise sales or, as we like to say, 'make really banging cheese'.

The number of new artisan cheesemakers was augmented when it was decided to move the manufacturing operation out of Neal's Yard itself and into the countryside. This was partly because milk would be cheaper, but also because the focus in the shop was shifting onto maturing and selling rather than making cheese. Perry James and Beatrice Garroche set up a creamery in Sevenoaks in Kent to make yoghurt, crème fraîche and a soft fresh goat's cheese they called Perroche, a portmanteau of their names. In 1990, the pair decided to move on and a Neal's Yard monger, Charlie Westhead, was sent out to Sevenoaks and given two days' instruction. Although this was about as steep as a learning curve gets, Charlie must have done okay, because he is still making Perroche in his creamery in Herefordshire, as well as more mature cheeses like the mould-ripened goat's cheese Ragstone, and a crème fraîche that can go toe to toe with its Normandy rival any day. The Dairy's first full-time employee, Charlie is in some ways a typical new wave cheesemaker – he says it was a Sex Pistols concert that made him abandon thoughts of a traditional career and set off to London to find his fortune.

🧀 🧀 🧀

Looking into how cheese was made in Britain in the 1960s and 1970s, I was introduced to a woman called Val Bines, who gained a National Diploma in Dairying in 1961 and recalled teaching a block-Cheddar-making course at college to the 'up and coming new men' who would become foremen in the cheese factories of Birmingham. At the time she and her fellow teachers used raw milk in their cheesemaking classes, and these young men said, 'It's as if you were telling us all about tractors and now you want us to drive a horse and cart!' They were fascinated by new techniques and machinery and had little interest in any artisan tradition.

But, by the 1970s, the love of the modern had paled, and a desire to return to some idea of pre-industrial simplicity was on the rise. Counterculture types – and, according to Val, more mainstream folk, often inspired by the TV sitcom *The Good Life* – began having a go at self-sufficiency. Val also recalled that, in the gloomy economic climate of the early 1970s, lots of people were losing their jobs and redundancy packages were often generous enough to allow you to set yourself up on a smallholding somewhere and try making some cheese.

I wondered why these budding cheesemakers didn't choose to make traditional British varieties. Val thought this was down to two factors – memories of wartime 'mousetrap Cheddar' were still recent and people had begun travelling in Europe, discovering the funky washed-rinds of northern France, the piquant goat's cheeses of the south of France or the rustic sheep's cheeses of Spain.

Dougal Campbell, perhaps the most influential of these early 'renaissance cheesemakers', was a good example. After finishing a degree in Civil Engineering, he had set off to the Valais in the Swiss Alps to climb mountains. To prolong his stay, he got a job as an assistant cheesemaker. This steered him in a new direction, and in 1976 he set himself up on a farm in west Wales and began making a hard cow's milk cheese called Tyn Grug, using raw milk from a herd of fifteen cows with a hybrid of Alpine and Cheddar methods.

Campbell had unwittingly started a new tradition in British artisan cheesemaking when he then taught other aspiring cheesemakers – notably Todd and Maugan Trethowan, whom we met making Caerphilly, and the Jones brothers, who make Lincolnshire Poacher, a cheese I like to describe as the lovechild of Cheddar and Gruyère, since it has some of the sweetness and elasticity of an Alpine cheese with the savoury flavour and acidic bite of a Cheddar.

Meantime, there were other pioneering revivals of artisan and farmhouse cheesemaking, often at the edges of the British Isles. As we have seen, Mary Holbrook had begun making her cheeses in the mid-1970s at Sleight Farm, initially with just a couple of goats. Veronica Steele in Ireland was creating Milleens in County Cork. And, up in the hills of Lanarkshire in Scotland, another cheese was being conceived, that would come to be called Lanark Blue. Its story and that of its maker Humphrey Errington is in miniature the story of the triumphs and the tribulations of so many of the renaissance cheesemakers. But, before we get to Humphrey and his cheese, there's something else we have to talk about, which is that on the first of January 1973, Britain and Ireland joined that community of nations that we now refer to as the EU.

Whatever you think about the EU, it's worth remembering that it was set up, six years after the end of the Second World War to 'make war not only unthinkable but materially impossible'. So far, in continental Europe at least, the EU's record on that one is pretty solid. Of course, it has its problems, too.

Take the aspect of the EU which most affects cheesemakers: the infamous Common Agricultural Policy, or CAP, which has been part of the EU since the Treaty of Rome in 1957, long before we joined. To increase productivity, provide a decent standard of living for rural workers and guarantee food security, tariffs were put on imports from outside Europe and producers within the community were supported with subsidies.

This worked, in the sense that production increased, living standards did rise and food supplies have remained secure. But the policy also caused massive problems. For one thing, it produced huge surpluses – the infamous wine lakes and butter mountains. The system also tended to favour larger farms, which had the staff and managerial expertise to cope with complex regulations. Another problem for British cheesemakers was the rather ham-fisted way those regulations were implemented. In contrast, the French government found a way to protect smaller cheesemakers from the burden of the milk quota, which tells you as much about the French love of cheese as it does about the EU. On the brighter side, in the early 1980s, a cheesemaker called Elliot Hume, quoting EU anti monopoly regulations at the MMB, forced them to sell him milk even as a small- scale cheesemaker. On the whole, though, smaller farms have not done well under CAP, and despite recent attempts to remedy some of its problems (reducing subsidies, increasing the focus on sustainability and food safety, eliminating the surpluses), many family enterprises across Europe have disappeared, obliging rural workers to head to the cities for work.

Agenda 2000, announced in 1997, was intended to remedy some of the problems with the CAP, reducing subsidies, increasing focus on sustainability and food safety and attempting to halt rural decline. Since then the mountains have tumbled and the lakes dried up; food safety and sustainability are still deeply problematic, but at least we're talking about those issues and, though rural life in Britain at least is still sadly under threat, I'd say that's as much a result of decades of central government neglect as anything to do with the EU. But enough about politics – let's get back to Humphrey and his cheese.

Lanark Blue, like many of Britain's renaissance cheeses, takes inspiration from a traditional French cheese – in this case, Roquefort – but is rooted firmly in its local terroir, the hills of Lanarkshire in Lowlands Scotland. It is a soft, spicy cheese of extraordinary deliciousness, with a character entirely its own.

Its maker, Humphrey Errington, was not from a cheesemaking or farming family. He read History at Cambridge, where he formulated the slightly tongue-in-cheek theory that a diet of herring and oatmeal was an unexplored cause of the Scottish Enlightenment. He then did time with an Edinburgh shipping firm before, in 1972, chucking it in to buy a hill farm near Beattock, in the region of Dumfries and Galloway, to raise cattle and Cheviot sheep. A few years later he moved to a 'drier and less stony' farm at Walston Braehead in Lanarkshire. Having a keen interest in the farming history of his region, he turned to the *Statistical Account of Scotland* to see what his forbears had been producing. The *Account* had been compiled by a pillar of the eighteenth-century Scottish Enlightenment known as 'Agricultural' Sir John Sinclair, an MP and keen 'improver' who coined the term 'statistics'. For the Accounts, he sent detailed questionnaires to every minister of every parish in Scotland – a kind of benevolent version of the Domesday Book.

For Humphrey, the *Statistical Account* 'opened up an astonishing picture'. He discovered that in the eighteenth century the main cash income of the hill farms of the Upper Clyde Valley came from cheesemaking, specifically sheep's cheesemaking. That's a surprise when you consider that Dunlop, the most famous Scots cheese, is made from cow's milk, and that since the nineteenth century the Scottish cheesemaking industry had made mainly Cheddar. Furthermore, Humphrey discovered that the cheese of the region was more often than not a blue, and was well regarded. Walter Scott wrote in his introduction to *The Cook and Housewife's Manual*, published in 1826, 'we have had the pleasure of eating Scotch cheese...as good as Stilton, and taken for it'.

An 1805 account suggests the cheese could have given a Cabrales – a characterful blue cheese from northern Spain – a run for its money, recording that it was known as 'under the wool cheese', since 'from the position of the ewe, whatever drops from her falls into the milking pail'. Thankfully the makers would have strained the milk into the vat to get rid of the 'solids', but, well... they can put it better than me: 'the cheese is peculiarly dark in

Contented Errington ewes having their breakfast at home in Lanarkshire.

colour, and has a peculiar haute gout'. If this was the same cheese Walter Scott admired, he must have had a pretty jaded palate.

Dunlop aside, the two best-known traditional farmhouse cheeses of Scotland must be Caboc, a rich soft cheese made without rennet and rolled in oats, and a similar but skimmed-milk cheese called Crowdie. But, as small soft cheeses, these wouldn't travel, whereas Dunlop, that magical Ayrshire cheese developed in the seventeenth century by Mrs Gilmour, could. It was not only larger and firmer than Caboc and Crowdie but, being made with whole milk, far tastier than the other rock-hard skimmed-milk cheeses made on Scottish farms at the time. (The fact that Suffolk Bang was popular in Scotland tells you all you need to know about those.)

In the late eighteenth and early nineteenth centuries, a craze for making Dunlop set in, which meant that its overall quality and reputation sank. It was then that the Ayrshire Deputation went down to Somerset to see Mr Harding, who in turn came up to teach the Scots his method. It was the beginning of a form of cheese imperialism that in the 1870s would see the position of the indigenous Dunlop severely threatened by Cheddar. Then, during the Second World War, the Scottish Milk Marketing Board, like its English counterpart, pretty much closed down farmhouse cheesemaking, and its resumption was actively discouraged after the war. And by the 1970s, traditional cheesemaking was all but gone from Scotland. Indeed, in 1972, the Company of Scottish Cheesemakers awarded its annual farmhouse trophy to J. Brian Finlay in perpetuity because there were no other cheesemakers to compete with him. Even he gave up in 1974.

Against all the odds, however, those two small, soft cheeses, Caboc and Crowdie, did survive. They were made, and still are, in Tain, a town twenty miles or so north of Inverness, by a woman called Susannah Stone, and by her son Rory. Mrs Stone claims direct descendance from the fabled inventor of Caboc – Mariota de l'Ile, daughter of a fifteenth-century chieftain of the MacDonald clan. Susannah started making Crowdie when her husband Reggie

Caboc and Crowdie – two of Scotland's oldest cheeses, rolled in oats.

asked her for some like his mother used to make. She used a whole churn of their milk, strained though a linen pillowcase into their bathtub. There was too much cheese for the family to eat and so they took some down to the local shop. Forty years later, their business, Highland Fine Cheeses, is going strong, and their range has been added to by the formidable Strathdon Blue and the rather disturbingly named Blue Murder, Fat Cow and Minger.

But I have digressed. Back in 1980s Lanarkshire, Humphrey Errington was worried about being overdependent on European subsidies for conventional sheep farming and, saddened by the loss of rural employment (a process he felt had been accelerated during the years of Mrs Thatcher's government), he decided to take inspiration from local farming history and give blue sheep's cheese a go. There were no cheesemakers left in the area to ask for advice, so Humphrey looked to the makers of Roquefort in southern France, to whom he was introduced by Janet Galloway, a teacher of cheesemaking at the Ayr agricultural college.

While his cheese, Lanark Blue, might have originally been based on a Roquefort recipe, or at least as much as Humphrey could get out of its protective makers, it has its own character and appearance,

Selina Errington, rubbing and turning one of her cheeses.

with a slightly firmer texture and a darker ivory hue, as opposed to Roquefort's bone-white appearance. Errington is sure terroir is the main driver of that difference. The sheep farms in Aveyron, where Roquefort is made, are on limestone,while his farm is on 'old red sandstone and basalt', and that apparently makes all the difference.

Actually, there is an ongoing argument about how much terroir, as opposed to the practices of its maker, affects the character of a cheese. I suspect there will always be a bit of mystery around what factors really do contribute to a cheese's qualities, as Robin Congdon, a Devon-based contemporary of Errington, found out when he tried to make his version of Roquefort. Like Errington, Robin started making cheese in the early 1980s and, again, with no indigenous tradition to call on, he went to the caves of Roquefort for inspiration. He tried to replicate as many factors as he could: he bought the same breed of sheep, Lacaune, whose high-fat milk contributes to Roquefort's fondant-like texture; took cuttings of grasses and herbs from the fields they grazed in; scraped samples of mould from the walls of the cave where the cheeses matured; and even built a cave on his farm to replicate the air currents in the caves in France. His cheese is called Beenleigh Blue and it resembles Roquefort only in the sense that it is a blue cheese made from sheep's milk. Where Roquefort is as soft and creamy as butter, Beenleigh has a texture like moist fudge. Roquefort tends to be very intense, the peppery blue flavour and acidity at times combining to make one's eyes water. Most of the time Beenleigh is gentle, with a floral sweetness. That he had worked so hard to reproduce Roquefort and ended up with quite a different cheese might have been a bit frustrating for Robin but it's one for the terroir argument. Or, as he puts it, 'the cheesemaker only guides the milk in the direction it wants to go'.

Whether or not terroir contributes to the character of a cheese, the concept is a useful one when it comes to finding a drink to go with it, although you can only go so far with the idea. It was pleasing to find out that Humphrey likes a whisky with his Lanark Blue, but it turns out that not just any old whisky will do. Humphrey told me that in a tasting session with the Scottish Malt Whisky Society, they found that the Islay single malts were the best partners for the Lanark. This makes sense to me, as Lanark Blue is a hefty cheese and needs something of equal intensity to stand up to it. The gentler Lowland malts, while closer geographically, are a little too retiring for this rough-hewn child of the Lanarkshire hills, whereas the cheese's meaty umami, pepper and acidity are perfectly complemented by the briny smokiness of an Islay single malt.

Developing a cheese, of course, is not the same thing as running a successful cheese business. And Humphrey had his battles over the years, mainly due to his insistence on using unpasteurised milk. The Scottish Office, in pre-devolution days, tried to stop him; and they did this by, according to Humphrey, wilfully misinterpreting EU regulations in such a way as to cut off his farming subsidies – an example of a national government rather than the EU itself making life hard for farmers. Undeterred, Humphrey carried on, farming successfully without subsidies for thirty years, although it was a tough situation to be in. This wasn't the last time Humphrey and his family have had to go up against the authorities. As recently as 2019, the Erringtons had to fight another battle with the Scottish food standards authority over raw milk cheesemaking, this time allied with four other Scottish producers. Happily for them and for all of us, raw milk won the day. Errington Cheese has thrived over the years and not just through sheer grit. They were championed initially by the food writer Jane Grigson, and later by Jane Scotter, who was Randolph Hodgson's business partner in Neal's Yard Dairy before becoming a biodynamic farmer, and author, in Wales.

At first Humphrey tried to make only sheep's cheese, but he ran up against an age-old problem – that sheep's cheesemaking is seasonal, as ewes naturally give birth in spring and then give milk for seven or eight months. As the business started to grow, and he began to employ more people, he needed to keep them occupied year-round. After protracted and unsuccessful attempts to get half his sheep to lamb in autumn, he decided to make cow's milk cheese in the autumn and winter months, and the result was Dunsyre Blue. This is a little gentler than the Lanark and a bit like a cross between a Stilton and a Bleu d'Auvergne. He later added Maisie's Kebbuck, a white semi-soft cow's milk cheese (named after his mother-in-law, who didn't like blue cheese), and Cora Lynn, a hard sheep's cheese a little like a Manchego or Pecorino.

But, once more, I am getting ahead of myself. Let's go back to the 1980s and the currents of history.

🧀 🧀 🧀

In 1979, Margaret Thatcher's government was swept into power by years of industrial unrest that culminated in the 1978 'Winter of Discontent', with seemingly the whole nation on strike. The authoritarian, nationalistic Thatcher fought the Falklands War of 1982 and ruthlessly suppressed the Miners' Strike in 1984. But, in the cheese world, her government is remembered chiefly for the creation of a new British cheese.

Actually, to be fair, the cheese was created at the request of the MMB, and for a familiar reason – to use up surplus milk. A tender was put out to an advertising agency to come up with a concept and, reviewing what was on offer, Butler, Dennis, Garland decided in their wisdom that there was a gap in the market for a soft blue cheese. As part of their 'brand story', the agency came up with the idea of an imaginary English village and set up a national competition to name the village and cheese. These days, of course, the result would likely have been 'Cheesy McCheese Face', but the British were more serious in the 1980s and the name that won was 'Lymeswold'. A creamery in Somerset began making the cheese in 1982 and its creation was celebrated by then-Minister for Agriculture Peter Walker, claiming the cheese (renamed 'Westminster Blue' for export) would 'improve the balance of payments'. Which is surely the worst reason ever for making a cheese.

Lymeswold was, according to a *Daily Mail* article, Margaret Thatcher's favourite cheese. But few people followed her gastronomic tips. *Private Eye* mocked it mercilessly, referring to it as Slymeswold, and its demise in 1992 was greeted by the restaurant critic of the *Daily Telegraph*, John Withley, with 'unfettered joy'.

This little story highlights an issue I have with the MMB, which is its seeming lack of interest in the existing great cheeses of Britain. A better way to improve the balance of payments would have been to increase the exports of British cheeses such as Cheshire, Cheddar or Stilton that already had an international reputation. But the MMB itself was not to survive for very much longer. In 1994, the sixty-year-old body was stripped of its powers, and in 2002 it was wound up. Its Scottish incarnation held on another year.

You might expect me to wholeheartedly celebrate the demise of the MMB, given its rather draconian rule over milk sales and cheesemaking, but my feelings are complicated. In the Applebys' kitchen up in Shropshire, I spoke to Aunt Sarah, whose visits to small farms in her role as 'the War Ag Lady' had given her a more positive view of the MMB and its role in supporting dairy farming. She thought that dissolving the MMB was one of the more troublesome aspects of Margaret Thatcher's legacy. And, indeed, the period since its closure has been a rocky one for dairy farmers, as the milk price fluctuates with the fortunes of the market, just as it did in the 1930s. The domination of the supermarkets has not helped, either, as price wars have at times brought the price of a pint of milk below the cost of producing it. There are now fewer than half the number of dairy herds in Britain than there were in 1995. Herds have got larger and dairy farming more technical, creating higher yields, but this has been at the expense of the smaller herds and family-run farms. As to the effects of industrial-scale dairy farming on the environment, both on a local and global scale, and on the welfare of the animals, well, there's a whole other book in there.

In addition, the farming industry in the 1980s and '90s had a rash of food scares to deal with. There was a crisis with eggs in 1988, which led among other things to Health Minister Edwina Currie's resignation, and then the far more serious bovine spongiform encephalopathy, aka 'Mad Cow Disease', which led to a European ban on British beef from 1996 to 2006. But, for the dairy industry, by far the most problematic pathogen was listeria, and throughout the 1980s there was an explosion of reported cases. There are various bits of good news and bad news about this particular bacterium. First, it is a comparatively rare cause of disease in Britain; second, if you are in good health with a functional immune system, and not pregnant, there is not a great deal to worry about. If you are pregnant, or immunosupressed, though, listeria can be a serious threat.

Cheese has been unjustly demonised in the great listeria debate – you're just as likely to pick it up from a pre-cut sandwich. But that's not the kind of message a government minister will put out, and so when 'something had to be done' after a 1989 outbreak the government announced it was going to ban raw milk cheesemaking in Britain. It was a Sunday morning and Randolph Hodgson was at home listening to the radio when he heard the news. He was immediately galvanised into action and called up Radio 4, telling them that he was the president of the Specialist Cheesemakers Association and that he would give them an interview about why the ban was a terrible idea. Randolph then rang round the cheesemakers telling them that he had just formed the SCA and they all needed to get up to London so that they could stop this raw milk cheese ban.

Luckily for them, and all of us cheese fanciers, Randolph not only had his forceful personality and the backing of a bunch of independent-minded and extremely good cheesemakers, he had a powerful secret weapon – the cheese knowledge of Patrick Rance. In his perfectly timed *The French Cheese Book*, which had just been published, Rance had devoted a chapter to pointing out that to date all the cheese-related outbreaks of listeria had been traced back to heat-treated cheeses. Raw milk was not the issue. Armed with Rance's research, Randolph was able to persuade the minister that the ban was misguided. 'The forces of witless pasteurisation', in Rance's memorable phrase, had been held at bay.

The message, however, was out, and many people still feel they must avoid raw milk cheese and stick to pasteurised products. Actually, the important distinction is between hard cheeses (which are safer) and soft and blue cheeses (which are less so). Whether or not they are made from pasteurised milk is not the issue. A hard cheese, high in acidity and low in moisture, is not a place for pathogenic bacteria to live. Soft and blue cheeses, low in acidity and moist as anything, provide a more congenial environment for listeria. And here is a vital bit of information: these cheeses can be contaminated after pasteurisation, so if you need to be careful, avoid soft and blue cheeses, even if they are made from pasteurised milk.

Randolph's spontaneous formation of the SCA was a boon to British cheesemaking, not just for its lobbying activities but for the technical support it offers to cheesemakers. A similar role is performed in Ireland by the Association of Irish Farmhouse Cheesemakers (CAIS), which pipped the British to the post, being founded in 1983 by Veronica Steele and others, including ex-fashion designer Jeffa Gill and Anglo-Hungarian Giana Ferguson, who had married into an Irish farming family. There followed a flowering of washed-rind cheesemaking in County Cork in the late 1970s and early '80s: Jeffa made the unctuous and earthy Durrus, while Giana produced the springy-textured and delicate Gubbeen, whose rind, it was recently discovered, contains a unique and flavoursome bacterium now named *microbacterium gubbeenense*.

Also in Cork, in 1979, Helene and Dick Willems – originally from Holland – began making a Gouda-style cheese called Coolea, one of the sweetest cheeses I have ever tasted, with a flavour much

The stars of Cashel Blue – it all begins on a lane in Tipperary.

like salted caramel. Meanwhile, in neighbouring Tipperary, in 1980, Jane Grubb began making cheese on the family farm near the small town of Fethard. At first, just like the Irish cheesemakers of the 1930s, Jane made British-influenced cheeses: Balingarry, based on Caerphilly; and Fethard, a Cheshire-style. Then, in 1984, she introduced an entirely novel Irish cheese called Cashel Blue. With its rich buttery texture and only a hint of spiciness, the lovely Cashel Blue is so gentle that I often use it to woo back unfortunates who have been frightened off by more spiky blue cheeses like the utterly mental Spanish cheese Picos de Europa.

In the crowded field of cheesemakers with colourful backgrounds, American-born Bill Hogan – another County Cork producer – stands head and shoulders above the rest. In the 1960s he worked in the office of Martin Luther King, but after Dr King and Bobby

Kennedy were assassinated Bill decided it was time to leave the States. He headed down to Costa Rica, where he began working with a Swiss cheesemaker called Joseph Dubach, who as part of a Swiss international development initiative was teaching peasant farmers how to make cheese as a way to lift themselves out of poverty. After that, Bill made his way to Cork, where he made hard, rustic, Swiss-inspired cheeses called Desmond and Gabriel, with his business partner, Sean Ferry. All went well for a decade or so, until 2002, when the Irish Department of Agriculture closed them down after finding TB in one of the herds that supplied their milk. Bill, no stranger to civil disobedience, refused to surrender and hired a solicitor called Helen Collins, who herself has an impressive pedigree of resistance – she's the grand-niece of Irish revolutionary Michael Collins. The legal battle took almost six years, and took its toll on Bill's health and finances, but in the end they won.

The story of James Aldridge provides a sad coda to the subject of food scares. Wells Stores and Neal's Yard Dairy weren't the only cheesemongers keeping the flame alight in this era. Aldridge, formerly a scaffolder, had opened his shop in Beckenham in the late 1970s, experimenting with affinage, and creating – by washing Duckett's Caerphillies – a new cheese called Tornegus. Inspired by this, he decided to go the whole hog, sold his shop and set up a cheesemaking business in Surrey. There, Aldridge invented a number of cheeses, including Flower Marie, a snowy white cube of sheep's milk cheese (now made by Golden Cross Cheese Co. in East Sussex) and Lord of the Hundreds, a hard sheep's cheese (now made at The Traditional Cheese Dairy, again in East Sussex). But in 1998, when his business was at its peak, supplying Harrods and the House of Commons, disaster struck when a case of e. coli poisoning was thought to have been traced to a Caerphilly made by Chris Duckett. Fatefully for Aldridge, he had seven tons of Duckett's cheese maturing in his cellars. Even though his stock was tested and found to be safe, he was forced to destroy all of it – £50,000 worth of cheese. A campaign raised

£20,000 for his cause, and Aldridge received a message of support from Prince Charles, the patron of the SCA, but his business was in ruins. He died in 2001, but is remembered in the James Aldridge Memorial Award, for cheeses nominated and judged by fellow SCA members. Two of this book's signature cheeses, Appleby's Cheshire and Stichelton, have won it, as, rather touchingly, has St James cheese, made by his onetime protégé, Martin Gott.

🐄   🐄   🐄

In 1992, Neal's Yard Dairy moved out of the yard and into the adjacent street, Short's Gardens. Not only was the shop larger, it had space for a cold room and that indispensable requirement for the serious affineur, a cellar. By having the cheese maturing underneath and literally in the shop, the Dairy was showing how much craft, experience and effort goes into making and finishing proper cheeses..

Others, too, were recognising the worth of British and Irish cheese. In 1994, New Zealand-born Juliet Harbutt, who had opened her wine and cheese shop, Jeroboams, in 1983, launched the British Cheese Awards. This was the first competition specifically to celebrate British cheeses and it has done much to forward the cause. Much as I have with the title of this book, its organisers employed a somewhat Gordian approach to the problem of what to call the awards, as Irish cheeses have not only entered but won the accolade of supreme champion several times over the years. In fact, the Celtic fringe made a good showing in the very first years, with top prize going to both Milleens and Celtic Promise. The latter is made by the Savage family, more founder members of the cheese renaissance, who came over to Wales from Holland in 1982.

In the late 1980s, Ann-Marie Dyas quit her career in advertising and marketing to open the Bath Fine Cheese Company, and joined Rance, Randolph and Aldridge in their quest to preserve the cheeses or Britain and Ireland. Over the next decade, ever

Juliet Harbutt at the British Cheese Awards, which she established in 1994. The latest event attracted 1,008 entries from 148 cheesemakers.

more people joined the campaign. In 1993, Iain Mellis opened the first of his Scottish cheese shops in the perfect environment of a 'small, damp, cave-like shop' in Edinburgh's Old Town. Mellis now has something of a Scottish cheese empire, with shops in Glasgow, Aberdeen and St Andrews. Over in Ireland, having begun with a modest market stall in Galway in 1995, Seamus and Kevin Sheridan founded Sheridans cheesemongers. There are now branches in Galway, Meath, Waterford and Dublin, from whose counters they champion the cause of Irish cheese as well as fancy imports.

The fancy foreign business is, of course, going stronger than ever in Britain. Patricia Michelson, founder of French cheese shop La Fromagerie (and author of the *World's Best Artisan Cheeses*), wins the Modest Beginnings cup for coming back from a skiing holiday with a wheel of Beaufort, which she sold out of her garden shed. This must have blown her luggage allowance sky-high, as a whole wheel weighs around forty-five kilos. Patricia opened her first shop in Highbury Park in 1992, where she matured French and other foreign cheeses in its cellars, adding to the portfolio over the years with shops in Marylebone and Bloomsbury. Notwithstanding the French name and the impressive Continental selection, British and Irish cheesemakers also feature strongly. At last count, the stock included almost a hundred cheeses from the British Isles.

On 9 November 1999 a parliamentary committee on agriculture sat to consider the state of cheesemaking in Britain. Among the witnesses it called was Mr Arthur Cunynghame, chair of the Specialist Cheesemakers Association and owner of the venerable Paxton & Whitfield – Winston Churchill's cheese shop of choice. If the committee were cheese fanciers, what they heard would have pleased them considerably. Although dairy farmers were struggling with the current milk price at below the cost of production, and regulations were still making life difficult for small-scale producers, cheese was back from the brink.

From the postwar low of 162, the number of cheesemakers in the UK had risen to 350 and the chair asked if there was any likelihood of the return of a 'glorious golden age of specialist cheesemaking'. Mr Cunynghame spoke of the renaissance of the last twenty years and, when pressed to guess how many new cheesemakers might appear over the next decade said, 'A thousand would be a realistic number to aim for.'

CHAPTER TEN

Postmodern cheese

Let a thousand cheeses bloom

2000–

OBVIOUSLY, ON A PERSONAL LEVEL, the most important thing that happened in 2000 was my first taste of Caerphilly at Borough Market, the epiphany that led me to become a cheesemonger. This was only a couple of years after Borough's debut as a retail market, but it was already bustling, as more and more people began to seek out local and authentic food. It wasn't just cheese, of course. A similar renaissance had been taking place with all sorts of food and drink products – notably beer, which, on a similar trajectory to cheese, had escaped its factory shackles to become 'Real Ale' in the 1980s before mutating into 'Craft Beer' in the new millennium.

Borough was part of a movement of farmers' markets and farm shops in Britain, which took off in a big way in the new millennium. Nowadays the Farm Retail Association lists more than three hundred farmers' markets – the majority in England, but with a good showing in Scotland, a fair scattering in Wales, two in Ireland, one in Northern Ireland and one on the Isle of Man – truly a movement spanning the British Isles.

Outlets such as Bath Farmers' Market, which opened in 1997 and gave Mary Holbrook her first outlet, and Perth Market, founded in 1999, were a godsend for small artisan producers. And there were many older markets, too, that were revived or given a new lease of life. York Market, established in 1086, shortly after the Harrying of the North, was one such, while the website for Ely Farmers' Market, which reopened for business in 2000, proudly boasts 'established 1216'. Caerphilly Market in Wales and Kilkenny in Ireland are of a similar vintage, while in Belfast the lovely Victorian covered market, St George's, has been thriving since renovation in 1999. Many of these markets had been brought to the point of extinction by competition from the supermarkets in the 1970s and '80s.

Farmers' markets tend to require traders to sell only food whose provenance is guaranteed. At Borough I was selling Todd's cheese – he would drive down from the farm at Llanddewi every week with a van-load for us to sell over the weekend. One notable Sunday, in the hot summer of 2001, we set up a stall together for his Caerphilly at Columbia Road flower market in Hackney. As it was a traditional market, the Royal Oak pub in its midst was allowed to open early to serve the traders.Todd and I had quite a few cooling pints throughout the day and somehow forgot to unload the van fully. Next week we discovered some boxes of Caerphilly that had spent a week in the van. This normally restrained and delicate cheese had become feisty and peppery, with a bouquet of ammonia and a rich creamy texture all the way through, as the overexcited mould rind had entirely broken down the cheese. We tried it, rather liked it and put it on one end of the stall with a sign saying 'Van Matured Caerphilly'. The customers really liked it. Indeed, twelve years later, at Borough, a chap came to the stall and said hopefully, 'I know this is a long shot, but I don't suppose you have any of the van-matured do you? I loved that cheese.'

I've often wondered how often cheese 'product diversification' actually occurs when someone has had a few too many pints. I'm also tempted to categorise that magic batch of Caerphilly under

Simon and Tim Jones and their Lincolnshire Poacher.

the term 'postmodern cheese'. For, after the renaissance of modern cheeses, postmodern has very definitely arrived on the table in the past couple of decades. What I mean by this is a playful mixing of styles and influences, a healthy iconoclasm about established varieties, and a crossing and recrossing of the boundaries between the science, craft and art of cheese.

Actually you could make a case for dating the origins of postmodern cheese to 17 February 1992, when Dougal Campbell turned up with a sachet of starter and a Schweppes tonic bottle full of rennet to make cheese with Simon Jones at Ulceby Grange Farm in Lincolnshire. On that day, Lincolnshire Poacher was born, and, probably as a result of Campbell's cheese apprenticeship in the

Swiss Alps, it turned out as a combination of Alpine and British cheese culture. Jones and his head cheesemaker Richard Tagg use a mixture of traditional British methods – for example, the process known as Cheddaring, in which the curd is set firmly and then cut into blocks and stacked – with some Swiss tweaks, such as heating the milk to a higher temperature than you would for Cheddar, and

Maggie Maxwell ironing one of her Gouda-shaped Doddington cheeses.

cutting the curd into smaller particles. The result is a cheese with some of the sharpness and savoury beefy notes of Cheddar but with some sweetness and even a note of chocolate that you will find in mountain cheeses like Gruyère or Comté.

Sometimes, if you are very lucky, Lincolnshire Poacher will have a pronounced pineapple flavour, which can be startling when you first come across it. I asked Richard if he knew where the pineapple flavour came from and he said, with some frustration, that he didn't, but it wasn't for want of trying to find out. He brought out a stack of notebooks, in which he'd recorded details like which field the cows were grazing in and the weather on a given day of cheesemaking, to try and work out what conditions correlated with the appearance of the pineapple. But the mystery remains.

There were other harbingers of postmodern cheese in the old century. In 1993, in the Cheviot Hills, Maggie Maxwell, the third generation of her family at Doddington Farm, began making a cheese she describes as a cross between Cheddar and Leicester; it combines the umami flavour and acidic bite of the former with the smoother texture of the latter. Maggie spent some of her cheesemaking apprenticeship in Holland and I notice a caramel sweetness in her cheese, too, much like that of an aged Gouda, which it resembles with its rounded edges and burgundy-coloured wax. But, for all its influences, this raw milk cheese, as its maker is proud to point out, is very much a product of Northumbria, and gets much of its character from the unique microflora living in the local pastures. Here is a cheese that combines three different cheesemaking traditions with its own unique terroir.

🧀 🧀 🧀

But let us return to the twenty-first century. In 2008, Bill Oglethorpe, the Zambian-born Boer who taught me all I knew of affinage in the Neal's Yard cellars, set up a business of his own called Kappacasein,

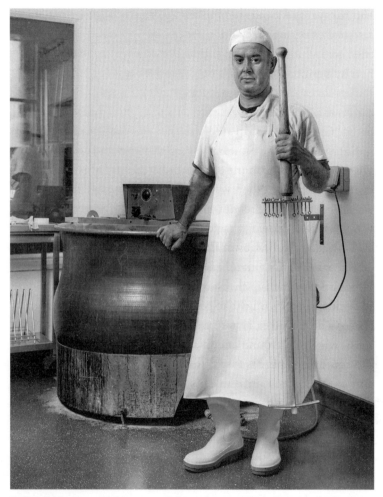

Bill Oglethorpe, with his vat and cheese harp, making Swiss style cheeses under the railway arches in Bermondsey.

named after the protein that is responsible for coagulating milk. His dairy is an old railway arch in Bermondsey, where, in an old-style copper vat, he makes a very traditional Swiss-style cheese called Bermondsey Hardpress. Bill describes the method for his cheese as 'traditional alpage Gruyère in a mature hardpress' and in his south London redoubt claims to get 'some of the more piquant and barnyardy flavours reminiscent of the French Abondance'. Bill also makes Bermondsey Frier, a Halloumi-style cheese that is nice fried, and alludes to the eleventh-century monastery that existed in nearby Bermondsey Square until the Dissolution, and Ricotta, an Italian cheese made from re-cooking the whey produced when he makes his other cheeses. So, just to recap: that's a Zambian making Swiss-, Greek- and Italian-style cheeses in a railway arch in London.

But it's not just Bill's cultural influences that are a bit of a mash-up. On the one hand he is one of the most rigorous cheesemakers I've ever come across. When we made cheese together in his arch, I was about to add the rennet when Bill, having checked the acidity with his titratable acidity meter, stopped me, produced a stopwatch and initiated a countdown. He records the length of time until his curd begins to coagulate, and monitors changes in the time to better understand his cheesemaking process. On the other hand, to decide when it's time to to get the curd out of the whey and into moulds, he just takes a handful of curd and squeezes it into a solid mass, wiggles it around and takes a bite, listening for the pitch of the squeak against his teeth. There's historical precedent for this sort of thing. The Cantal makers of the Auvergne, a truly ancient cheese whose forebears are mentioned in Pliny's *Naturalis Historia*, check when their curd is ready by squeezing a handful of curd and throwing it; the level of stickiness the cheesemaker feels as the curd leaves the hand tells them what they need to know.

Same, but different, is the story of Dave Holton, universally known as Aussie Dave for his place of birth and, for a brief period during a tangle with malaria, as Mossie Dave. He began his cheesemaking career in 2007 in the Yarra Valley in Victoria, Australia, where, curiously enough, he made a cheese inspired by Persian Feta. Then, in 2010, Dave met a Neal's Yard alumnus called Laurie Gutteridge, who was running a cheese shop in Melbourne. Having listened to Laurie's descriptions of Dairy life, he came over to London for a ten-day stint as a Christmas temp. This 'I'm just here for Christmas' thing has happened to a lot of Dairy mongers, and six months later Dave had made the move to affinage in the cellars, rubbing down and turning Cheshires and Lancashires, which keeps you fit but is not otherwise demanding. Things changed when Dave went on a French exchange, working at Hervé Mons' caves in Saint-Haon-le-Châtel in the Auvergne-Rhône Alpes. This turned him on to soft cheese. What sparked Dave's attention was how much attention they need – how soft, volatile cheeses can change 'in front of your eyes' and thus make the affineur's role one of substance.

Dave then set up his own company, Blackwoods Cheese, with a partner, Tim Jarvis, starting out by making Graceburn, an oil-marinated Feta like the one he had made back in Australia. But his soft cheese moment in France had instilled ambitions, and he and Tim decided to try making a cheese based on Langres, from the Champagne-Ardennes region. This creation was to be a lactic, Geotrichum-rinded, washed-rind cheese – 'lactic' referring to a slow coagulation relying on the acidity from the starter rather than rennet; Geotrichum denoting a wrinkly looking rind with a cabbagey flavour; and washed-rind you know all about from the monks. I couldn't help suggesting to Dave that he'd made a rod for his own back, to which he responded that they had decided to make the cheese because 'it was a tricky make and tricky to mature as well'. They called their creation Edmund Tew, after one of the convicts transported to Australia for stealing cheese in 1829. In the summer, when the milk they get from Commonwork Organic Farm in Kent is at its richest, they also make a soft, fresh cow's cheese called William Heaps (an 1838 cheese convict), best eaten only a few days old. They have no current plans to add further cheeses to the range, but there are apparently plenty more names from the 'transported to Australia for stealing cheese' category to choose from.

These newly created postmodern cheeses are far from clones. Edmund Tew, for example, doesn't look like a Langres – it's smaller, and, whereas the French cheese is a bright orange from the washing and a bit of extra colouring, Edmund is a creamy off-

Aussie Dave and Tim Jarvis on the make, creating their Edmund Tew cheeses.

white with highlights of terracotta. Its flavour is malty and fresh on the inside, a bit gentler than a ripe and funky Langres. The differences aren't just down to a different terroir. Dave and his fellow cheesemakers worked hard to develop the recipe and make it their own. Blackwoods Cheese was originally based in a lock-up in Brockley, and Dave, still doing a shift at Neal's Yard's maturing rooms in Bermondsey, would finish work there, drive down to Kent to pick up milk, and begin the cheesemaking that evening, coming back at 4 a.m. the next morning to ladle curd, a work schedule that Dave described laconically as 'pretty intense'. I wondered if Dave had changed the recipe to fit better with his life, but he pointed out that he's changed his life to fit the cheese, having moved house and dairy down to the farm in Kent where the milk is produced. That means they can collect milk in the morning and be ladling curd that afternoon, and even that seemingly small change will have altered how they make and mature the cheese.

🧀 🧀 🧀

In Gwynedd, north Wales, Dr Carrie Rimes makes, among other things, a sheep's milk cheese called Brefu Bach – 'Little Bleat' in Welsh. She began her career – as did Dave Holton – in environmental science, her field being grassland conservation. Unlike Dave, she managed to resist the lure of cheesemaking for some decades, and this carries over into her new career as an artisan cheesemaker. I don't think I've met anyone who speaks with such infectious enthusiasm about pasture. One of the first things she mentioned about her initial steps in cheesemaking were the 'beautiful, beautiful flower-rich meadows' in the Auvergne, where she learnt to make cheese with Raphaël Lefroc on his farm near La Chaise-Dieu.

Carrie did come from a farming background, though, having grown up on a small mixed farm in Devon. The farm had eighteen head of cattle, a flock of fifty sheep, chickens and pigs. This might sound like an idyllic environment, but, as Carrie said, in the 1970s it was hard to make a living out of farming on that scale. Rather than expand and intensify, her father decided to sell off the stock and retire, but Carrie's mother kept a couple of cows and carried on dairying. Even with just the two cows, there was still a huge amount of milk and, though they made 'stacks of clotted cream, and so many milk puddings I never wanted to see another one', there was still loads of surplus milk. So, of course, 'the obvious thing was to make cheese'.

The family had no history of cheesemaking – Devon is more famous for its clotted cream than its cheese – and Carrie and her mother looked for recipes in the *Farmers' Weekly* recipe book, *Farmer's Fare*, first published in 1935. This charming and eminently practical book is a repository of traditional farmers' kitchen cheese recipes. Carrie and her mother found one they liked the look of, punched some holes in cake tins to make cheese moulds and gave it a go. Things didn't go well. The cheeses were 'awful'. But it sparked in Carrie a lifelong passion to find the secret and magic of cheesemaking.

With hindsight, and as a professional cheesemaker, Carrie knows what the problem was with that first experiment. They were using skimmed milk, which, as the farmers of East Anglia discovered, doesn't tend to make good cheese. Also, their milk had been cooked, to produce clotted cream, and cooked milk has little chance of making good cheese.

Decades later, after her son had left home, Carrie felt it was now or never for cheesemaking, gave up her job, and enlisted in the WOOFING (World Wide Opportunities on Organic Farms) movement. This gave her the chance to make cheese on farms in the Auvergne and then the Pyrenees – where she worked at a 'tiny place' with no electricity and hand-milked herds of cows and sheep. She also made cheese in the Cévennes, in south-central France, where the sheep grazed in the chestnut forests, and among the flowery meadows and herb-rich uplands of the Montagne Noire, further south.

This working tour of some of France's major cheesemaking regions, each with their own traditional methods, using the milk from different local breeds, must have been a solid and thorough grounding in the craft of cheesemaking. And, if that wasn't enough, the next year Lefroc, the Auvergnat farmer, begged Carrie to come back and run his dairy – 'a rash move from his point of view', Carrie said, 'but there's nothing like being shoved in the deep end.' She ended up staying there for two years, making a sort of cross between Tomme and Saint-Nectaire, one of the traditional cheeses of the Auvergne, with milk from a 'motley collection of fifteen traditional-breed cows' who grazed on 'those beautiful, beautiful meadows'. Lefroc, like all the cheesemakers in the area, made lactic cheeses: small, soft and slow-setting fresh cheeses called *fromages blancs*, and a small mould-ripened cheese which Lefroc called Petit Bibi after his previous head cheesemaker.

Eventually, Carrie decided it was time to go home to Wales and begin cheesemaking on her own account. But, of course, she had to decide what cheese to make. With her love of lactic cheesemaking, Petit Bibi, or something like it, was the obvious choice But there was to be one major difference. In France, Carrie had made the Petit Bibi with cow's milk, but in Wales using sheep's milk seemed an obvious choice. Amazingly, Carrie recalls, there was no-one else making sheep's milk cheese in Wales at the time.

Sheep's and cow's milk have a quite different constitution: in sheep's milk the fat particles are smaller and more homogenous,

A Lleyn sheep – a traditional Welsh breed – back in the cheesemaking fold.

and this meant that Carrie had to adapt the recipe she had learnt in France. She also discovered that it's harder to make cheese with early-season sheep's milk – so hard that traditional producers in France don't even bother (they feed all of the early milk to the lambs). Carrie, however, persevered and worked out how to change her method to fit the season. In this, she acknowledges gratefully, she had the help of a modern institution, the Llangefni Food Technology Centre in Anglesey, set up in 1999 to 'develop Wales and the UK's reputation for producing and manufacturing innovative food and drink'. She also had a useful bursary from the Specialist Cheesemakers Association, named after Dougal Campbell.

Carrie had another problem to deal with, which was that no one seemed to be milking sheep in Wales, so at first she had to buy her milk from England. Then, on a Welsh TV farming programme, she said (in Welsh, of course) that it would be a great thing if people began milking sheep again in Wales. Not long after, a local farmer called Alan Parry Jones rang up and said he had been thinking about it. Seven months later, he rang again to say he had an offer of twenty Friesland ewes for milking, and should he buy them? Carrie said yes, knowing she would have to commit to taking all this milk. Recently, Jones has begun to change his flock over to a native Welsh breed called Lleyn, which Carrie says produce less milk – but what they give is 'lovely stuff, they're grass fed, out there grazing and it seems to work really well'. So, not only has Carrie had a hand in bringing sheep's milk back to Wales, she has helped to get a traditional breed back in the business.

All this work and a natural bent for cheesemaking paid off when Carrie's cheese, Brefu Bach, won a gold medal at the British Cheese Awards in 2016. But Carrie and her cheese need no external accolades, like generations of cheesemakers before her, 'her cheese is her judge and jury'. Brefu Bach is startlingly sweet, honeyed, with a delicate vegetal note from its *Geotrichum* rind and a luscious texture. It is an excellent cheese, made in Wales by a Devonian woman who learnt her cheesemaking from French producers, and then made their traditional recipe her own.

🧀 🧀 🧀

Renegade Monk, our next cheese, is postmodern par excellence. As a blue washed-rind, it fits into no previously existing category of cheese, as far as I know. Its creator Marcus Fergusson describes it as 'a sort of homage to those stinky Burgundian cheeses', and of course the second part of the name refers to, as Marcus says, 'a European monastic tradition of cheesemaking'. Marcus and Penny, his wife and co-conspirator, didn't want to go down the route of naming the cheese after a local village, and yet the Renegade hints at their location, just outside of Templecombe in Somerset, once a holding of the Knights Templar, the original renegade monks. Renegade is also a cheeky riposte to any scepticism from the cheese establishment about the viability of such a hybrid.

When you unwrap a Renegade Monk you may be reminded of an Époisses, the famous Burgundian washed-rind. It's a yellow-orange disk about five inches across with a wrinkly texture to the rind from the *Geotrichum*. And when you taste it...well, fellow cheesemonger and cheese judge Charlie Turnbull describes it as 'a vicious little cheese', which Marcus rightly took as a compliment. This is not to say that eating a Renegade is an unpleasant experience, but it is an intense and intriguing one. On the nose there are the funky and gamey aromas you would expect from a stronger washed-rind, fresh yeast, lots of salty umami, and a pronounced sweetness, as well as the piquant pepperiness of the blue. The finish is long. In a cheese and beer pairing session, my craft beer pals struggled to find a suitable partner among a large collection of barley wines, Belgian tripels and rich thick stouts, and so we ate a lot of Renegade. I woke the next morning with a gently persistent memory of its flavour still on my palate.

Renegade Monk – available at your local shop, if you live near Feltham's Farm.

A significant part of Renegade Monk's claim to postmodernity is that this cheese wasn't adapted from an existing style but was consciously designed from the outset. After Marcus quit his London job in corporate communications and the family moved to a small farm in Somerset, Marcus and Penny had to decide what to do with their new life. At twenty-two acres, the farm was too small to be economically viable and so they decided to develop a niche, high-value product (another of the many ways of saying 'cheese').

Having established this, they then had to plan what sort of cheese to make. There are two obvious ways you might do this. One would be to begin by making a very simple soft fresh cheese to get the hang of things, and then, in a sort of recapitulation of the last six thousand years of cheesemaking, develop a style from there. The other would be to look at the kind of cheese made in your area, 'the cheese the land wants you to make', in the words of Veronica Steele. Marcus did neither. Being in the very heart of Cheddar-making country, he felt 'there was no point in making Cheddar at all'. And in opposition to the idea of building from simple foundations, he wanted to 'throw everything I could at the cheese'.

Bold as it was, this approach seems to have worked. Although I wouldn't advise it for the faint-hearted, starting at the complex end of cheesemaking with a novel combination of two of the most ticklish styles to make – a washed-rind and a blue – has the advantage of speed, if you can pull it off. Marcus left his London job at the end of 2015 and sold his first Renegade Monk in March 2017. He began with a one-day course at River Cottage, then got a job with Bath Soft Cheese Company at their Park Farm dairy. Owned by the Padfield family since 1914, Park Farm originally produced Cheddar and, after a long cheeseless period, have since 1990 been making soft cheeses. Rejected at first because of his CV ('you'd be bored to death here', said Graham Padfield), Marcus confessed that he was planning to make cheese and would work for free. The Padfields took him on in a gesture typical of the open-spirited nature of so many cheesemakers; they were rewarded when he turned his hand to toning up their social media presence. After another course at the School of Artisan Food, based on the Welbeck Estate where Joe Schneider makes his Stichelton, and taught by the demandingly brilliant microbiologist-cheesemaker Paul Thomas, Marcus began making Renegade Monks in his kitchen, maturing them in a broken fridge that maintained a perfect temperature of twelve degrees.

These original cheeses developed blue veining right through them, but no environmental health officer in the world was going to let Marcus sell the products of his kitchen, and so, with the sage advice of Paul, Marcus built a dairy. Although he did what he could to make the transfer seamless, making the cheeses in the old place and bringing them through to mature, the end result is inevitably different. Renegade Monk no longer develops the blue

veining, but the flavour is still there. As Marcus says, 'you taste it
in the back of your nose', a phrase that immediately caused me to
identify the sensation I'd been experiencing: eating a Renegade
Monk is a bit like being dumped by a big wave.

Six months into production, Renegade won Best Artisan Soft
Cheese at the Global Cheese Awards, beating his old mentor Bath
Soft Cheese, a fact that apparently caused Graham Padfield much
amusement. Marcus is now planning to add some more cheeses
to his stable, and to expand, having secured an EU grant to build
a bigger dairy. It seems they also might be going into charcuterie,
since Penny has calculated that they will need up to a hundred
pigs to consume the whey from their expanded production. In
this she is following the advice given by Columella two thousand
years ago to anyone starting up cheesemaking for profit – that one
should pay attention to the ratio of pigs to pounds of cheese.

It's hard to know where to place Joe Schneider and his Stichelton in
the traditional/modern/postmodern cheese schema. You could see
it as a return to a previous tradition, or a recent offshoot. Perhaps
we should classify it as 'Modern Traditional', a category that has
been getting increasingly populated in recent years. In 2013,
another new Stilton style was born. Its maker was Mike Thomson,
who had his cheese epiphany at the Arcadia Deli in Belfast, and,
like Marcus Fergusson, went on the cheesemaking course at the
School of Artisan Food, before spending time at Neal's Yard Dairy,
at Manor Farm in Somerset where Montgomery's Cheddar is made,
and at Sparkenhoe Farm with the Clarke family. Having paid his
dues, Thomson went back to Newtonards in County Down, where
on an industrial estate, on 26 November 2013, he made his first
cheese – a raw milk blue with a very familiar shape and flavour
profile. Living outside the three Stilton counties – Nottinghamshire,

Mike Thomson with his Young Buck – Northern Ireland's answer to Stilton.

Leicestershire or Derbyshire – he was never going to be able to call it a Stilton, whether or not he pasteurised his milk. So, with admirable cheek, he named it Young Buck. Within the year he had bagged a silver medal from the Irish Cheese Awards.

In 2017 the Clarkes at Sparkenhoe Farm also started making a raw milk blue cheese. Their farm *is* in Leicestershire, so if it wasn't for the raw milk, this would have been the first new Stilton for a hundred years. Instead, this new addition to the burgeoning category of 'Modern Traditionals' that I have just invented, is called Sparkenhoe Blue.

The Clarkes are part of another movement in cheese that has been gathering momentum, in a completely different direction to postmodern cheese, but to be celebrated with equal joy. This is the

'Return of the Territorials'. In 2005, after a fifty-year absence from the cheeseboard, David and Jo Clarke brought back raw milk, cloth-bound farmhouse Red Leicester. When this first came into the Dairy, I found it peculiarly hard to get customers to give it a second glance, so poor was the reputation of its factory-made incarnation. But if you put a chunk on the end of a knife and got people to taste it, everyone wanted some. Sparkenhoe Red Leicester's deep orange colour is a harbinger of the rich yet subtle flavour of this wonderful cheese.

Farmhouse or Pickled Wensleydale, extinct since the post-war years, has also returned, in the form of the creamy blue-veined Stonebeck, handcrafted in Nidderdale, Yorkshire, with raw milk from a herd of just fifteen Northern Dairy Shorthorns. It is made by Andrew and Sally Hattan at their ecologically managed Low Riggs Farm, with pastures full of wildflowers, to a recipe researched from Wensleydale history and an interview with a 101-year-old cheesemaker. So the future of Wensleydale no longer rests entirely on the shoulders of Hawes Creamery. And the Hattans aren't alone. Over in Bedale, Andy Ridley is making a moist, open-textured cheese called Richard III that was originally made near Middleham (birthplace of the king) by a cheesemaker called Suzanne Stirke from her mother's old recipe.

That such extinct traditions of cheesemaking can be brought back to life is a joyful thing – and it is a trend that has happened to Double Gloucester, too. In Chedworth – in Gloucestershire, of course – Neil Robinson and Dominique Lizé-Beaulieu are making Chedworth Double Gloucester. Organic, and cloth-bound, like its traditional forebears, this cheese reverses a trend for the better-quality Double Gloucester cheeses to be dyed orange with annatto. Chedworth, which has a delicate buttery flavour, is the purest white.

Another thing I'm very excited about is the resurgence of East Anglia. Happily refuting the old idea that you can't make good cheese on Suffolk land, Jonathan and Dulcie Crickmore are making Baron Bigod at Fen Farm near Bungay. Unlike the old Suffolk Bang, this is not a cheese you could sharpen knives on, but a luxuriantly creamy Brie style, with flavours of mushroom, cabbage, cream and pepper. Dulcie and Jonathan also make rich, full-cream butter, and seem to be doing okay. Let's hope they don't make too much. Julie Cheyney, maker of the fudgey little cow's milk St Jude cheeses, moved her whole operation to Fen Farm because of its herd of French Montbéliarde cows, famed for the richness and quality of their milk. That's the kind of devotion you can expect from a great cheesemaker. And these are not the only cheeses driving the Anglian resurgence. In Norfolk, Catherine Temple is making the cow's milk Binham Blue, and Ferndale Farm Cheeses make Norfolk Dapple, a hard cloth-bound cow's cheese in a Cheddar style with a deep sunset-yellow colour.

Cheddar did not escape the attrition of the twentieth century. Rance counted 333 farms in the south-west making Cheddar in 1939. By 1974, three hundred had been lost and numbers dwindled through that decade. In Somerset, Montgomery's, Keen's, and Westcombe held the line, joined in Devon by Quickes. From the 1990s onwards, these stalwarts have been joined by newer cheeses from the rest of Britain. There is Hafod, the Welsh Cheddar, which we waved at in passing; and, to the east, Lincolnshire Poacher. Off the wet and windy west coast of Scotland, the Reade family make a Cheddar named after the Isle of Mull, on which they live. There isn't a lot of grass up there and the cattle get much of their nourishment from draff, the spent barley mash used to make Tobermory whisky on the isle's distillery. When I eat Isle of Mull, I can taste the peat and iodine notes I would expect from a single malt like this. I recommend trying the two together.

Most happily, on the Cheddar revival front, my old friends the Trethowans, who make the Caerphilly that got me into all this cheese malarkey in the first place, have for the last year been making a Cheddar called Pitchfork, which won a gold medal on its first appearance at the 2018 World Cheese Awards. Dropping in on the family on my way to Westcombe, I sat down with Todd and tried some. Moist, firm, subtle, with a gentle acidity, a little

Anglia resurgent: Jonathan Crickmore with his Baron Bigod.

sweetness and a hint of nuttiness, it would make those Cheddar giants F.J. Lloyd and Edith Cannon proud. Having moved their dairy from their old home in Llanddewi Brefi to Somerset, Todd points out that this must be the first new artisanal Somerset Cheddar for something like a hundred years.

🧀 🧀 🧀

Not only are there more markets, more new cheeses to sell in them and more curious customers to buy them, there are much broader outlets now for farmhouse and artisan cheeses. Supermarkets that once contributed to the disappearance of farmhouse cheeses by prioritising easily packaged produce, have recognised people's desire for more interesting fare. Waitrose, in particular, has dedicated cheese counters where you can buy freshly cut pieces from people with an enthusiasm and knowledge about proper cheese. And even on their regular shelves you can buy pre-cut pieces of some proper good cheeses, like Keen's Cheddar, Gorwydd Caerphilly and Appleby's Cheshire.

While I would always prefer to buy cheese from an independent retailer, where you have more chance of a nice chat over some samples, the appearance of interesting British cheeses in supermarkets has been a boon to their makers and their fans alike. This blessing, however, has been a mixed one. For the cheesemakers, the large orders from a supermarket can make a business, as long as they are not suddenly dropped without warning, and left with just a few months to find a replacement outlet. A cruel blow that has recently fallen on several cheesemakers I know, this should remind us to support smaller independently owned cheesemongers as much as we can, so that they can help keep cheesemakers like this in business.

Another significant trend in cheesemaking is a concern for sustainability, a concept that has shifted from hippie to mainstream since the new millennium. On the whole, the better the cheese, the better it is for the planet. Smaller herds, fed mostly on grass, hay and silage, produce vastly less methane than the huge herds with a diet consisting mostly of maize and other products unsuited to the cow's digestive system, and happier, healthier animals produce tastier more interesting cheese. Small mixed farms where exhausted arable fields are replenished when the animals are turned out on them to graze are a great way to preserve the health and vitality of topsoil, an issue that is becoming increasingly pressing.

Historically, cheesemaking has always had an elegance about it that suits the concept of sustainability, and before the introduction of artificial fertilisers it was a part of a virtuous circle, with grass-fed cows producing milk to make cheese, the whey from which was fed to pigs, whose dung fed the fields that grew the grass. Today, cheesemakers like Dave Holton, who minimises his waste production and water use, and Marcus Fergusson, who uses solar energy and ground-source heating to power and heat his dairy, and feeds his whey to grateful pigs, are enriching that tradition. It's nice to think that, when you buy an Edmund Tew or even a Renegade Monk to bring to a friend's dinner party, you're not just spreading the word of proper cheese, but championing the virtues of sustainability.

🧀 🧀 🧀

On 3 February 2019, after a short illness, Mary Holbrook, god-mother of British goat's cheese, maker of Sleightlett, and the first person I ever made cheese with, died on her farm just outside the village of Timsbury in Somerset. It was just turning from winter to spring, the goats had kidded, and the new cheesemaking season was about to begin.

Mary's funeral was held on an unseasonably warm and sunny day in February and my wife Imogen and I travelled from London to Bath and then into the deep countryside around the Mendip Hills to celebrate Mary's long and rich life. She was eighty-two when she died. The parish church of Timsbury, where the service was held, aptly named St Mary's, was packed with generations of cheesemakers, cheesemongers, farmworkers, customers and friends.

Of course, Mary's life was about so much more than cheese, and her niece Catherine spoke about her doctorate in Byzantine art, her love of music, her charity work and involvement in the local farmers' market in Bath. The parish priest in his eulogy reminded us of Mary's love of the land, and I thought about how she showed me the new saplings she was planting around the farm, cheerfully saying she wouldn't live to see them full grown, but adding, 'you've got to give something back'. It was a sad day but also a joyful one.

Just as there is a joyfulness in celebrating a long life well lived, there is also joy in seeing the legacy that someone has left. In Mary's case there was much to celebrate. First, the farm itself. Sleight Farm, as a small mixed farm, shouldn't by all accounts be a viable business, but under Mary's stewardship, and thanks to the market for her cheeses, it has survived and prospered. The call has gone out for a cheesemaker to come and take over the running of the dairy, and happily it looks as if the farm might carry on, producing the cheeses that Mary developed there. Under a new head cheesemaker they will probably develop a new character, and perhaps even some new cheeses will appear.

After Mary's funeral we gathered at the Royal British Legion bar, in a corrugated-iron building just down the road from the church. I stood there in the unseasonal afternoon sunlight streaming in the windows, with a pint of Bath Ale in my hand, thinking about Mary and looking round at a room full of people who had all in one way or another been influenced by her. I talked to to Randolph about a Mrs Longstaff, whom he knew in the 1980s when she was one of the few surviving farmhouse cheesemakers in the Dales, and to Charlie Westhead about his first faltering steps in cheesemaking. Dave Holton, who had also made cheese with Mary was there, and Owen Bailey, who worked with Mary looking after cheese in the maturing rooms at Neal's Yard Dairy. I made plans to go and see Martin Gott, who in 2006 began making the washed-rind St James on his farm in Cumbria and who learnt much about cheesemaking down at Timsbury.

In one corner of the bar, a huddle of cheesemakers and farmers discussed Brexit. I imagined similar groups of people having similar conversations in this very village down the ages: farmers, Cheddar makers and factors discussing the new American imports; yeomen and buyers from London talking about the competition from Cheshire; the reeve, the bailiff and some villeins from the local manor working out what to do with all the land made untenanted by the Great Mortality.

Mary Holbrook at Sleight Farm, with her happy, inquisitive goats.

Saying goodbye to our friends, we caught the bus back to Bath, a lovely trip through the Mendips, passing the patchwork of fields and hedgerows, made even more beautiful on this sunny and warm afternoon. I was thinking how I had come up with the idea for this book while I was making cheese with Mary, those simple Sleightlett cheeses that could have been made in the same way and in the same countryside six thousand years ago. At the time, my idea of cheese history was more linear and more progressive. I imagined that cheeses like Sleightlett were the ur-cheese and that all the other styles, mould ripened, washed-rinds, blues and hard cheeses had developed out of these, as cheeses and cheesemaking become more complex and sophisticated.

Now, that thought amuses me. I don't believe for a moment that Edith Cannon nor her cheeses were any less sophisticated than Bill Oglethorpe and his, nor was she a smarter and better cheesemaker than her forebears on Salisbury Plain six thousand years before her. Now, I see not only cycles in cheesemaking, from the boom times of the seventeenth and eighteenth centuries to the struggle with factories and imports in the nineteenth and twentieth, but also reflections and repetitions, as when Veronica Steele found the cheese the land wanted her to make, or Robin Congdon realised the direction his milk wanted to go in.

Whatever the next six thousand years have in store for the British Isles, I'm confident that we'll have plenty of cheese.

Some favourite cheeses

At last count, there are about 800 different cheeses being produced on a regular basis in the British Isles. Some are only available in small batches, sold locally. But most can be found at specialist cheese shops. Below are some personal favourites. You can also find an ever-expanding version of this list on my website, *www.CheeseTastingCo.uk*, along with links to the producers and a directory of specialist shops.

Fresh cheeses

This style of cheese employs the simplest and most low-tech method. Milk is soured and set and the resulting curd ladled into moulds with little if any more intervention. Served at anything from a day to not much more than a week old, these young cheeses have a delicate clean flavour such that they are best eaten earlier in your cheese session before more mature stronger styles. So as not to overwhelm their gentle flavour I would pair them with more subtle drinks. Crispy floral white wines or light jammy reds make considerate partners. Their soft texture also responds well to a quality lager or, if you're feeling expansive, champagne.

Caboc and Crowdie

Made by the Stone Family at Blarliath Farm, near Tain, Ross, Scotland.

Pasteurised cow's milk, veg. rennet.

Crowdie, made with skimmed milk, is a light soft cheese. Its more opulent sister cheese, Caboc, enriched with extra cream and rolled in oats, has an enticing yellow colour and tastes like slightly tangy clotted cream. According to legend this cheese was first made by Mariota de l'Ile for her father, the chief of the MacDonald Clan – luxury full cream cheeses were the perks of the rich in the old days. Happily in this more democratic age, Caboc is available to all.

Perroche

Made by Charlie Westhead and his team at Neal's Yard Creamery, near Dorstone, Herefordshire, England.

Pasteurised goat's milk, veg. rennet.

A cheese so simple and delicate that it welcomes added flavourings. Perroche comes rolled in herbs like rosemary or dill, or in a plain version, to which you could add your own flavours – smoked paprika, roasted garlic or crumbled honeycomb are three of my favourites. That is not to say that, with its citrussy flavour and moussy texture, it cannot be enjoyed as nature intended. Big bold New World reds can work with this cheese, its bright acidity bringing out their dark fruit notes.

Sleightlett

Made on Sleight Farm, near Bath, Somerset, England.

Unpasteurised goat's milk, animal rennet.

Small snowy discs with a dusting of ash, these cheeses are best enjoyed before they have had time to develop a rind and, like most goat's milk cheeses they are only available for a limited season – from early spring to autumn. Although they are firmer and more strongly flavoured than Perroche, Sleightletts have only the merest hint of goatiness about them, making them excellent starter cheeses for the novice goat fancier.

Mould-ripened cheeses

This style of cheese is ripened by a layer of mould that is encouraged to grow on the outside of the cheese, forming the rind. Actually there tend to be a whole unruly gang of microbial organisms on the rind – moulds, yeasts and bacteria all jostling for position on the more interesting cheeses. The most widely recognised is the mould *Penicillium camemberti*, responsible for the felty-white coat familiar to us from the more industrial versions of Camembert and Brie. Where the surface of the cheese is pure white and flat, *Penicillium camemberti* has been added in considerable quantity so that it will outcompete any other opportunistic microorganisms and produce a consistent flavour and appearance. I suggest seeking out the uglier fruits of the family, whose wrinkled, brainy appearance and orange flecks denote the presence of *Geotrichium candidum*, which adds cabbagey flavours, and *Coryneform* bacteria, which adds an element of funk. As these cheeses ripen they produce ammonia, the more intense the ammoniac aroma, the riper your cheese is (make your own judgement about how ripe is too ripe). The presence of a firmer chalky band in the centre of the cheese is a sign of youth but doesn't necessarily mean it is underripe; French affineurs call that chalky stripe *l'âme du fromage*, the soul of the cheese.

Monsieur Androuet, the guv'nor of French cheese writing, suggests pairing Brie with 'fruity, lively reds: Beaujolais-Villages, Pommard, Volnay Savigny-les-Beaune', and Camembert with the 'suave, fruity and elegant wines of Burgundy, Bordeaux and Côtes-du-Rhône'. All those options should keep you occupied for a while with their British Isles relatives.

Baron Bigod

Made by Jonny Crickmore and his team on Fen Farm, near Bungay, Suffolk, England.

Unpasteurised cow's milk, animal rennet.

The original Bigod was a Norman lord who also Earl of Norfolk. A fitting name, then, for a Norfolk cheese based on the most famous French cheese of all time – Brie. The Crickmores' herd of Montbéliarde cows, a French breed famed for the quality of their milk, graze on the rich and varied pastures of Stow Fen. Breed and terroir contribute to the rich, golden yellow colour of this outstanding cheese.

Brefu Bach

Made by Carrie Rimes, Ffarm Moelyci, Bangor, Gwynedd, Wales.

Unpasteurised sheep's milk, animal rennet.

Displaying a honeyed sweetness common to many soft sheep's cheeses, this meltingly creamy cheese gets its character from the local pastures and in part from a local breed of sheep called Lleyn, brought back to cheesemaking after a long hiatus. *Brefu Bach* means 'little bleat' in Welsh.

Flower Marie

Made by Kevin and Alison Blunt on Greenacres Farm, near Hailsham, Sussex, England.

Unpasteurised sheep's milk, veg. rennet.

Flower Marie was developed by the late cheesemonger and affineur James Aldridge, who taught the Blunts how to make it in the 1990s. A cheese as pretty as its name, these pillowy white cubes look like little fluffy clouds as they grow their rinds in the cellar. When young they have a refreshing acidity, and as they age this softens into a rich creaminess.

Kevin and Alison also make **Golden Cross** – a dense, nutty goat's cheese log made from unpasteurised milk with vegetable rennet. It's made along the lines of a Loire valley St Maure.

Ragstone

Made by Charlie Westhead and his team at Neal's Yard Creamery, near Dorstone, Herefordshire, England.

Pasteurised goat's milk, veg. rennet.

The wrinkly rind of a Ragstone suggests the presence of *Geotrichium*, the yeasty mould with a vegetal flavour. Ragstone has a texture somewhere between fluffy and dense and, as it ages, bright fresh flavours round out and are joined by a slight goaty tang.

Charlie also makes **Dorstone**, another mould-ripened goat's cheese that has a more moussy open texture and a bright acidity, and **Finn**, a luxuriant double cream cow's cheese named after his dog.

St George

Made by Lyn and Jenny Jenner on Nut Knowle Farm, Hailsham, Sussex, England.

Pasteurised goat's milk, veg. rennet.

Nut Knowle are stalwarts of London and Sussex farmers' markets, offering a dozen or so proper goat's cheeses. St George is their Camembert-style flagship, equally good fresh, or mature and a bit runny, with a nice bloomy rind.

They also do lovely, seasonal fresh garlic-wrapped cheeses, the washed-rind **Martlet Gold**, and a fine blue goat's cheese called **Blue Knowle**.

St Jude

Made by Julie Cheyney on Fen Farm near Bungay, Suffolk, England.

Unpasteurised cow's milk, animal rennet.

Small, fudgey and perfectly formed, clean and fresh with just a hint of cowiness, St Jude is consistently one of my favourite cheeses. Lovely in the springtime with a glass of pink fizz.

Tunworth

Made by Stacey Hedges and Charlotte Spruce at Hampshire Cheeses on Scratchface Lane, Herriard, Hampshire, England.

Pasteurised cow's milk, animal rennet.

'The best Camembert in the world', says Raymond Blanc. Quite a claim, but when you taste this feisty cheese with its wrinkly rind and unctuous cabbagey paste you will see what he means. A great cheese for a cheeseboard, Tunworth can also be baked in its box for extra indulgence. Add a sliver or two of garlic, a sprig of rosemary and a glug of a fruity white wine, stick it in the oven for half an hour, dip bread into molten cheese goo, be happy.

Tymsboro

Made on Sleight Farm, near Bath in Somerset, England.

Unpasteurised goat's milk, animal rennet.

A flat-topped pyramid based on the iconic Valençay from France, Tysmboro with its thick blue-green eiderdown of mould rind is salty, peppery, goaty and delicious. This must be the most well-known of the late Mary Holbrook's cheeses. When you try it, you will see why she became known as the godmother of British goat's cheese.

Wigmore

Made by Anne and Andy Wigmore at Village Maid Cheeses, Riseley, Berkshire, England.

Unpasteurised sheep's milk, veg. rennet.

Forget everything I said about seeking out wrinkly cheeses with orange flecks, this smooth-surfaced cheese is a pure unblemished white, and it is delicious. While the curd is still in the vat, Anne Wigmore runs off some of the acidic whey and replaces it with hot water. This washing step creates a sweeter, creamier flavour and a wonderful silky texture.

Washed-rind cheeses

Washed-rinds are the Marmite of the cheese world. Pungent and sticky, they either appeal or repel. Actually, a washed-rind's bark is usually worse than its bite and, once past their aroma (described worshipfully by the French as *les pieds de dieu* or 'the feet of god'), you will be rewarded with a splendid array of flavours – umami, smoke, brine, cream, cabbage and a hint of the barnyard. Many washed-rinds are washed in various sorts of booze, but all are first washed in brine. The salty water keeps off mould and encourages the pink, sticky bacterial rind that gives them flavour.

Pairing such forthright cheeses with drinks can be a bit of a challenge. A red Burgundy can be a good complement; sweet, heady barley wines and super-rich old-style porters combine with its texture to create a sumptuous mouthfeel; and champagne cleanses the palate.

Cardo

Made on Sleight Farm, near Bath, Somerset, England.

Unpasteurised goat's milk, veg. rennet.

Cardo is delicate for a washed-rind cheese, with a hint of bitterness from the cardoon thistle rennet that gives backbone to the flavour. Yet another thoroughbred from the stable of Mary Holbrook, Cardo is a rare thing, indeed – a washed-rind goat's cheese.

Celtic Promise

Made by John Savage-Onstwedder and his team on Glynhynod Farm, Llandysul, Ceredigion, Wales.

Unpasteurised cow's milk, veg. rennet.

Two-times supreme champion at the British Cheese Awards, this firm, buttery cheese has a fruity flavour that might come from the cider it is washed in. An off-dry cider would be a good partner for it, or a glass of Dà Mhìle Welsh whisky, which is distilled at the very same farm.

Durrus

Made by Jeffa Gill in Coomkeen, near Bantry, County Cork, Ireland.

Pasteurised cow's milk, animal rennet.

On the wet and salty Atlantic coast, West Cork is a good place to make washed-rinds, but it's not just the atmosphere. Growing on fertile chocolatey soil, the lush pasture produces excellent milk for cheesemaking, and of course Jeffa's forty years of experience helps, too. Durrus has a creamy texture and an earthy flavour with just a hint of white chocolate.

Edmund Tew

Made by Dave Holton and his team at Blackwoods Cheese Company, near Chiddingstone, Kent, England.

Unpasteurised cow's milk, animal rennet.

Named after a convict transported for stealing cheese, and based on a Langres from the Champagne region, this wrinkled, pudgy little cheese has notes of malt, yeast and funk in its flavour. I like it with a Belgian-style saison beer.

Gubbeen

Made by Giana Fergusson at Gubbeen House, Schull, County Cork, Ireland.

Pasteurised cow's milk, animal rennet.

Gubbeen means 'little mouthful' in Irish, which nicely signals its delicacy; this springy-textured cheese is very gentle and would make a great introduction to the wonderful world of washed-rinds, as well as a perfect cheese to start the day with. I personally have never been able to confine myself to a single little mouthful, though. I like it melted with a garlicky pickle.

Milleens

Made by Quinlan Steele at Milleens Far, Eyries, County Cork, Ireland.

Pasteurised cow's milk, animal rennet.

With its smoky and meaty flavours, there is a tang of bacon about this brilliant cheese. It would make a fantastic tartiflette, the Alpine dish of potatoes, melted cheese, bacon, butter and cream, but it is just as at home on a cheeseboard accompanied with a hunk of sourdough and a glass of something authoritative.

Renegade Monk

Made by Marcus Fergusson on Feltham's Farm near Templecombe, Somerset, England.

Pasteurised cow's milk, veg. rennet.

Is it a washed-rind? Is it a blue? This modern, genre-bending cheese, named for the renegade Templar monks as much as for its maverick status, has a raucous flavour with an eye-watering hit of ammonia. Not for the faint-hearted, but a whole lot of fun.

St James

Made by Nicola Robinson and Martin Gott on Holker Farm, Cartmel, Cumbria, England.

Unpasteurised sheep's milk, animal rennet.

Although its square shape is reminiscent of Italian Taleggio, St James owes more of a debt to Lancashire in that the milk is left to sour slowly overnight. Martin Gott first learnt to make cheese with Graham Kirkham, celebrated maker of Kirkham's Lancashire, before he and Nicola went to work with Mary Holbrook in Somerset. The cheese is named after James Aldridge, heroic monger of the 1970s and beyond, who originally inspired Martin to make cheese.

Stinking Bishop

Made by Charles Martell on Hunt Court Farm near Dymock, Gloucestershire, England.

Pasteurised cow's milk, veg. rennet.

Fittingly, given its name, Stinking Bishop smells pretty funky, and yet like many washed-rinds, the aroma belies its milder flavour. Surprisingly the cheese isn't named for its odour, but after a variety of pear used to make the Perry it is washed in. The pear itself is named for a nineteenth-century farmer whose behaviour was so appalling that locals called him Stinking Bishop.

Blue cheeses

Blue cheeses get their characteristic piquant flavour from the addition of blue mould, *Penicillium roqueforti*, which most modern cheesemakers buy in powder form and add to the milk in the vat. Then, during maturation, the cheeses are pierced to allow air in that encourages the mould to grow. The flavour in a blue cheese comes from the ripening action of the mould rather than the flavour of the mould itself. Therefore, look for cheeses with an even distribution and fairly low proportion of blue to cheese for a balanced and complex flavour, or enjoy the intensity of a heavily blued cheese. Most blue cheeses are soft or semi-soft, the open texture allowing the blue mould to spread more easily throughout the cheese.

Traditionally the British have enjoyed blue cheese, especially Stilton, with port. But only the more expensive vintage ports have the subtlety needed not to overwhelm the cheese, and I prefer to eat them with sweet sticky dessert wine or a rich dark porter.

Beenleigh Blue

Made by Ben Harris and Robin Congdon near Totnes in Devon, England.

Pasteurised sheep's milk, veg. rennet.

Sweet, fruity and fudge-textured, younger Beenleighs are delicate and slightly floral, sometimes reminding me of tutti-frutti ice cream. Older cheeses can pack a heftier punch. Their original maker, Robin Congdon, declared that 'the cheesemaker only guides the milk in the direction it wants to go'.

Binham Blue

Made by Catherine Temple on Copys Green Farm, near Wells-next-the-Sea, Norfolk, England.

Pasteurised cow's milk, veg. rennet.

Sweet and delicate, with restrained blueing, Binham Blue is closer to a Gorgonzola Dolce than a Stilton, while the rich milk of Temple's Swiss Brown cows gives the cheese an indulgent creamy texture. The cattle are grass-fed on the lush local meadows, and the milk is heated using biomass fuel.

Cashel Blue

Made by Geurt Van Den Dikkenberg and the Grubb Family on Beechmount Farm, County Tipperary, Ireland.

Pasteurised cow's milk, veg. rennet.

With its buttery texture, this gentle yet complex cheese is a great way to introduce people to the blues. Tiring of turning hundreds of cheeses, Louis Grubb invented a system in which whole shelves can be spun in one go, just one aspect of his dairy's ingenuity and attention to detail.

Cashel's sister cheese, **Crozier Blue**, is more strongly flavoured, its peppery heat coming from the sheep's milk used to make it.

Colston Bassett Stilton

Made by Billy Kevan and his team in Colston Bassett, Nottinghamshire.

Pasteurised cow's milk, animal rennet.

As well as being hand-ladled, this fine Stilton owes its luxuriant texture and rounded sweetness to the animal rennet used to set the milk. Alongside the malty and umami flavours common to many great blue cheeses, Colston Bassett Stilton can show a startling note of bubblegum. Colston Bassett also has a long, unbroken tradition: Billy Kevan is only its fourth head cheesemaker in the last hundred years.

Dorset Blue Vinny

Made by the Davies Family on Woodbridge Farm, near Sturminster Newton, Dorset.

Pasteurised cow's milk, veg. rennet.

Revived after its postwar demise, this traditional Dorset cheese is made with skimmed milk. The Davies family skim by hand so that, while Vinny is harder than most blue cheeses, it retains a moist, giving texture. Thankfully they have forgone the other tradition, of blueing the cheese by dragging a bit of harness tack through the vat. Dark veins permeate the cheese evenly, conferring a strong blue flavour on this characterful cheese.

Lanark Blue

Made by the Errington family near Carnwath in South Lanarkshire, Scotland.

Unpasteurised sheep's milk, animal rennet.

Scotland's answer to Roquefort, this strong salty blue gets its character from the red sandstone and basalt soils on which the Erringtons farm. Lanark also revives a long-lost local tradition of making blue sheep's cheeses that according to Walter Scott were 'as good as Stilton'. If you were feeling bold, you could pair this cheese with a smoky, saline, Islay single malt.

The Erringtons also make a cow's milk version called **Dunsyre Blue**.

Sparkenhoe Blue

Made by Jo and David Clarke on Sparkenhoe Farm, near Nuneaton, Warwickshire, England.

Unpasteurised cow's milk, animal rennet.

Sparkenhoe Blue has a dense, chewy texture and the light shade of the blue mould imparts a subtlety to the flavour. Restrained yet complex, this is a welcome addition to the growing family of raw milk Stilton-style cheeses adorning cheese counters and cheeseboards throughout the British Isles.

Stichelton

Made by Joe Schneider and his team at Collingthwaite Farm, Nottinghamshire, England.

Unpasteurised cow's milk, animal rennet.

A raw milk Stilton-style cheese, Stichelton has a luscious fondant texture and a rich, complex flavour, with notes of malt and Marmite. This comes from a combination of happy healthy cows, raw milk and the skill and diligence of its makers. By law all Stilton must be pasteurised, so this cheese gets its name from the old Anglo-Saxon spelling of its disputed home town, Stichelton.

Young Buck

Made by Mike Thomson in Newtonards, near Belfast, County Down, Ireland.

Unpasteurised cow's milk, animal rennet.

Made in Northern Ireland – rather than the traditional Stilton counties of Nottinghamshire, Leicestershire or Derbyshire – this cheese can't be called Stilton; hence its rather cheeky name. And it is doubly disqualified, like Stichelton, as it is made with unpasteurised milk. This endows Young Buck with a pleasingly robust flavour, a hint of minerality and considerable length.

Semi-soft

Semi-soft cheeses are the result of more interventions during the make than tend to occur for soft cheese, which include heating the curd and cutting it to release more whey. The category is a broad church which contains others within it – firmer blue cheeses like the Stiltons covered above, for example – as well as a cheese like Gorwydd Caerphilly, with its velvety rind that is both semi-soft and mould-ripened.

Cornish Yarg

Made by Catherine Mead at Lynher Dairies, near Truro, Cornwall, England.

Pasteurised cow's milk, animal rennet.

Based on a Caerphilly recipe, nettle-wrapped Cornish Yarg is a strong contender for most beautiful cheese in the world with its deep green colour, highlights of white mould and the fern-like patterns of the leaves. The leaves inhibit mould growth and preserve the cheese's firmness and fresh acidity. Yarg was developed from a 17th century recipe in the 1980s by Bodmin cheesemakers Jenny and Alan Gray, and the name, as authentically Cornish as it sounds, is 'Gray' backwards.

Lynher Dairies also make **Cornish Kern**, a dense-textured Gouda-style cheese with a crystalline crunch.

Duckett's Caerphilly

Made by Tom Calver and his team on Westcombe Farm, Evercreech, Somerset, England.

Unpasteurised cow's milk, animal rennet.

For some years Chris Duckett was a keeper of the flame – the only person still making a traditional farmhouse Caerphilly, an accident of history meaning that Somerset rather than Wales was the repository of Caerphilly tradition. Tom Calver took over the recipe, returning the cheese to its original raw milk status when Chris passed away in 2009. With only a narrow strip of creamy breakdown, Duckett's is quite firm for a Caerphilly and has a clean flavour with a hint of minerality.

Dunmanus

Made by Jeffa Gill in Coomkeen, near Bantry, County Cork, Ireland.

Unpasteurised milk, animal rennet.

Dunmanus is only made in summer, when the cows are out grazing on the luscious and salty pastures of Dunmanus Bay. With its semi-soft texture and thin grey rind, this cheese is reminiscent of an Alpine Tomme. And, like a Tomme, its milder flavour makes it good for ploughman's lunches, melting or just hearty snacking. The Fergusons keep it out of the fridge in their kitchen and call it a 'table cheese'.

Gorwydd Caerphilly

Made by the Trethowan family at Trethowan's Dairy, near Weston-Super-Mare, Somerset, England.

Unpasteurised cow's milk, animal rennet.

Gorwydd Caerphilly is the reason I became a cheesemonger, so don't expect me to be objective. Of course, I think it is one of the greatest cheeses in the world. But you don't have to take my word for it. Gorwydd has won so many awards over the years it's becoming a bit embarrassing. Take the 2005 World Cheese Awards, for example, when the Trethowans scooped up a gold for Caerphilly, won Best Welsh Cheese and overall Best British Cheese. With distinct textures and flavours from its rind (velvety mushrooms), its breakdown (cabbagey cream) and its centre (crumbly citrus), you get three cheeses for the price of one.

Maisie's Kebbuck

Made by the Errington Family near Carnwath in Lanarkshire, Scotland.

Unpasteurised cow's milk, animal rennet.

This smooth, white, cloth-bound cheese, reminiscent of a Wensleydale, is clean and fresh with a herbaceous hint. Kebbuck (also spelled Caboc) is a Scots dialect word for a whole cheese.

Richard III Wensleydale

Made by Andy Ridley at Rostock Dairy, Barton, Lancashire, England.

Pasteurised cow's milk, animal rennet.

If you think Wensleydale is a hard cheese, you might be surprised to see it in this category, but Richard III is based on a prewar style, when the cheese was much more moist and soft. So much so that in the 1930s much of the cheese was blue and considered by its fans the equal of Stilton. This cheese was originally made by Susan Stirke to her mother's old recipe in Middleham, a Yorkshire market town that was the childhood home of Richard III.

Seator's Orkney

Made by Anne Seator on Grimbister Farm, Kirkwall, Orkneys, Scotland.

Unpasteurised cow's milk, veg. rennet.

You can age Seator's to the point where it develops a mould rind and more creamy texture, but I like it when it is still young, crumbly and lactic with a citrussy tang. Anne Seator's mother Hilda originally made this cheese without using any started culture at all – a truly ancient way to make cheese.

Hard cheeses

To create hard cheese, the curd is heated to a higher temperature and, for many British cheeses, cut into blocks; these are just turned in the case of crumbly cheeses, or turned and stacked for even harder cheeses like Cheddar. The blocks are then milled into small pieces and salted before being put into moulds. Removing more moisture means that the cheeses can be matured for longer to develop more intense and more complex flavours.

Applebys Cheshire

Made by Garry Gray and the Appleby family on Hawkstone Abbey Farm, near Shrewsbury, Shropshire, England.

Unpasteurised cow's milk, animal rennet.

Sunset pink, at least for Southerners (a white version is sold in the North), this moist and crumbly cheese has a delicate flavour with a hint of minerality. When it's absolutely banging, Sarah Appleby refers to it as 'juicy'. Lovely.

Bermondsey Hard Pressed

Made by Bill Oglethorpe and his team at Kappacasein Dairy, London, England.

Unpasteurised cow's milk cheese, animal rennet.

This impeccably authentic Alpine-style cheese is made in a railway arch in Bermondsey. Like its cousins from the Swiss and French Alps, it has a supple texture and a sweet and spicy flavour.

Bill and his team also make a Halloumi style called **Bermondsey Frier** and a **Ricotta** from the whey that is a by-product of their cheesemaking.

Coolea

Made by Dickie Willems at Coolea Farmhouse Cheeses Ltd, in Macroom, County Cork, Ireland.

Pasteurised cow's milk, animal rennet.

With its caramelised sugar flavour, this is the sweetest cheese that I know. It is based on a Gouda recipe that Dickie Willems' Dutch parents began making as a sort of hobby when they moved to Ireland in the late 1970s. Victims of their own success, they sold so much that they had to turn the cheesemaking into a business.

Doddington

Made by Maggie Maxwell on Doddington Farm, near Wooler, Northumberland, England.

Unpasteurised cow's milk, animal rennet.

Maggie Maxwell says that Doddington is a hybrid of Leicester (with its dense, slightly creamy texture) and Cheddar (for its savoury tang). Her cheeses have rounded edges and a deep-red rind, like Edam, which makes sense as she learnt to make cheese in Holland. Doddington also has some of the sweetness of a classic Gouda.

Dunlop

Made by Ann Dorward on Clerkland Farm, near Dunlop, Ayrshire, Scotland.

Pasteurised cow's milk, animal rennet.

When young, Dunlop has a smooth texture and a sweet, nutty flavour. As the cheese ages, it hardens and develops a sharper flavour. It is made from the milk of the local Ayrshire breed and represents a tradition reaching back to the seventeenth century, when one Barbara Gilmour came back from Ireland with a recipe for full-cream cheese. Her cheese was so good, the locals accused her of witchcraft.

Hafod

Made on Holden Farm near Lampeter, Ceredigion, Wales.

Pasteurised cow's milk, animal rennet.

Hafod is based on a recipe from Dora Saker's *Practical Cheddar Cheese-making* book, published in 1917. Its low and slow make results in a mild yet complex, moist soft cheese. It is so soft, you may find it hard to believe it really is a Cheddar.

Hawes Wensleydale

Made at Wensleydale Creamery, Hawes, Yorkshire, England.

Pasteurised cow's milk, animal rennet.

The fact that I've included a Wensleydale in two different cheese categories – semi-soft and hard – encapsulates the story of this cheese. Hawes Wensleydale (and I personally prefer their Kit Calvert special edition) is more reminiscent of the harder cheeses made during the Second World War. The texture is firmer than prewar styles and the flavour is clean and fresh with a hint of green herbs.

Isle of Mull Cheddar

Made by the Reade family on Sgriob-ruadh Farm on the Isle of Mull, Argyll, Scotland.

Unpasteurised cow's milk, animal rennet.

The Reades' cattle are fed partly on draff – the spent barley mash used to make whisky – and their Cheddar has a paler colour than its southern counterparts, where the animals eat more grass. I also believe that the draff imparts some of the flavours of a single malt. It certainly goes well with the local Tobermory whisky.

Keen's Cheddar

Made by the Keen family on Moorhayes Farm, near Wincanton, Somerset, England.

Unpasteurised cow's milk, animal rennet.

Keen's is a Cheddar with authority, as befits a cheese that has been made on the same farm by the same family for five generations. Its relatively high moisture content encourages vigorous bacterial activity during ripening, resulting in a mouth-tingling acidity and a bit of wild sulphuric flavour alongside classic Cheddary earthiness.

Kirkhams Lancashire

Made by Graham Kirkham on Beesley Farm, near Goosnargh, Lancashire, England.

Unpasteurised cow's milk, animal rennet.

'Butter crumble' is what Graham Kirkham calls the texture of his cheese, and that's a perfect description. The flavour is buttery, too, with just a hint of acidity to give it some edge, and Kirkhams makes great cheese on toast (crumbled not grated). Graham's mother, Ruth Kirkham, began making Lancashire on their farm in 1978, a harbinger of the farmhouse revival.

Lincolnshire Poacher

Made by Simon Jones and Richard Tagg on Ulceby Grange Farm, near Alford, Lincolnshire, England.

Unpasteurised cow's milk, animal rennet.

The lovechild of Cheddar and Gruyère, Poacher owes its savoury and nutty flavour to its Somerset cheesemaking tradition and its sweetness and supple texture to Alpine methods. Sometimes, if you are lucky, there can be a pronounced pineapple flavour. Nobody knows why.

Lord of the Hundreds

Made by the Dyball family at the Traditional Cheese Dairy, near Stonegate, Sussex, England.

Unpasteurised sheep's milk, animal rennet.

Similar to a young unpressed Pecorino, Lord of the Hundreds has a deep, comforting flavour with notes of honey and hazelnuts. The recipe was originally developed by James Aldridge, an iconic figure among cheesemakers.

Martell's Double Gloucester

Made by the Martell family on Hunt Court Farm near Dymock, Gloucestershire, England.

Unpasteurised cow's milk, veg. rennet.

In 1973, when Charles Martell handmilked his three Gloucester cows to make his first batch of Double Gloucester, it was the first time this succulent, richly coloured cheese had been made in the county for around twenty years.

Martell actually began making cheese in order to bring Gloucester cows back from the edge of extinction. And, in 1978, he also began making **Single Gloucester**, a lighter cheese with a gentle lactic flavour.

Montgomery's Cheddar

Made by Jamie Montgomery and Steve Bridges on Manor Farm, North Cadbury, Somerset, England.

Unpasteurised cow's milk, animal rennet.

Everything about a Monty's is impressive. The cheese comes in tall, imposing cylinders with a grey-brown cloth coat, and upon opening they present a deep orange-yellow colour, a foretaste of delights to come. Elegance, complexity and balance characterise the texture – a combination of dense friability and moisture – while its flavour takes in brothiness, earth and a perfect edge of acidity. This is truly one of the great Cheddars – indeed, one of the great cheeses of the world.

Norfolk Dapple

Made by Ellie Betts on Ferndale Farm, Little Barningham, Norfolk, England.

Unpasteurised cow's milk, animal rennet.

With its pretty dappled rind, soft creamy texture and sweet nutty flavour, Norfolk Dapple shows that the terroir of East Anglia produces excellent cheese. As a small mixed farm, Ferndale confounds expectations in this age of large-scale agribusiness. Small is still beautiful.

Pitchfork Cheddar

Made by the Trethowan Family at Trethowan's Dairy, near Weston-Super-Mare, Somerset, England.

Unpasteurised cow's milk, animal rennet.

The new kid on the block, Pitchfork is Somerset's first new artisan Cheddar for perhaps a hundred years. It is elegant, clean, with a pliant texture and reserved acidity, and already a bit of a classic, winning Best Traditional Cheddar at the British Cheese Awards in 2019.

Quicke's Cheddar

Made by Malcolm Mitchell and the Quicke family on Home Farm, Newton St Cyres, Devon, England.

Pasteurised cow's milk, animal rennet.

The Quicke family have been farming their land for more than four hundred years, and it's obvious from their cheeses that they have put this experience to good use. Sir John Quicke brought Cheddar-making back to the farm in the 1970s, and his daughter Mary carries on his legacy with an infectious and inspiring enthusiasm. There's a cheese for every palate, from the buttery creaminess of their younger Cheddar to the depth and intensity of their two-year-old Vintage Clothbound.

Sparkenhoe Red Leicester

Made by Jo and David Clarke on Sparkenhoe Farm, near Nuneaton, Warwickshire, England.

Unpasteurised cow's milk, animal rennet.

In 2005, when Jo and David Clarke started making this cheese, proper cloth-bound farmhouse Red Leicester had been absent from our cheeseboards for fifty years. There was a little worry at first that this traditional territorial cheese's reputation had been undermined by the rather bland offerings of the factory, but this proved to be unfounded. Handmade with raw milk, Sparkenhoe is a treat: give anyone a taste, and they will be immediately seduced by its rounded acidity and mellow savoury flavour.

Spenwood

Made by Anne Wigmore at Village Maid Cheese, Riseley, Berkshire, England.

Unpasteurised sheep's milk, veg. rennet.

Inspired by a Sardinian Pecorino that Anne Wigmore tasted while she was sailing to Australia – cheesemakers do that sort of thing – Spenwood has a nutty flavour with a hint of caramel. It's a bit harder than many Pecorino-style cheeses and makes a delicious alternative to Parmesan in a risotto.

Westcombe's Cheddar

Made by Tom Calver and his team on Westcombe Farm, Evercreech, Somerset, England.

Unpasteurised cow's milk, animal rennet.

Westcombe is quite soft for a Somerset Cheddar, and its flavour is mellow. Sweet and nutty flavours intertwine with an acidic bite. There's no lack of complexity and depth in this traditional cloth-bound Cheddar, though. Tom Calver calls it a 'five mile cheese' – as in, you can still taste it five miles down the road.

SOURCES

Further reading

Below is a list of the source texts that I found most useful in writing the *Cheesemonger's History*. Books precede papers, and those with an asterisk are highly recommended if your interest in cheese history is whetted. For a longer, annotated list see my website *www.CheeseTastingCo.uk*

GENERAL BOOKS

* V. Cheke, *The Story of Cheesemaking in Britain* (Routledge & Kegan Paul, 1959).

* G.E. Fussell, *The English Dairy Farmer* (Frank Cass, 1966).

* Juliet Harbutt (ed.), *The World Cheese Book* (Dorling Kindersley, 2015).

* P. Kindstedt, *Cheese and Culture, A History of Cheese and Its Place in Western Civilisation* (Chelsea Green, 2012).

* B. and P. Percival, *Reinventing the Wheel, Milk, Microbes and the Fight For Real Cheese* (Bloomsbury, 2017).

* P. Rance, *The Great British Cheese Book* (Papermac, 1983).

* P. Thomas, *Home-Made Cheese: From Simple Butter, Yogurt and Fresh Cheeses to Soft, Hard and Blue Cheeses, an Expert's Guide to Making Successful Cheese at Home* (Lorenz, 2016).

* J. Squire (ed.) *Cheddar Gorge: A Book of English Cheeses* (1937; reissued by Harper Collins, 2018).

CHAPTER ONE

T. Darvill, *Prehistoric Britain* (Routledge, 2010).

F. Pryor, *Farmers in Pre-Historic Britain* (The History Press, 2011).

M. S. Copley et al., 'Direct chemical evidence for widespread dairying in prehistoric Britain' (*Proceedings of the National Academy of Sciences of the USA*, Vol. 100, No. 4, 2003).

A. Curry, 'Archaeology: The Milk Revolution' (*Nature*, 31/7/13).

J. Smyth and R. Evershed, 'Milking the Megafauna: Using organic residue analysis to understand early farming practice' (*Journal of Environmental Archaeology*, 2015).

CHAPTER TWO

* J. Alcock, *Food In Roman Britain* (The History Press, 2001).

L. I. M. Columella, *On Agriculture, Volume II: Books 5–9* (Harvard University Press, 1954).

G. De La Béyodère, *Roman Britain, a New History* (Thames & Hudson, 2013).

* Michael Wood, *In Search of the Dark Ages* (BBC Books, 2006).

R.W. Davies, 'The Roman Military Diet' (*Britannia*, Vol. 2, 1971).

D.A. Harvey, 'Rectitudines Singularum Personarum and Gerefa' (*The English Historical Review*, V. 108, 1993).

G. Hawkes, 'Food and Foodways in Roman Britain, a study in contact and culture change' (Doctoral thesis, University of Leicester, 2003).

R. Reece, 'Town and Country, the End of Roman Britain' (*World Archaeology*, Vol. 12, No. 1, 1980).

CHAPTER THREE

* C. Dyer, *Making a Living in the Middle Ages* (Yale University Press, 2009).

N. Harris (ed.), *Privy Purse Expenses of Elizabeth of York* (W. Pickering, 1830).

R. Rosewell, *The Medieval Monastery* (Shire, 2012).

E. Searle and B. Ross, (eds.), *Accounts of the Cellarers of Battle Abbey 1275–1513* (Sydney University Press, 1967).

* R.A.L. Smith, *Canterbury Cathedral Priory – A study in monastic administration* (Cambridge University Press, 1943).

C.M. Woolgar, D. Serjeantson, and T. Waldron (eds), *Food in medieval England: diet and nutrition* (Oxford University Press, 2006).

CHAPTER FOUR

J. Davies, *A History of Wales* (Penguin, revised ed., 2007).

B. Gummer, *The Scourging Angel* (Vintage, 2010).

E.A. Lewis, *Welsh Port Books: With An Analysis Of The Customs Revenue Accounts Of Wales For The Same Period* (Honourable Society of Cymmrodorion, 1927).

* D. Oschinsky, *Walter of Henley and other treatises on estate management and accounting* (Clarendon Press, 1971).

E. Robo, 'The Black Death in the Hundred of Farnham' (The *English Historical Review*, Vol. 44, 1929).

* W.M. Stern, 'Where, oh where, are the cheesemongers of London?' (*London Journal*, Vol. 5, No. 2, , 1979).

CHAPTER FIVE

* C.F. Foster, *Cheshire Cheese and Farming in the North West in the 17th and 18th Centuries* (Arley Hall Press 1998).

P.G. Maxwell-Stuart, *The British Witch: The Biography* (Amberley Publishing, 2014).

I. Mortimer, *The Time Travellers Guide to Elizabethan England* (Vintage, 2012).

S. Hickey, 'Fatal Feeds?: Plants, livestock losses and witchcraft accusations in Tudor and Stuart Britain' (*Folklore*, Vol. 101, No. 2, 1990).

CHAPTER SIX

R. Porter, *English Society in the Eighteenth Century* (Penguin, 1990).

* V. Yarnspinner, *Nottingham Rising: The Great Cheese Riot of 1766 & the 1831 Reform Riots* (Loaf on a Stick Press, 2014).

D. Valenze, 'The Art of Women and the Business of Men: Women's Work and the Dairy Industry c.1740–1840' (*Past and Present*, Vol. 130, 1991).

CHAPTER SEVEN

R.C. Allen, *The Industrial Revolution, A Very Short Introduction* (Oxford University Press, 2017).

* I. Beeton, *The Book of Household Management* (S.O. Beeton, 1861).

J. Flanders, *Inside the Victorian Home: A Portrait of Domestic Life in Victorian England* (W. W. Norton & Co., 2005).

F.J. Lloyd, *Observations on Cheddar Cheese Making* (William Clowes, 1892).

J. Bourke, 'Dairywomen and Affectionate Wives: Women in the Irish Dairy Industry 1890–1914' (*Agricultural History Review*, Vol. 38 No. 2 1990).

D. Taylor, 'Growth and Structural Change in the English Dairy Industry, c.1860–1930' (*Agricultural History Review*, 1987).

A. Voelcker, 'On Poisonous Cheese' (*Journal of the Royal Agricultural Society of England*, Vol. 23, No. 49, 1862).

CHAPTER EIGHT

K. Calvert, *Kit Calvert of Wensleydale, The Complete Dalesman* (Dalesman Publishing Co. Ltd., 1981).

K. Knight, *Spuds, Spam and Eating for Victory: Rationing in the Second World War* (The History Press, 2011).

P.J. Atkins, 'The pasteurisation of England: the science, culture and health implications of food processing, 1900–1950', in *Food, Science, Policy and Regulation in the Twentieth Century: International and Comparative Perspectives* (Routledge, 2000).

'Ministry of Agriculture, Food and Fisheries, Report on the Marketing of Dairy Produce in England and Wales, Part 1, Cheese' (*Economic Series*, Vol. 22, HMSO, 1930).

CHAPTER NINE

C. Bickerton, *The European Union: A Citizen's Guide* (Pelican, 2016).

B. Miles, *London Calling* (Atlantic Books, 2010).

* N. Saunders, *The Neal's Yard Story* (Institute for Social Inventions, 1987).

J. Gray, 'The Common Agricultural Policy and the Re-Invention of the Rural in Europe' (*Sociologia Ruralis*, Vol. 40, No. 1, 2000).

CHAPTER TEN

I didn't read anything; I just talked to the cheesemakers.

Acknowledgements

Without the cheesemakers, I wouldn't have had anything to write about, and my gratitude to all of them, not just those mentioned in this book, is boundless. There are too many to fit in here so let me confine myself to this: if you make cheese, thank you, and please carry on. If I were to single out any for special thanks it would be the late Mary Holbrook, the first cheesemaker to let me get my hands into a vat, and in whose kitchen I came up with the germ of the idea for this book. Thanks Mary, I hope there are goats and cheese vats wherever you are now.

Special thanks, too, to Gorwydd Caerphilly and the craft and dedication of its makers, Todd, Maugan and Kim Trethowan, since it was the first taste of that cheese that set me on the path; and to Jess for introducing me to the Trethowans and their cheese and, almost twenty years later, to Jill and Mark Hatch who patiently answered my questions about Neolithic cheesemaking.

I'm hugely grateful to those cheesemakers who let me into their dairies or allowed me to bombard them with questions over the phone: Quinlan Steele of Milleens; Sarah and Paul Appleby, Aunt Sarah and Garry Gray of Appleby's Cheshire; Joe Schneider of Stichelton Dairy; Tom Calver of Westcombe Dairy; cheese educator Val Bines; Humphrey Errington of Errington's Cheese; Carrie Rimes of Cosyn Cymru; Marcus Fergusson of Felton's Farm; and Dave Holton of Blackwood's Cheese Company.

I also want to say a heartfelt thanks to the cheesemongers who made me what I am: Cathi, Sylvie, Viv, Matt Owen, Evin,

Chris George, Bill and of course Randolph Hodgson, without whom, etc. And to all those friends in the writing fraternity who offered advice, support, or an empathic ear, in particular Alex von Tunzelman, Robyn Young and Kate Williams.

This book would have never made it out of the back-of-a-fag-packet stage without the initial enthusiasm and tireless championing from my agent and cornerman David Luxton. It would have been a lot longer and less readable without the skill and experience of my brilliant editor, Mark Ellingham, and the diligence and rigour of Jonathan Buckley, and suggestions from Nat Jansz. Thanks for the arresting cover design and lavish endpaper map to David Wardle of Bold & Noble; to Henry Iles for the text design and layout and the photo treatments; to the eagle-eyed Nikky Twyman for correcting my wayward spelling and grammar, and saving my bacon; and to Bill Johncocks for the thoroughness of the index. On the marketing, publicity and sales front, thanks to Flora Willis, Anna-Marie Fitzgerald and Jane Pickett, and to Claire Beaumont and her team. In fact I want to thank everyone at Profile; there can't be many publishing houses where you are greeted with such hospitality and friendliness even when you don't bring cheese.

Straddling effortlessly that fraught boundary between friendship and professionalism, Nausicaa Ramerino and Tam Cooper did a great job of translating some medieval Italian cheese writing. I am also blessed with too many wonderful friends to thank individually for their loyal and occasionally tough advice ('just get up earlier, Ned', being a fine example). Thank you all. I do want to mention two people, Rosalind Graves Cooper and Gabriella Oakley who, a very long time ago indeed, knew that I could and would before I did.

My dad, Greg Palmer, took me into the stacks of the British Library to 'help' him at the National Archive when I was very small. That's probably where all this started. My mum, Ann Palmer, showed me how to string a sentence together and most of the time picked my pen up when I chucked it across the room.

And then there is my first reader, sternest critic and biggest fan, my best friend and wife, the brilliant writer Imogen Robertson. Thanks Imo.

Photo credits

Thanks to all the cheesemakers, and photographers, who have provided images for this book. It wouldn't be half as much fun without them. In a book that includes archive photos, we have made every effort to identify the photographers, but this has not always been possible; the author and publishers would be grateful for information on any omissions or errors and will correct these in any future editions.

CHAPTER ONE

p.10 Hamish Renton/Fourth & Church; p.15 Historica Graphica Collection/Heritage Images/Getty Images; p.19 Andrew Matthews/ Press Association; p.23 House of Bruar; p.30 Emli Bendixen.

CHAPTER TWO

p.38 Village Maid; p.40 Ned Palmer; p.43 Andia/Universal Images Group via Getty Images; p.49 The Print Collector/Alamy Stock Photo; p.53 Village Maid; p.56 Universal Images Group/Getty Images; p.59 WikiCommons; p.62 Sarah Jordan/ Bread & Flowers; p.65 Village Maid; p.68 Village Maid.

CHAPTER THREE

p.72 Quinlan Steele/Milleens; p75 Matt Cardy/Stringer/Getty Images; p.78 WikiCommons; p.80 Hemis/Alamy Stock Photo; p.82 La Fromagerie, London; p.85 WikiCommons; p.87 Professor J. J. N. Palmer, George Slater/University of Hull/opendomesday.org; p.92 Juan Jackson; p.96 Alinari Archives/Getty Images; p.101 WikiCommons; p.105 Milleens; p.109 Dan Linehan; p.111 Milleens.

CHAPTER FOUR

p.114 Trethowans; p.119 WikiCommons; p.123 Universal

History Archive/Getty Images; p.129 WikiCommons; p.132 Alinari Archives/Getty Images; p.136 WikiCommons; p.138 Chris Lawrence/Alamy Stock Photo; p.140 Stefan Johnson/St Johns; p.144 Dan Bliss/Paxton & Whitfield; p.147 & p.148 Andre Pattenden/Trethowans Dairy.

CHAPTER FIVE

p.152 Appleby's; p.157 WikiCommons; p.162 WikiCommons; p.172 WikiCommons; p.178 Ned Palmer; p.181 Appleby's; p.183 Ned Palmer.

CHAPTER SIX

p.188 Stichelton Dairy; p.193 WikiCommons; p.198 Collection of Trevor Hickman; p.205 Stichelton Dairy; p.208 Harry Darby/ Stichelton Dairy; p.212 Practical Cheesemaking; p.214 Stichelton Dairy.

CHAPTER SEVEN

p.216 ©brond.co.uk; p.219 Viewpoint Photography/Pong Cheese Ltd; p.223 iStock; p.224 Alamy Images; p.226 Ned Palmer; p.229 Val Cheke; p.234 the Sage Family; p.238 Harper's Magazine;

p.242 Alamy Images; p.247 WikiCommons.

CHAPTER EIGHT

p.250 Hawes Wensleydale; p.255 Douglas Miller/Stringer/Getty Images; p.262 National Archives; p.266 © The Sainsbury Archive, Museum of London Docklands; p.269 E.H. Shepard/Cheddar Gorge; p.274 Dales Countryside Museum collection; p.278 Hawes Wensleydale.

CHAPTER NINE

p.282 Errington Cheese; p.284 flickr; p.287 & p.288 Mark Edwards; p.291 Patrick Rance; p.293 Mark Edwards; p.299 Errington Cheese; p.301 Highland Fine Cheeses; p.302 Errington Cheese; p.309 Cashel Farmhouse Cheesemakers; p.312 Juliet Harbutt/www.thecheeseweb. com.

CHAPTER TEN

p.314 Helen Cathcart/Alamy Stock Photo; p.317 F. W. Read & Sons; p.318 Doddington Dairy; p.320 Tom Bunning; p.323 Toby Allen Photos; p.326 WikiCommons; p.329 Marcus Feltham/Feltham's Farm Ltd; p.332 Mike's Fancy Cheese; p.335 Fen Farm Dairy; p.339 Emli Bendixen.

Index

Italic page references indicate illustrations

A

goat's milk cheeses and 34–7,
207, 296
Tymsboro 28, *30*, 41, 344
see also Sleightlett
Holden, Patrick 254, 352
'Hollande cheese' 131–3
Holton, Dave 321, 324, 337, 338
Home-made Cheese, by Paul
Thomas 177
Homer's *Odyssey* 47
Hooke, Robert 222, 231
Hopkins, Matthew 161, *162*
horse collars, adoption 122
Houghton, John 192
*(The Book of) Household
Management,* by Mrs Beeton
217–18, 246–9, *247*
hubba-bubba flavours 199, 348
Hume, Elliot 297
the Hundred Years' War 123–4,
137
Husbandry, by Walter of Henley
98
hygiene 45, 106, 109–10,
164–6, 191
Hywell Dda, King in Wales 69

I

imported cheeses
American 174, 238–9, 245
from continental Europe 265,
267, 312
from the Dominions 245,
257–9, 263
to Roman Britain 54–5
the Industrial Revolution 8, 192
Ireland
Beara Peninsula 73, 103–10,
105, 293
and the Black Death 118

Ceide field system 26
changing status of women
236–7
cheeses of, award winning
311, 332
cheeses of, in *Cheddar Gorge*
270
English Civil War and 185
famine of 1845-49 105, 239
folklore 158
monasticism in 77–84
Norman influence 85
public transport in 103–4
separation from European
mainland 25
union with Great Britain 193
Young Buck 332, 349
see also Milleens
Irish Cheese Awards 332
Irish Farmhouse Cheesemakers
Association (CAIS) 81, 110,
308
iron deficiency 18
Italian cheeses, popularity
265–6

J

James, cargo ship 169
James, Perry 294
James (VI and) I 155, 158
James II 191
Jarvis, Tim 322, *323*
Jenks, Jorian 254
Jenner, Lyn and Jenny 344
Jervaulx Abbey, Yorkshire 88,
90, 96, 102
Jill (Hatch) 16–17, *19,* 21
Joe (Schneider, of Stichelton)
203–13, *205, 208, 214,* 330,
348

A CHEESE
MONGER'S
MAP
OF THE
BRITISH
ISLES
___